Enduring
Issues
in
Criminology

Other Books in the Enduring Issues Series:

Enduring Issues in Criminology

Ron Boostrom

David L. Bender, *Publisher*
Bruno Leone, *Executive Editor*

Bonnie Szumski, *Series Editor*

Ron Boostrom, Professor of Criminal Justice
Administration, School of Public
Administration and Urban Studies,
San Diego State University, *Book Editor*

Greenhaven Press, Inc., San Diego, CA 92198-9009

Library of Congress Cataloging-in-Publication Data

Enduring issues in criminology: opposing viewpoints / Ron Boostrom, book editor.
    p.   cm.   — (Enduring issues series)
    Includes bibliographical references and index.
    ISBN 1-56510-255-X (pbk.: alk. paper) — ISBN 1-56510-256-8 (lib. bdg.: alk. paper)
    1. Criminology. I. Boostrom, Ron, 1936-   . II. Series.
HV6025.E57   1995
364—dc20   94-24935
                                                                    CIP

Copyright © 1995 by Greenhaven Press, Inc.
P.O. Box 289009, San Diego, CA 92198-9009
Printed in the U.S.A.

Contents

Chapter 3: What Causes Criminal Behavior?

Chapter 4: How Should Society React to Crime?

Chapter 5: What Is the Future of Criminology?

Foreword

"When a thing ceases to be a subject of controversy, it ceases to be a subject of interest."

William Hazlitt

The Enduring Issues Series is based on the concept that certain fundamental disciplines remain interesting and vibrant because they remain controversial, debatable, and mutable. Indeed, it is through controversy that these disciplines were forged, and through debate that they continue to be defined.

Each book in the Enduring Issues Series aims to present the most seminal and thought-provoking issues in the most accessible way—by pitting the founders of each discipline against one another. This running debate style allows readers to compare and contrast major philosophical views, noting the major and minor areas of disagreement. In this way, the chronology of the formation of the discipline itself is traced. As American clergyman Lyman Beecher argued, "No great advance has ever been made in science, politics, or religion, without controversy."

In an effort to collect the most representative opinions of these disciplines, every editor of each book in the Enduring Issues Series has been chosen for his or her expertise in presenting these issues in the classroom. Each editor has chosen the materials for his or her book with these goals in mind: 1) To offer, both to the uninitiated and to the well read, classic questions answered by the leading historical and contemporary proponents. 2) To create and stimulate an interest and excitement in these academic disciplines by revealing that even in the most esoteric areas there are questions and views common to every person's search for life's meaning. 3) To reveal the development of ideas, and, in the process, plant the notion in the reader's mind that truth can only be unearthed in thoughtful examination and reexamination.

The editors of the Enduring Issues Series hope that readers will find in it a launching point to do their own investigation and form their own opinions about the issues raised by these academic disciplines. Because it is in the continued contemplation of these questions that these issues will remain alive.

Introduction

Crime is a primary concern of the American people. The problems involved in dealing with crime and criminals that occupy much of the energy of politicians at all levels of government are a major focus of study for many social scientists as well. As politicians and the media have identified the crime problem as at the forefront of public concern, an increasing number of researchers and theorists from a variety of social science disciplines have turned their attention to the study of crime, criminality, and criminal justice. An expanding variety of practitioners of criminology from various disciplinary backgrounds has created many differences of opinion about exactly what criminologists should study, how they should study it, and how the results of their studies should be used.

The discipline of criminology, the scientific study and analysis of crime, criminality, and society's reaction to crime, has been growing and developing in the United States since 1909, when the first formal organization to recognize and encourage the study of criminology was established in Chicago. Criminology was established and developed not only by lawyers, jurists, and other practitioners in criminal justice, but also by social scientists with various theoretical and research interests. Thus many debates have arisen about what topics should be the focus and concern of criminologists.

Some criminologists maintain that the field should limit itself to only those acts that clearly violate the existing criminal law and to only those people found guilty of violating the existing criminal law. They maintain that the study of the criminal law violator is what makes criminology a unique social science discipline. From their perspective, when criminologists study other types of deviance or rule-violating behavior they are blurring the boundaries between criminology and other disciplines that study human behavior, such as sociology or psychology. For instance, they claim that those criminologists who have specialized in the study of "white-collar crime" are actually straying from the study of criminal behavior by including the study of those charged with violations of the civil code and regulatory statutes that are noncriminal in the strict definition of the word.

Other criminologists argue for broadening study to include individuals and groups who commit acts not prosecuted under the criminal law who nevertheless cause harm to society. They argue that the "white-collar" violator who is subject to civil law sanctions or fines by government regulatory agencies should be studied because these violators are responsible for much social harm, often doing more damage to society than the "street criminal" who is the traditional subject of criminologists.

Some experts believe that the research and conclusions of criminologists should be judged by their usefulness in controlling crime. These criminologists take it for granted that the problems studied by criminology are the practical social problems for which they can suggest practical solutions that should be incorporated into social policy by politicians and criminal justice managers. This approach tends to broaden the study of crime to include the relationship between criminal behavior, poverty, race, class differences, and the uses of political power. This social problems approach has been favored by most American criminologists since the study of criminology was first developed in the United States.

Other criminologists take issue with this approach, suggesting that criminology should be more detached from politics. They claim that the study of criminology should not be influenced by those who hold positions of power in the political state but should be guided only by the tenets and methods of social science. For instance, some criminologists have included human rights violations as a legitimate area of study. They view criminology as encompassing all forms of victimization and look for the similarities between values and practices that justify family violence and values and practices that justify national foreign policies. They claim that the "power elite" in the United States, which does not want these connections drawn, is therefore guilty of impeding the scientific social study of criminal behavior and criminal victimization for political reasons.

All of these debates and differences of opinion within criminology have resulted in conflicts about what criminologists should study, how they should go about their studies, and what should be done with the results of criminological studies. These differences of opinion reflected in the viewpoints in this book point to the fact that criminology is still a developing and dynamic discipline.

The criminologist who has done more than any other over the years in attempting to resolve these debates is Edwin H. Sutherland, generally regarded as the most influential American criminologist. Attempting to bring some organization and coherence to the study of criminology, Sutherland wrote the first criminology textbook that defined criminology's scope and subject matter. First published in 1924, this text has since gone through numerous editions. It influenced generations of American criminologists as they struggled to come to terms with how to approach the vast subject of crime, criminal behavior, and crime control.

Sutherland defined the object of criminology as "the development of a body of general and verified principles and other types of knowledge regarding the process of law, crime, and reaction to crime." The study of criminology, according to Sutherland, includes (a) the process of making and administering law and criminal justice; (b) the scientific analysis of the causes of crime; and (c) the social reaction to lawbreaking (crime control measures).

It is Sutherland's definition of criminology that drives the selections. The first chapter, What Should Criminologists Study?, provides a foundation for considering differing views in the chapters that follow on the functions of criminal law and the administration of justice, the causes of crime, the social reactions to crime, and the future of criminology.

Reading these viewpoints will provide you with an understanding of the main ideas in criminology and how they have evolved. Do you think criminals are abnormal deviants who should be locked away indefinitely? Do you think that criminals are otherwise normal people who have used bad judgment and should be taught a lesson? Maybe you think criminals and delinquents should be rehabilitated, reformed, and reintegrated into the community rather than warehoused for purposes of punishment. Do you think the criminal justice system needs to be restructured and reformed? Do you think that citizens should be more involved in and responsible for crime prevention and control? You will find that criminologists have debated all of these viewpoints over the years. Keep an open mind as you read the following viewpoints and perhaps they will suggest some new directions for your own study and understanding of these fascinating social issues.

CHAPTER

1

What Should Criminologists Study?

Chapter Preface

Efforts to create a specialized discipline of criminology began at the turn of the century in the United States. American reformers experimented with many practical penal innovations. Reformatories created in the last century became places to study, as well as to confine, the criminal. Many practitioners in criminal justice, reformers, and legal scholars began to get interested in creating a specialized discipline to study crime and criminals and to recommend changes in crime control methods.

The person most responsible for beginning the organization of a specialized discipline to study crime and criminality was John Henry Wigmore, dean of the law school of Northwestern University. In 1909 Wigmore convened a conference in Chicago to celebrate the fiftieth anniversary of Northwestern Law School. This first conference of eminent criminologists, criminal lawyers, and penal and legal reformers resulted in the founding of an American Institute of Criminal Law and Criminology. It also led to publication of the *Journal of Criminal Law and Criminology*. Scholars concerned with the study of crime, criminality, and criminal law could now publish their findings and communicate with one another. Other major developments resulting from this gathering of scholars included publication of a series on modern European criminology and committees to study and lobby for criminal justice reforms, to study the improvement and use of criminal statistics, and to further the teaching of criminology and criminalistics in colleges and universities. This mobilization of effort and creation of a community of scholars interested in crime began a tradition of criminological study, linked to criminal justice reform efforts, that is still with us today.

This chapter reveals that American criminology is a dynamic discipline with many conflicts about what should be studied, how it should be studied, and how the results of this study should be used in practice. These differences of opinion have been a part of criminology since its inception.

Criminology began with a focus on the criminal and the factors that account for criminal behavior. Developed by sociologists, the discipline gradually began to concern itself with the social conditions that account for crime. In recent years, the field of criminology has become increasingly concerned with understanding the criminal justice system, victims of crime, and with analyzing community social controls and their impact on crime and crime prevention.

Some criminologists have maintained the original focus of criminology. They attempt to understand the causal factors that lead to criminality and delinquency. They may view criminality as abnormal and search for the peculiar factors that lead to "deviant behavior." Others view criminality, delinquency, and deviance as natural phenomena and look for the controls that will keep the majority of people from committing crimes.

It may seem confusing that criminologists do not agree with one another about the focus of their study and the ways in which their results might be used. However, this allows criminology to remain a dynamic and changing area of study. This is one of the factors that makes the field of criminology interesting to those who study crime and criminal behavior.

Criminologists Should Study Political Ideology

WALTER B. MILLER

Criminology was originally conceived at the beginning of this century. The research and theory developed by criminologists were intended to help solve the crime problem in society. Some criminologists have explicitly rejected the idea that criminologists should have a responsibility to suggest practical solutions to crime. However, most American criminologists have accepted the idea that criminology can or should have policy relevance. In an effort to specify conservative and liberal, or "right" and "left," assumptions about crime, methods of dealing with crime, and the criminal justice system, Walter B. Miller indicates that commitment to ideology has an important part to play in developing effective social policy. Liberals on the political left provide innovative ideas. Conservatives on the political right provide an

Excerpted from Walter B. Miller, "Ideology and Criminal Justice Policy: Some Current Issues," *The Journal of Criminal Law and Criminology* 64 (1973): 142-54, published by Northwestern University School of Law.

appreciation for the importance of tradition. If the two sides can maintain a respect for one another and a willingness to consider the others' views, they may be able to effectively reduce crime. According to Miller, crime control policy can be improved by making the assumptions of liberals and conservatives more explicit so they can be dealt with more openly. Walter B. Miller was a criminologist and sociologist at Harvard University.

QUESTIONS

1. Who or what is to blame for our crime problem in society, according to liberals and conservatives?
2. Do those on the political left and those on the political right differ in their views on the factors that cause crime? How?
3. How can the justice system be reformed to better deal with the crime problem, in the opinion of those on the political left and the political right?

■ ■ ■

The major contention of this presentation is that ideology and its consequences exert a powerful influence on the policies and procedures of those who conduct the enterprise of criminal justice, and that the degree and kinds of influence go largely unrecognized. Ideology is the permanent hidden agenda of criminal justice.

The discussion has two major aims. First, assuming that the generally implicit ideological basis of criminal justice commands strong, emotional, partisan allegiance, I shall attempt to state explicitly the major assumptions of relevant divergent ideological positions in as neutral or as nonpartisan a fashion as possible. Second, some of the consequences of such ideologies for the processes of planning, program, and policy in criminal justice will be examined. . . .

Ideological Positions

Right: Crusading Issues

Crusading issues of the right differ somewhat from those of the left; they generally do not carry as explicit a message of movement toward new forms, but imply instead that things should be

16

reconstituted or restored. However, the component of the message that says, "Things should be different from the way they are now," comes through just as clearly as in the crusading issues of the left. Current crusading issues of the right with respect to crime and how to deal with it include the following:

1. *Excessive leniency toward lawbreakers.* This is a traditional complaint of the right, accentuated at present by the publicity given to reform programs in corrections and policing, as well as to judicial activity at various levels.
2. *Favoring the welfare and rights of lawbreakers over the welfare and rights of their victims, of law enforcement officials, and the law abiding citizen.* This persisting concern is currently activated by attention to prisoners' rights, rehabilitation programs, attacks on police officers by militants, and in particular by a series of well-publicized Supreme Court decisions aimed to enhance the application of due process.
3. *Erosion of discipline and of respect for constituted authority.* This ancient concern is currently manifested in connection with the general behavior of youth, educational policies, treatment of student dissidents by college officials, attitudes and behavior toward law-enforcement, particularly the police.
4. *The cost of crime.* Less likely to arouse the degree of passion evoked by other crusading issues, resentment over what is seen as the enormous and increasing cost of crime and dealing with criminals—a cost borne directly by the hard working and law abiding citizen—nevertheless remains active and persistent.
5. *Excessive permissiveness.* Related to excessive leniency, erosion of discipline, and the abdication of responsibility by authorities, this trend is seen as a fundamental defect in the contemporary social order, affecting many diverse areas such as sexual morality, discipline in the schools, educational philosophies, child-rearing, judicial handling of offenders, and media presentation of sexual materials.

Right: General Assumptions

These crusading issues, along with others of similar import, are not merely ritualized slogans, but reflect instead a more abstract set of assumptions about the nature of criminal behavior, the causes of criminality, responsibility for crime, appropriate ameliorative measures, and, on a broader level, the nature of man and of a proper kind of society. These general assumptions provide the basic charter for the ideological stance of the right as a whole, and a basis for distinguishing among the several subtypes along the points of the ideological scale. Major general assumptions of the right might be phrased as follows:

1. The individual is directly responsible for his own behavior. He is not a passive pawn of external forces, but possesses the capacity to make choices between right and wrong—choices which he makes with an awareness of their consequences.

2. A central requirement of a healthy and well functioning society is a strong moral order which is explicit, well-defined, and widely adhered to. Preferably the tenets of this system of morality should be derived from and grounded in the basic precepts of a major religious tradition. Threats to this moral order are threats to the very existence of the society. Within the moral order, two clusters are of particular importance:

   a. Tenets which sustain the family unit involve morally-derived restrictions on sexual behavior, and obligations of parents to maintain consistent responsibility to their children and to one another.

   b. Tenets which pertain to valued personal qualities include: taking personal responsibility for one's behavior and its consequences; conducting one's affairs with the maximum degree of self-reliance and independence, and the minimum of dependency and reliance on others, particularly public agencies; loyalty, particularly to one's country; achieving one's ends through hard work, responsibility to others, and self-discipline.

3. Of paramount importance is the security of the major arenas of one's customary activity—particularly those locations where the conduct of family life occurs. A fundamental personal and family right is safety from crime, violence, and attack, including the right of citizens to take necessary measures to secure their own safety, and the right to bear arms, particularly in cases where official agencies may appear ineffective in doing so.

4. Adherence to the legitimate directives of constituted authority is a primary means for achieving the goals of morality, correct individual behavior, security, and other valued life conditions. Authority in the service of social and institutional rules should be exercised fairly but firmly, and failure or refusal to accept or respect legitimate authority should be dealt with decisively and unequivocally .

5. A major device for ordering human relations in a large and heterogeneous society is that of maintaining distinctions among major categories of persons on the basis of differences in age, sex, and so on, with differences in religion, national background, race, and social position of particular importance. While individuals in each of the general categories should be granted the rights and privileges appropriate thereto, social order in many circumstances is greatly facilitated by maintaining both conceptual and spatial separation among the categories.

Left: Crusading Issues

Crusading issues of the left generally reflect marked dissatisfaction with characteristics of the current social order, and carry an insistent message about the desired nature and direction of social reform. Current issues of relevance to criminal justice include:

1. *Overcriminalization.* This reflects a conviction that a substantial number of offenses delineated under current law are wrongly or inappropriately included, and applies particularly to offenses such as gambling, prostitution, drug use, abortion, pornography, and homosexuality.

2. *Labeling and Stigmatization.* This issue is based on a conception that problems of crime are aggravated or even created by the ways in which actual or potential offenders are regarded and treated by persons in authority. To the degree a person is labeled as "criminal," "delinquent," or "deviant," will he be likely to so act.

3. *Overinstitutionalization.* This reflects a dissatisfaction over prevalent methods of dealing with suspected or convicted offenders whereby they are physically confined in large institutional facilities. Castigated as "warehousing," this practice is seen as having a wide range of detrimental consequences,

many of which are implied by the ancient phrase "schools for crime." Signalled by a renewed interest in "incarceration," prison reform has become a major social cause of the left.

4. *Overcentralization.* This issue reflects dissatisfaction with the degree of centralized authority existing in organizations which deal with crime—including police departments, correctional systems, and crime-related services at all government levels. Terms which carry the thrust of the proposed remedy are local control, decentralization, community control, a new populism, and citizen power.

5. *Discriminatory Bias.* A particularly blameworthy feature of the present system lies in the widespread practice of conceiving and reacting to large categories of persons under class labels based on characteristics such as racial background, age, sex, income level, sexual practices, and involvement in criminality. Key terms here are racism, sexism, minority oppression and brutality.

Left: General Assumptions

As in the case of the rightist positions, these crusading issues are surface manifestations of a set of more basic and general assumptions, which might be stated as follows:

1. Primary responsibility for criminal behavior lies in conditions of the social order rather than in the character of the individual. Crime is to a greater extent a product of external social pressures than of internally generated individual motives, and is more appropriately regarded as a symptom of social dysfunction than as a phenomenon in its own right. The correct objective of ameliorative efforts, therefore, lies in the attempt to alter the social conditions that engender crime rather than to rehabilitate the individual.

2. The system of behavioral regulation maintained in America is based on a type of social and political order that is deficient in meeting the fundamental needs of the majority of its citizens. This social order, and the official system of behavioral regulation that it includes, incorporates an obsolete morality not applicable to the conditions of a rapidly changing technological society, and disproportionately

geared to sustain the special interests of restricted groups, but which still commands strong support among working class and lower middle class sectors of the population.

3. A fundamental defect in the political and social organization of the United States and in those components of the criminal justice enterprise that are part of this system is an inequitable and unjust distribution of power, privilege, and resources—particularly of power. This inequity pervades the entire system, but appears in its more pronounced forms in the excessive centralization of governmental functions and consequent powerlessness of the governed, the military-like, hierarchical authority systems found in police and correctional organization, and policies of systematic exclusion from positions of power and privilege for those who lack certain preferred social characteristics. The prime objective of reform must be to redistribute the decision-making power of the criminal justice enterprise rather than to alter the behavior of actual or potential offenders.

4. A further defect of the official system is its propensity to make distinctions among individuals based on major categories or classes within society such as age, sex, race, social class, criminal or non-criminal. Healthy societal adaptation for both the offender and the ordinary citizen depends on maintaining the minimum separation—conceptually and physically—between the community at large and those designated as "different" or "deviant." Reform efforts must be directed to bring this about.

5. Consistent with the capacity of external societal forces to engender crime, personnel of official agencies play a predominantly active role, and offenders a predominantly reactive role, in situations where the two come in contact. Official agents of behavioral regulation possess the capacity to induce or enhance criminal behavior by the manner in which they deal with those who have or may have engaged in crime. These agents may define offenders as basically criminal, expose them to stigmatization, degrade them on the basis of social characteristics, and subject them to rigid and arbitrary control.

6. The sector of the total range of human behavior currently included under the system of criminal sanctions is excessively broad, including many forms of behavior (for

example, marijuana use, gambling, homosexuality) which do not violate the new morality and forms which would be more effectively and humanely dealt with outside the official system of criminal processing. Legal codes should be redrafted to remove many of the behavioral forms now proscribed, and to limit the discretionary prerogatives of local authorities over apprehension and disposition of violators. . . .

For the right, the paramount value is order—an ordered society based on a pervasive and binding morality—and the paramount danger is disorder—social, moral and political. For the left, the paramount value is justice—a just society based on a fair and equitable distribution of power, wealth, prestige, and privilege—and the paramount evil is injustice—the concentration of valued social resources in the hands of a privileged minority.

Few Americans would quarrel with either of these values since both are intrinsic aspects of our national ideals. Stripped of the passion of ideological conflict, the issue between the two sides could be viewed as a disagreement over the relative priority of two valuable conditions: whether *order with justice,* or *justice with order* should be the guiding principle of the criminal justice enterprise.

These are ancient philosophical issues, and their many aspects have been argued in detail for centuries. Can both order and justice be maximized in a large, heterogeneous, pluralistic society? Can either objective be granted priority under all circumstances? If not, under what circumstances should which objective be seen as paramount? It might appear that these issues are today just as susceptible to rational discussion as they have been in the past; but this is not so, because the climate militates against such discussion. . . .

Academic Criminologists: Probably the most important point to make here is that the day-to-day ideological environment of the average academic criminologist, viewed within the context of the total society, is highly artificial; it reflects the perspectives of a deviant and unrepresentative minority. Academic criminology, reflecting academic social science in general, is substantially oriented toward the left, while the bulk of American people are oriented toward the right.

Furthermore, the members of the large liberal academic majority do proportionately more writing and speechmaking than those of the small conservative minority, so that their impact on the ideological climate exceeds even their large numbers. If the proportion of right-oriented persons in academic criminology comes close to being just the reverse of that in the general population, then this marked ideological divergence certainly has implications for those situations in which academicians come in contact with the public, particularly where they interact with representatives of other criminal justice branches. It also has an important impact on their own perceptions of the ideological positions of the public and other criminal justice professionals. . . .

Consequences of Ideology

If, as is here contended, many of those involved in the tasks of planning and executing the major policies and procedures of our criminal justice system are subject to the influence of pervasive ideological assumptions about the nature of crime and methods of dealing with it—assumptions which are largely implicit and unexamined—the question then arises: what are the consequences of this phenomenon?

While both the crusading issues and graded ideological positions presented earlier were phrased to convey the tone of urgent imperatives, the assumptions from which they arise were phrased in relatively neutral terms as a set of general propositions about the nature, causes, and processes of coping with crime. So phrased and so regarded, these assumptions are susceptible to rational consideration. Their strengths and weakness can be debated, evidence can be employed to test the degree of validity each may possess, contradictions among them can be considered, and attempts made to explain or reconcile differences among them. Formulated and used in this manner, the question arises: why are they characterized here as "ideological?"

The scale of ideology presented comprises a single major parameter—substantive variation along a left-right scale with respect to a set of issues germane to crime and the criminal justice process. But there is an additional important parameter which must also be considered: that of intensity—the degree of emotional charge which attaches to the assumptions. It is the capacity of these positions to evoke the most passionate kinds of reactions and to become infused with deeply felt, quasi-religious significance that constitutes the crucial element in the difference between testable assumptions and ideological tenets. This dimension has the power to transform plausibility into ironclad certainty, conditional belief into ardent conviction, the reasoned advocate into the implacable zealot. Rather than being looked upon as useful and conditional hypotheses, these assumptions, for many, take the form of the sacred and inviolable dogma of the one true faith, the questioning of which is heresy, and the opposing of which is profoundly evil. . . .

It cannot be doubted that the United States in the latter 20th century is faced with the necessity of confronting and adapting to a set of substantially modified circumstances, rooted primarily in technological developments with complex and ramified sociological consequences. It does not appear too far-fetched to propose that major kinds of necessary social adaptation in the United States can occur only through the medium of ardently ideological social movements—and that the costs of such a process must be borne in order to achieve the benefits it ultimately will confer. If this conception is correct, then ideological intensification, with all its dangers and drawbacks, must be seen as a necessary component of effective social adaptation, and the ideologists must be seen as playing a necessary role in the process of social change.

Criminologists Should Study Convicted Criminals

PAUL W. TAPPAN

In this classic statement, Paul Tappan argues that criminology must focus on adjudicated crimes and criminals. Criminology is specifically the study of the law violator, according to Tappan. It should not be confused with other types of study that include broad concern with social control and conduct norms. Antisocial behavior that is not a clear violation of the existing criminal law is not the proper focus for the study of criminology. Tappan says that only those acts and those persons sanctioned by the criminal law are within the province of criminological study. Those criminologists who insist on studying groups who commit acts disliked by the criminologist but who are outside the boundaries of the criminal law are doing a disservice to criminology. Tappan reasons that vague, all-inclusive concepts are a blight on the development of criminology as an objective, social scientific discipline. Paul

Paul W. Tappan, "Who is the Criminal?," *American Sociological Review* 12 (1947): 96-102.

W. Tappan was a professor of sociology and law at the University of California, Berkeley. He died in 1964. He wrote extensively on crime, delinquency, and corrections.

QUESTIONS

1. Why do some scholars argue that convicted criminals represent too narrow a focus for those who study crime and criminals?
2. Do you agree with Tappan that those who argue for studying socially injurious conduct and violations of broad conduct norms are going beyond the boundaries of legitimate criminology? Why or why not?
3. What is the "juristic view" of criminology favored by Tappan?

■   ■   ■

What is crime? As a lawyer-sociologist, the writer finds perturbing the current confusion on this important issue. Important because it delimits the subject matter of criminological investigation. A criminologist who strives to aid in formulating the beginnings of a science finds himself in an increasingly equivocal position. He studies the criminals convicted by the courts and is then confounded by the growing clamor that he is not studying the real criminal at all, but an insignificant proportion of non-representative and stupid unfortunates who happened to have become enmeshed in technical legal difficulties. It has become a fashion to maintain that the convicted population is no proper category for the empirical research of the criminologist. Ergo, the many studies of convicts which have been conducted by the orthodox, now presumably outmoded criminologists, have no real meaning for either descriptive or scientific purposes. Off with the old criminologies, on with the new orientations, the new horizons!

This position reflects in part at least the familiar suspicion and misunderstanding held by the layman sociologist toward the law. To a large extent it reveals the feeling among social scientists that not all anti-social conduct is proscribed by law (which is probably true), that not all conduct violative of the criminal code is truly anti-social, or is not so to any significant extent (which is also undoubtedly true). Among some students the opposition to the traditional definition of crime as law violation arises from their desire to discover and study wrongs which are absolute and eternal rather than mere violations of a statutory and case law system which vary in time and place; this is essentially the old metaphysical search for the law of nature. They consider the dynamic and relativistic nature of law to be a barrier to the growth of a scientific system of hypotheses possessing universal validity.

Recent protestants against the orthodox conceptions of crime and criminal are diverse in their views: they unite only in their denial of the allegedly legalistic and arbitrary doctrine that those convicted under the criminal law are the criminals of our society and in promoting the confusion as to the proper province of criminology. It is enough here to examine briefly a few of the current schisms with a view to the difficulties at which they arrive.

Some Criminologists Study Anti-Social Conduct

A number of criminologists today maintain that mere violation of the criminal law is an artificial criterion of criminality, that categories set up by the law do not meet the demands of scientists because they are of a "fortuitous nature" and do not "arise intrinsically from the nature of the subject matter." The validity of this contention must depend, of course, upon what the nature of the subject matter is. These scholars suggest that, as a part of the general study of human behavior, criminology should concern itself broadly with all anti-social conduct, behavior injurious to society. We take it that anti-social conduct is essentially any sort of behavior which violates some social interest. What are these social interests? Which are weighty enough to merit the concern of the sociologist, to bear the odium of crime? What shall constitute a violation of them?— particularly where, as is so commonly true in our complicated and unintegrated society, these interests are themselves in conflict? Roscoe Pound's suggestive classification of the social interests served by law is valuable in a juristic framework, but it solves no problems for the sociologist who seeks to depart from legal standards in search of all manner of anti-social behavior.

27

However desirable may be the concept of socially injurious conduct for purposes of general normation or abstract description, it does not define what is injurious. It sets no standard. It does not discriminate cases, but merely invites the subjective value-judgments of the investigator. Until it is structurally embodied with distinct criteria or norms—as is now the case in the legal system—the notion of anti-social conduct is useless for purposes of research, even for the rawest empiricism. The emancipated criminologist reasons himself into a cul de sac: having decided that it is footless to study convicted offenders on the ground that this is an artificial category— though its membership is quite precisely ascertainable, he must now conclude that, in his lack of standards to determine anti-sociality, though this may be what he considers a real scientific category, its membership and its characteristics are unascertainable. Failing to define anti-social behavior in any fashion suitable to research, the criminologist may be deluded further into assuming that there is an absoluteness and permanence in this undefined category, lacking in the law. It is unwise for the social scientist ever to forget that all standards of social normation are relative, impermanent, variable. And that they do not, certainly the law does not, arise out of mere fortuity or artifice.

Some Criminologists Study Violations of Conduct Norms

In a differing approach certain other criminologists suggest that "conduct norms" rather than either crime or anti-social conduct should be studied. There is an unquestionable need to pursue the investigation of general conduct norms and their violation. It is desirable to segregate the various classes of such norms, to determine relationships between them, to understand similarities and differences between them as to the norms themselves, their sources, methods of imposition of control, and their consequences. The subject matter of this field of social control is in a regrettably primitive state. It will be important to discover the individuals who belong within the several categories of norm violators established and to determine then what motivations operate to promote conformity or breach. So far as it may be determinable, we shall wish to know in what way these motivations may serve to insure conformity to different sets of conduct norms, how they may overlap and reinforce the norms or conflict and weaken the effectiveness of the norms.

We concur in the importance of the study of conduct norms and their violation and, more particularly, if we are to develop a science of human behavior, in the need for careful researches to determine the psychological and environmental variables which are associated etiologically with nonconformity to these norms. However, the importance of the more general subject matter of social control or "ethology" does not mean that the more specific study of the law-violator is non-significant. Indeed, the direction of progress in the field of social control seems to lie largely in the observation and analysis of more specific types of non-conformity to particular, specialized standards. We shall learn more by attempting to determine why some individuals take human life deliberately and with premeditation, why some take property by force and others by trick, than we shall in seeking at the start a universal formula to account for any and all behavior in breach of social interests. This broader knowledge of conduct norms may conceivably develop through induction, in its inevitably very generic terms, from the empirical data derived in the study of particular sorts of violations. Too, our more specific information about the factors which lie behind violations of precisely defined norms will be more useful in the technology of social control. Where legal standards require change to keep step with the changing requirements of a dynamic society, the sociologist may advocate—even as the legal profession does—the necessary statutory modifications, rather than assume that for sociological purposes the conduct he disapproves is already criminal, without legislative, political, or judicial intervention.

White Collar Crime

Another increasingly widespread and seductive movement to revolutionize the concepts of crime and criminal has developed around the currently fashionable dogma of "white collar crime." This is actually a particular school among those who contend that the criminologist should study antisocial behavior rather than law violation. The dominant contention of the group appears to be that the convict classes are merely our "petty" criminals, the few whose depredations against society have been on a small scale, who have blundered into difficulties with the police and courts through their ignorance and stupidity. The important criminals, those who do irreparable damage with impunity, deftly evade the machinery of justice, either by remaining "technically" within the law or by exercising their intelligence, financial prowess, or political connections in its violation. We seek a definition of the white collar criminal and find an amazing diversity, even among those flowing from the same pen, and observe that characteristically they are loose, doctrinaire, and invective. When Professor E. H. Sutherland launched the term, it was applied to those individuals of upper socioeconomic class who violate the criminal law, usually by breach of trust, in the ordinary course of their business activities. This original usage accords with legal ideas of crime and points moreover to the significant and difficult problems of enforcement in the areas of business crimes, particularly where those violations are made criminal by recent statutory enactment. From this fruitful beginning the term has spread into vacuity, wide and handsome. We learn that the white collar criminal may be the suave and deceptive merchant prince or "robber baron," that the existence of such crime may be determined readily "in casual conversation with a representative of an occupation by asking him, 'What crooked practices are found in your occupation?' "

Confusion grows as we learn from another proponent of this concept that, "There are various phases of white-collar criminality that touch the lives of the common man almost daily. The large majority of them are operating within the letter and spirit of the law. . ." and that "In short, greed, not need, lies at the basis of white-collar crimes." Apparently the criminal may be law obedient but greedy; the specific quality of his crimes is far from clear.

Another avenue is taken in Professor Sutherland's more recent definition of crime as a "legal description of an act as socially injurious and legal provision of penalty for the act."

Here he has deemed the connotation of his term too narrow if confined to violations of the criminal code; he includes by a slight modification conduct violative of any law, civil or criminal, when it is "socially injurious."

In light of these definitions, the normative issue is pointed. Who should be considered the white collar criminal? Is it the merchant who, out of greed, business acumen, or competitive motivations, breaches a trust with his consumer by "puffing his wares" beyond their merits, by pricing them beyond their value, or by ordinary advertising? Is it he who breaks trust with his employees in order to keep wages down, refusing to permit labor organization or to bargain collectively, and who is found guilty by a labor relations board of an unfair labor practice? May it be the white collar worker who breaches trust with his employers by inefficient performance at work, by sympathetic strike or secondary boycott? Or is it the merchandiser who violates ethics by undercutting the prices of his fellow merchants? In general these acts do not violate the criminal law. All in some manner breach a trust for motives which a criminologist may (or may not) disapprove for one reason or another. All are within the framework of the norms of ordinary business practice. One seeks in vain for criteria to determine this white collar criminality. It is the conduct of one who wears a white collar and who indulges in occupational behavior to which some particular criminologist takes exception. It may easily be a term of propaganda. For purposes of empirical research or objective description, what is it?

Whether criminology aspires one day to become a science or a repository of reasonably accurate descriptive information, it cannot tolerate a nomenclature of such loose and variable usage. A special hazard exists in the employment of the term, "white collar criminal," in that it invites individual systems of private values to run riot in an area (economic ethics) where gross variation exists among criminologists as well as others. The rebel may enjoy a veritable orgy of delight in damning as criminal most anyone he pleases; one imagines that some experts would thus consign to the criminal classes any successful capitalistic business man; the reactionary or conservative, complacently viewing the occupational practices of the business world might find all in perfect order in this best of all possible worlds. The result may be fine indoctrination or catharsis achieved through blustering broadsides against the "existing system." It is not criminology. It is not social science. The terms "unfair," "infringement," "discrimination," "injury to society," and so on, employed by the white collar criminologists cannot, taken alone, differentiate criminal and non-criminal. Until refined to mean certain specific actions, they are merely epithets.

Vague, omnibus concepts defining crime are a blight upon either a legal system or a system of sociology that strives to be objective. They allow judge, administrator, or—conceivably—sociologist, in an undirected, freely operating discretion, to attribute the status "criminal" to any individual or class which he conceives nefarious. This can accomplish no desirable objective, either politically or sociologically.

Worse than futile, it is courting disaster, political, economic, and social, to promulgate a system of justice in which the individual may be held criminal without having committed a crime, defined with some precision by statute and case law. To describe crime the sociologist, like the lawyer-legislator, must do more than condemn conduct deviation in the abstract. He must avoid definitions predicated simply upon state of mind or social injury and determine what particular types of deviation, in what directions, and to what degree, shall be considered criminal. This is exactly what the criminal code today attempts to do, though imperfectly of course. More slowly and conservatively than many of us would wish: that is in the nature of legal institutions, as it is in other social institutions as well. But law has defined with greater clarity and precision the conduct which is criminal than our anti-legalistic criminologists promise to do; it has moreover promoted a stability, a security and dependability of justice through its exactness, its so-called technicalities, and its moderation in inspecting proposals for change.

The Juristic View

Having considered the conceptions of an innovating sociology in ascribing the terms "crime" and "criminal," let us state here the juristic view: Only those are criminals who have been adjudicated as such by the courts. Crime is an intentional act in violation of the criminal law (statutory and case law), committed without defense or excuse, and penalized by the state as a felony or misdemeanor. In studying the offender there can be no presumption that arrested, arraigned, indicted, or prosecuted persons are criminals unless they also be held guilty beyond a reasonable doubt of a particular offense. Even less than the unconvicted suspect can those individuals be considered criminal who have violated no law. Only those are criminals who have been selected by a clear substantive and a careful adjective law, such as obtains in our courts. The unconvicted offenders of whom the criminologist may wish to take cognizance are an important but unselected group; it has no specific membership presently ascertainable. Sociologists may strive, as does the legal profession, to perfect measures for more complete and accurate ascertainment of offenders, but it is futile simply to rail against a machinery of justice which is, and to a large extent must inevitably remain, something less than entirely accurate or efficient.

Criminal behavior as here defined fits very nicely into the sociologists' formulations of social control. Here we find *norms* of conduct, comparable to the mores, but considerably more distinct, precise, and detailed, as they are fashioned through statutory and case law. The *agencies* of this control, like the norms themselves, are more formal than is true in other types of control: the law depends for its instrumentation chiefly upon police, prosecutors, judges, juries, and the support of a favorable public opinion. The law has for its *sanctions* the specifically enumerated punitive measures set up by the state for breach, penalties which are additional to any of the sanctions which society exerts informally against the violator of norms which may overlap with laws. *Crime* is itself simply the breach of the legal norm, a violation within this particular category of social control; the criminal is, of course, the individual who has committed such acts of breach.

Much ink has been spilled on the extent of deterrent efficacy of the criminal law in social control. This is a matter which is not subject to demonstration in any exact and measurable fashion, any more than one can conclusively demonstrate the efficiency of a moral norm. Certainly the degree of success in asserting a control, legal or moral, will vary with the particular norm itself, its instrumentation, the subject individuals, the time, the place, and the sanctions. The efficiency of legal control is sometimes confused by the fact that, in the common overlapping of crimes (particularly those *mala in se*) with moral standards, the norms and sanctions of each may operate in mutual support to produce conformity. Moreover, mere breach of norm is no evidence of the general failure of a social control system, but indication rather of the need for control. Thus the occurrence of theft and homicide does not mean that the law is ineffective, for one cannot tell how frequently such acts might occur in the absence of law and penal sanction. Where such acts are avoided, one may not appraise the relative efficacy of law and mores in prevention. When they occur, one cannot apportion blame, either in the individual case or in general, to failures of the legal and moral systems. The individual in society does undoubtedly conduct himself in reference to legal requirements. Living "beyond the law" has a quality independent of being non-conventional, immoral, sinful. Mr. Justice Holmes has shown that the "bad man of the law"—those who become our criminals—are motivated in part by disrespect for the law or, at the least, are inadequately restrained by its taboos.

From introspection and from objective analysis of criminal histories one can not but accept as axiomatic the thesis that the norms of criminal law and its sanctions do exert some measure of effective control over human behavior; that this control is increased by moral, conventional, and traditional norms; and that the effectiveness of control norms is variable. It seems a fair inference from urban investigations that in our contemporary mass society, the legal system is becoming increasingly important in constraining behavior as primary group norms and sanctions deteriorate. Criminal law, crime, and the criminal become more significant subjects of sociological inquiry, therefore, as we strive to describe, understand, and control the uniformities and variability in culture.

We consider that the "white collar criminal," the violator of conduct norms, and the anti-social personality are not criminal in any sense meaningful to the social scientist unless he has violated a criminal statute. We cannot know him as such

34

unless he has been properly convicted. He may be a boor, a sinner, a moral leper, or the devil incarnate, but he does not become a criminal through sociological name-calling unless politically constituted authority says he is. It is footless for the sociologist to confuse issues of definition, normation, etiology, sanction, agency and social effects by saying one thing and meaning another.

Conclusion

To conclude, we reiterate and defend the contention that crime, as legally defined, is a sociologically significant province of study. The view that it is not appears to be based upon either of two premises: 1. that offenders convicted under the criminal law are not representative of all criminals and 2. that criminal law violation (and, therefore, the criminal himself) is not significant to the sociologist because it is composed of a set of legal, non-sociological categories irrelevant to the understanding of group behavior and/or social control. Through these contentions to invalidate the traditional and legal frame of reference adopted by the criminologist, several considerations, briefly enumerated below, must be met.

    1. Convicted criminals as a sample of law violators:

    a. Adjudicated offenders represent the closest possible approximation to those who have in fact violated the law, carefully selected by the sieving of the due process of law; no other province of social control attempts to ascertain the breach of norms with such rigor and precision.

    b. It is as futile to contend that this group should not be studied on the grounds that it is incomplete or non-representative as it would be to maintain that psychology should terminate its description, analysis, diagnosis, and treatment of deviants who cannot be completely representative as selected. Convicted persons are nearly all criminals. They offer large and varied samples of all types; their origins, traits, dynamics of development, and treatment influences can be studied profitably for purposes of description, understanding, and control. To be sure, they are not necessarily representative of all offenders; if characteristics observed among them are imputed to law violators generally, it must be with the qualification implied by the selective processes of discovery and adjudication.

c. Convicted criminals are important as a sociological category, furthermore, in that they have been exposed and respond to the influences of court contact, official punitive treatment, and public stigma as convicts.

2. The relevance of violation of the criminal law:

a. The criminal law establishes substantive norms of behavior, standards more clear cut, specific, and detailed than the norms in any other category of social controls.

b. The behavior prohibited has been considered significantly in derogation of group welfare by deliberative and representative assembly, formally constituted for the purpose of establishing such norms; nowhere else in the field of social control is there directed a comparable rational effort to elaborate standards conforming to the predominant needs, desires, and interests of the community.

c. There are legislative and juridical lags which reduce the social value of the legal norms; as an important characteristic of law, such lag does not reduce the relevance of law as a province of sociological inquiry. From a detached sociological view, the significant thing is not the absolute goodness or badness of the norms but the fact that these norms do control behavior. The sociologist is interested in the results of such control, the correlates of violation, and in the lags themselves.

d. Upon breach of these legal (and social) norms, the refractory are treated officially in punitive and/or rehabilitative ways, not for being generally anti-social, immoral, unconventional, or bad, but for violation of the specific legal norms of control.

e. Law becomes the peculiarly important and ultimate pressure toward conformity to minimum standards of conduct deemed essential to group welfare as other systems of norms and mechanics of control deteriorate.

f. Criminals, therefore, are a sociologically distinct group of violators of specific legal norms, subjected to official state treatment. They and the non-criminals respond, though differentially of course, to the standards, threats, and correctional devices established in this system of social control.

g. The norms, their violation, the mechanics of dealing with breach constitute major provinces of legal sociology. They are basic to the theoretical framework of sociological criminology.

Criminologists Should Study Social Conditions

HERMAN AND JULIA SCHWENDINGER

There have been many recent attempts to broaden the boundaries of criminology beyond the traditional concerns of
conservatives and liberals. The areas most often targeted for
expansion are victimization and concerns for various human
rights violations. The statement by the Schwendingers reproduced here was one of the first declaring solidarity with the
oppressed whose rights and needs may be violated by the
political state. Those who make the law may structure law
and justice to satisfy demands for power and control.
According to the Schwendingers, in this kind of situation
criminology has the responsibility to uncover the criminality
of social systems and political states. Violations of human
rights such as imperialism, war, racism, sexism, and poverty
can be, and should be, analyzed as crimes against humanity.
Criminologists should use their research and theorizing to
join the battle against oppression and inhumanity wherever
they find it. According to the Schwendingers, legalistic definitions of the subject matter of criminology, such as that argued
for by Tappan, interfere with responsibilities of criminologists

From Herman and Julia Schwendinger, "Defenders of Order or Guardians of
Human Rights?" In *Critical Criminology*, Ian Taylor, Paul Walton, and Jock
Young, eds. London: Routledge & Kegan Paul, 1975. Reprinted by permission
of the publisher.

to examine human rights violations and to call for their redress. Herman and Julia Schwendinger are criminologists and sociologists on the faculty of the State University of New York at New Paltz. They pioneered the development of "critical criminology," a type of criminology which looks critically at social conditions related to crime and criminality.

QUESTIONS

1. What moral issues are involved in the way that our society defines the crime problem, according to the authors?
2. Do the authors think that it makes sense to define social systems as criminal or do they think that only individuals can be criminal? Why or why not?
3. According to the authors, in defining the problem of crime, does it make sense to assess the amount of "social injury" caused, whether or not it has been called a crime by the police and prosecutor? Explain.

■ ■ ■

There Are Criminal Social Systems

Perhaps there are no statements more repugnant to traditional legal scholars than those which define social systems as criminal. But this repugnance reflects the antiquarian psychologistic and technocratic character of the legal tradition. This tradition is blind to the fact that extensive social planning makes it possible to evaluate, mitigate or eliminate the *social* conditions which generate criminal behaviour. It is no longer sufficient to justify the restriction of criminology to the study of those institutions which define, adjudicate and sanction *individual* criminals. It has become evident that any group which attempts to control or prevent criminal behaviour by the activity of the traditional institutions of criminal justice alone is incapable of accomplishing this end.

As a rule, criminal behaviour *does* involve individual moral responsibility and the assessment of psychological relationships, such as the motivated character of the criminal act.

However, the science of crime has gone beyond the centuries-old notion that crime can be conceived as a function of the properties of atomistic individuals alone. Social scientists today are intensely involved in scrutinizing social relationships which generate criminal behaviour. This activity is reflected in the *real definitions* of crime which have been and are being developed by sociologists, economists, anthropologists and political scientists. . . .

If crime is defined by scientists in terms of the *socially* necessary and sufficient conditions for its existence, what would be more logical than to call these social conditions criminal? After all, crime has been traditionally defined by legalists on the basis of nominalist definitions or descriptive definitions which refer to the ways in which agents of the State react to criminal behaviour. To be sure, some legalists have used ethical terms such as 'public wrongs' or 'social injury' in earmarking criminal behaviour. But isn't a real definition of crime vastly superior to a nominalist definition or a definition which does not even define crime but merely refers to how the State reacts to it? And isn't a scientist justified in making a logically implied, normative evaluation of what he considers to be the cause of crime? And given the acceptance of criminal institutions and social-economic relationships as real definers of crime, what more ultimate claim can social scientists use to justify their unique role as criminologists, than to use the term crime to identify social systems which can be regulated or eliminated in order to control or prevent crime? What better term than crime can be used to express their *normative* judgments of the conditions which generate criminal behaviour?

It can be argued that the term 'criminogenic' be used to designate the social conditions which cause crime. But this term obfuscates the main point being made here: that the *social conditions* themselves must become the *object* of social policy and that it is not an individual or a loose collection of atomistic individuals which is to be controlled, but rather the social relationships between individuals which give rise to criminal behaviour. (Even if we put everybody involved in criminal behaviour at any one time behind bars, there is no guarantee that a new generation of criminals would not emerge given the maintenance of social conditions which originally made these individuals criminal.) In this context, the term crime as a label for social systems becomes a warrant not for controlling atomistic individuals, or preventing an atomistic act, but rather for the regulation or elimination of social relationships, properties of social systems, or social systems taken as a whole.

Are Imperialistic War, Racism, Sexism and Poverty Crimes?

Once human rights rather than legally operative definitions are used to earmark criminal behaviour, then it is possible to ask whether there are violations of human rights which are more basic than others and to designate these rights as most relevant to the domain of criminology. Basic rights are differentiated because their fulfillment is absolutely essential to the realization of a great number of values. Although the lower boundary of this number is not specified here, the sense of what is meant can be ascertained by considering security to one's person as a basic right. Obviously a danger to one's health or life itself endangers all other claims. A dead man can hardly realize *any* of his human potentialities.

Similar assessments can be made of the right to racial, sexual and economic equality. The abrogation of these rights certainly limits the individual's chance to fulfill himself in many spheres of life. These rights, therefore, are basic because there is so much at stake in their fulfillment. It can be stated, in the light of the previous argument, that individuals who deny these rights to others are criminal. Likewise, social relationships and social systems which regularly cause the abrogation of these rights are also criminal. If the terms imperialism, racism, sexism and poverty are abbreviated signs for theories of social relationships or social systems which cause the systematic abrogation of basic rights, then imperialism, racism, sexism and poverty can be called crimes according to the logic of our argument.

It is totally irrelevant, in this light, to consider whether leaders of imperialist nations are war-criminals by virtue of legal precedent or decisions by war-tribunals. Nor is it relevant to make note of the fact that property rights which underlie racist practices are guaranteed by law. It is likewise unimportant that sexual inequality in such professions as sociology is maintained by references to the weight of tradition. Neither can persistent unemployment be excused because it is ostensibly beyond the control of the State. What is important is that hundreds of thousands of Indo-Chinese persons are being denied their right to live; millions of black people are subjected to inhuman conditions which, on the average, deny them ten years of life; the majority of the human beings of this planet are subjected because of their sex; and an even greater number throughout the world are deprived of the commodities and services which are theirs by right. And no social system which systematically abrogates these rights is justifiable.

Is there wonder why we have raised questions about the legalistic definitions of crime when the magnitude of 'social injury' caused by imperialism, racism, sexism and poverty is compared to that wrought by individual acts which the State legally defines as crimes? Isn't it time to raise serious questions about the assumptions underlying the definition of the field of criminology, when a man who steals a paltry sum can be called a criminal while agents of the State can, with impunity, legally reward men who destroy food so that price levels can be maintained whilst a sizable portion of the population suffers from malnutrition. The USA is confronted with a grave moral crisis which is reflected above all in the technocratic 'benign neglect' shown in the unwillingness to recognize the criminal character of great social injuries inflicted on heretofore powerless people, merely because these injuries are not defined in the legal codes.

Modern Libertarian Standards

The limits of this viewpoint do not permit the detailing of operating standards which might be useful for earmarking the kinds of behaviour which should be of central interest to criminologists, but neither these standards, nor the notion of basic human rights itself, are more difficult to define than the operating standards and notions underlying legal conceptions of 'social injury' or 'public wrong'. The solution to this problem is also no less political. Indeed, it is time to recognize that all of the above concepts are brought to light and operationalized by the political struggles of our time. . . .

What is certain is that the legalistic definitions cannot be justified as long as they make the activity of criminologists subservient to the State. It is suggested that an alternative solution can be developed which is based on some of the traditional notions of crime as well as notions organized around the concept of egalitarianism. In this process of redefining crime, criminologists will redefine themselves, no longer to be the defenders of order but rather the guardians of human rights. In reconstructing their standards, they should make man, not institutions, the measure of all things.

Criminologists Should Study White Collar Crime

EDWIN H. SUTHERLAND

In this classic statement, first published in 1940, Edwin
Sutherland set a precedent that has influenced criminology to
this day. He created an emphasis within criminology on the
study of white collar crimes, which are usually committed by
those in positions of trust and power. In the process of docu-
menting the damage done by corporate and political crime,
Sutherland made the point that white collar crime does a lot
more financial harm to society than does common "street
crime." White collar, or corporate, crime can also cause more
injuries and deaths each year than street crimes. This point
has been documented in subsequent decades by other criminologists. Another point first made by Sutherland and often
repeated by other criminologists is that there is a separate
system for handling crimes of the upper classes. White collar
criminals are not regarded as real criminals by themselves, by

Edwin H. Sutherland, "White-Collar Criminality," *American Sociological Review*
5 (1940): 3-10.

the general public, by many in the criminal justice system, or by many criminologists. Since Sutherland first created the study of white collar crime, there has been a great deal of speculation in criminology about whether theories of crime meant to explain crimes of the lower classes can also explain crimes of the upper classes. Edwin Sutherland is generally considered the father of modern American sociological criminology and the American criminologist who made the greatest lasting contributions to the field of criminology.

QUESTIONS

1. How does Sutherland define white collar criminality?
2. Does Sutherland argue for going beyond the legalistic definition of crime favored by Tappan?
3. How should the study of white collar criminality influence our theories of criminal behavior, according to Sutherland?

■ ■ ■

Crime is in fact not closely correlated with poverty or with the psychopathic and sociopathic conditions associated with poverty, and an adequate explanation of criminal behavior must proceed along quite different lines. The conventional explanations are invalid principally because they are derived from biased samples. The samples are biased in that they have not included vast areas of criminal behavior of persons not in the lower class. One of these neglected areas is the criminal behavior of business and professional men, which will be analyzed in this paper.

The "robber barons" of the last half of the nineteenth century were white-collar criminals, as practically everyone now agrees. Their attitudes are illustrated by these statements: Colonel Vanderbilt asked, "You don't suppose you can run a railroad in accordance with the statutes, do you?" A. B. Stickney, a railroad president, said to sixteen other railroad presidents in the home of J. P. Morgan in 1890, "I have the utmost respect for you gentlemen, individually, but as railroad presidents I wouldn't trust you with my watch out of my sight." Charles Francis Adams said, "The difficulty in railroad management . . . lies in the covetousness, want of good faith, and low moral tone of railway managers, in the complete absence of any high standard of commercial honesty."

The present-day white-collar criminals are more suave and deceptive than the "robber barons.". . . Their criminality has been demonstrated again and again in the investigations of land offices, railways, insurance, munitions, banking, public utilities, stock exchanges, the oil industry, real estate, reorganization committees, receiverships, bankruptcies, and politics. Individual cases of such criminality are reported frequently, and in many periods more important crime news may be found on the financial pages of newspapers than on the front pages. White-collar criminality is found in every occupation, as can be discovered readily in casual conversation with a representative of an occupation by asking him, "What crooked practices are found in your occupation?"

White-collar criminality in business is expressed most frequently in the form of misrepresentation in financial statements of corporations, manipulation in the stock exchange, commercial bribery, bribery of public officials directly or indirectly in order to secure favorable contracts and legislation, misrepresentation in advertising and salesmanship, embezzlement and misapplication of funds, short weights and measures and misgrading of commodities, tax frauds, misapplication of funds in receiverships and bankruptcies. These are what Al Capone called "the legitimate rackets." These and many others are found in abundance in the business world.

In the medical profession, which is here used as an example because it is probably less criminalistic than some other professions, are found illegal sale of alcohol and narcotics, abortion, illegal services to underworld criminals, fraudulent reports and testimony in accident cases, extreme cases of unnecessary treatment, fake specialists, restriction of competition, and fee-splitting. Fee-splitting is a violation of a specific law in many states and a violation of the conditions of admission to the practice of medicine in all. The physician who participates in fee-splitting tends to send his patients to the surgeon who will give him the largest fee rather than to the surgeon who will do the best work. It has been reported that two thirds of the surgeons in New York City split fees, and that more than one half of the physicians in a central western city who answered a questionnaire on this point favored fee-splitting.

These varied types of white-collar crimes in business and the professions consist principally of violation of delegated or implied trust, and many of them can be reduced to two categories: misrepresentation of asset values and duplicity in the manipulation of power. The first is approximately the same as fraud or swindling; the second is similar to the double-cross. The latter is illustrated by the corporation director who, acting on inside information, purchases land which the corporation will need and sells it at a fantastic profit to his corporation. The principle of this duplicity is that the offender holds two antagonistic positions, one of which is a position of trust, which is violated, generally by misapplication of funds, in the interest of the other position. A football coach, permitted to referee a game in which his own team was playing, would illustrate this antagonism of positions. Such situations cannot be completely avoided in a complicated business structure, but many concerns make a practice of assuming such antagonistic functions and regularly violating the trust thus delegated to them. When compelled by law to make a separation of their functions, they make a nominal separation and continue by subterfuge to maintain the two positions.

An accurate statistical comparison of the crimes of the two classes is not available. The most extensive evidence regarding the nature and prevalence of white-collar criminality is found in the reports of the larger investigations to which reference was made. . . .

White-collar criminality in politics, which is generally recognized as fairly prevalent, has been used by some as a rough gauge by which to measure white-collar criminality in business. James A. Farley said, "The standards of conduct are as high among officeholders and politicians as they are in commercial life," and William Cermak, while mayor of Chicago, said, "There is less graft in politics than in business." John Flynn wrote, "The average politician is the merest amateur in the gentle art of graft, compared with his brother in the field of business." And Walter Lippmann wrote, "Poor as they are, the standards of public life are so much more social than those of business that financiers who enter politics regard themselves as philanthropists."

These statements obviously do not give a precise measurement of the relative criminality of the white-collar class, but they are adequate evidence that crime is not so highly concentrated in the lower class as the usual statistics indicate. Also, these statements obviously do not mean that every business and professional man is a criminal, just as the usual theories do not mean that every man in the lower class is a criminal. On the other hand, the preceding statements refer in many cases to the leading corporations in America and are not restricted to the disreputable business and professional men who are called quacks, ambulance chasers, bucket-shop operators, deadbeats, and fly-by-night swindlers.

Financial Costs

The financial cost of white-collar crime is probably several times as great as the financial cost of all the crimes which are customarily regarded as the "crime problem.". . .

The financial loss from white-collar crime, great as it is, is less important than the damage to social relations. White-collar crimes violate trust and therefore create distrust, which lowers social morale and produces social disorganization on a large scale. Other crimes produce relatively little effect on social institutions or social organization.

White-collar crime is real crime. It is not ordinarily called crime, and calling it by this name does not make it worse, just as refraining from calling it crime does not make it better than it otherwise would be. It is called crime here in order to bring it within the scope of criminology, which is justified because it is in violation of the criminal law. The crucial question in this analysis is the criterion of violation of the criminal law. Conviction in the criminal court, which is sometimes suggested as the criterion, is not adequate because a large proportion of those who commit crimes are not convicted in criminal courts. This criterion, therefore, needs to be supplemented. When it is supplemented, the criterion of the crimes of one class must be kept consistent in general terms with the criterion of the crimes of the other class. The definition should not be the spirit of the law for white-collar crimes and the letter of the law for other crimes, or in other respects be more liberal for one class than for the other. Since this discussion is concerned with the conventional theories of the criminologists, the criterion of white-collar crime must be justified in terms of the procedures of those criminologists in dealing with other crimes. The criterion of white-collar crimes, as here proposed, supplements convictions in the criminal courts in four respects, in each of which the extension is justified because the criminologists who present the conventional theories of criminal behavior make the same extension in principle.

Defining White-Collar Crime

First, other agencies than the criminal court must be included, for the criminal court is not the only agency which makes official decisions regarding violations of the criminal law. The juvenile court, dealing largely with offenses of the children of the poor, in many states is not under the criminal jurisdiction. The criminologists have made much use of case histories and statistics of juvenile delinquents in constructing their theories of criminal behavior. This justifies the inclusion of agencies other than the criminal court which deal with white-collar offenses. The most important of these agencies are the administrative boards, bureaus, or commissions, and much of their work, although certainly not all, consists of cases which are in violation of the criminal law. The Federal Trade Commission ordered several automobile companies to stop advertising their interest rate on installment purchases as 6 percent, since it was actually 11 1/2 percent. Also it filed complaint against *Good Housekeeping*, one of the Hearst publications, charging that its seals led the public to believe that all products bearing those seals had been tested in their laboratories, which was contrary to fact. Each of these involves a charge of dishonesty, which might have been tried in a criminal court as fraud. A large proportion of the cases before these boards should be included in the data of the criminologists. Failure to do so is a principal reason for the bias in their samples and the errors in their generalizations.

Second, for both classes, behavior which would have a reasonable expectancy of conviction if tried in a criminal court or substitute agency should be defined as criminal. In this respect, convictability rather than actual conviction should be the criterion of criminality. The criminologists would not hesitate to accept as data a verified case history of a person who was a criminal but had never been convicted. Similarly, it is justifiable to include white-collar criminals who have not been convicted, provided reliable evidence is available. Evidence regarding such cases appears in many civil suits, such as stockholders' suits and patent-infringement suits. These cases might have been referred to the criminal court but they were referred to the civil court because the injured party was more interested in securing damages than in seeing punishment inflicted. This also happens in embezzlement cases, regarding which surety companies have much evidence. In a short consecutive series of embezzlements known to a surety company, 90 percent were not prosecuted because prosecution would interfere with restitution or salvage. The evidence in cases of embezzlement is generally conclusive, and would probably have been sufficient to justify conviction in all of the cases in this series.

Third, behavior should be defined as criminal if conviction is avoided merely because of pressure which is brought to bear on the court or substitute agency. Gangsters and racketeers have been relatively immune in many cities because of their pressure on prospective witnesses and public officials, and professional thieves, such as pickpockets and confidence men who do not use strong-arm methods, are even more frequently immune. The conventional criminologists do not hesitate to include the life histories of such criminals as data, because they understand the generic relation of the pressures to the failure to convict. Similarly, white-collar criminals are relatively immune because of the class bias of the courts and the power of their class to influence the implementation and administration of the law. This class bias affects not merely present-day courts but to a much greater degree affected the earlier courts which established the precedents and rules of procedure of the present-day courts. Consequently, it is justifiable to interpret the actual or potential failures of conviction in the light of known facts regarding the pressures brought to bear on the agencies which deal with offenders.

Fourth, persons who are accessory to a crime should be included among white-collar criminals as they are among other criminals. When the Federal Bureau of Investigation deals with a case of kidnapping, it is not content with catching the offenders who carried away the victim; they may catch and the court may convict twenty-five other persons who assisted by secreting the victim, negotiating the ransom, or putting the ransom money into circulation. On the other hand, the prosecution of white-collar criminals frequently stops with one offender. Political graft almost always involves collusion between politicians and business men but prosecutions are generally limited to the politicians. Judge Manton was found guilty of accepting $664,000 in bribes, but the six or eight important commercial concerns that paid the bribes have not been prosecuted. James Pendergast, the late boss of Kansas City, was convicted for failure to report as a part of his income $315,000 received in bribes from insurance companies but the insurance companies which paid the bribes have not been prosecuted. In an investigation of an embezzlement by the president of a bank, at least a dozen other violations of law which were related to this embezzlement and involved most of the other officers of the bank and the officers of the clearing house were discovered but none of the others was prosecuted.

This analysis of the criterion of white-collar criminality results in the conclusion that a description of white-collar criminality in general terms will be also a description of the criminality of the lower class. The respects in which the crimes of the two classes differ are the incidentals rather than the essentials of criminality. They differ principally in the implementation of the criminal laws which apply to them. The crimes of the lower class are handled by policemen, prosecutors, and judges, with penal sanctions in the form of fines, imprisonment, and death. The crimes of the upper class either result in no official action at all, or result in suits for damages in civil courts, or are handled by inspectors, and by administrative boards or commissions, with penal sanctions in the form of warnings, orders to cease and desist, occasionally the loss of a license, and only in extreme cases by fines or prison sentences. Thus, the white-collar criminals are segregated administratively from other criminals, and largely as a consequence of this are not regarded as real criminals by themselves, the general public, or the criminologists.

This difference in the implementation of the criminal law is due principally to the difference in the social position of the two types of offenders. . . . The statement of Daniel Drew, a pious old fraud, describes the criminal law with some accuracy:

> Law is like a cobweb; it's made for flies and the smaller kinds of insects, so to speak, but lets the big bumblebees break through. When technicalities of the law stood in my way, I have always been able to brush them aside easy as anything.

What Is Criminal?

The preceding analysis should be regarded neither as an assertion that all efforts to influence legislation and its administration are reprehensible nor as a particularistic interpretation of the criminal law. It means only that the upper class has greater influence in moulding the criminal law and its administration to its own interests than does the lower class. The privileged position of white-collar criminals before the law results to a slight extent from bribery and political pressures, principally from the respect in which they are held and without special effort on their part. The most powerful group in medieval society secured relative immunity by "benefit of clergy," and now our most powerful groups secure relative immunity by "benefit of business or profession.". . .

The theory that criminal behavior in general is due either to poverty or to the psychopathic and sociopathic conditions associated with poverty can now be shown to be invalid for three reasons. First, the generalization is based on a biased sample which omits almost entirely the behavior of white-collar criminals. The criminologists have restricted their data, for reasons of convenience and ignorance rather than of principle, largely to cases dealt with in criminal courts and juvenile courts, and these agencies are used principally for criminals from the lower economic strata. Consequently, their data are grossly biased from the point of view of the economic status of criminals and their generalization that criminality is closely associated with poverty is not justified.

Second, the generalization that criminality is closely associated with poverty obviously does not apply to white-collar criminals. With a small number of exceptions, they are not in poverty, were not reared in slums or badly deteriorated families, and are not feebleminded or psychopathic. They were seldom problem children in their earlier years and did not appear in juvenile courts or child guidance clinics. The proposition, derived from the data used by the conventional criminologists, that "the criminal of today was the problem child of yesterday" is seldom true of white-collar criminals. The idea that the causes of criminality are to be found almost exclusively in childhood similarly is fallacious. Even if poverty is extended to include the economic stresses which afflict business in a period of depression, it is not closely correlated with white-collar criminality. Probably at no time within fifty years have white-collar crimes in the field of investments and of corporate management been so extensive as during the boom period of the twenties.

Third, the conventional theories do not even explain lower class criminality. The sociopathic and psychopathic factors which have been emphasized doubtless have something to do with crime causation, but these factors have not been related to a general process which is found both in white-collar criminality and lower class criminality and therefore they do not explain the criminality of either class. They may explain the manner or method of crime—why lower class criminals commit burglary or robbery—rather than false pretenses.

Criminologists Must Broaden Their Field of Study Beyond Crime and Criminals

CLIFFORD D. SHEARING

This viewpoint indicates that efforts to study crime and disorder often go beyond official crime and crime control. Shearing gives us the example of studying policing. This naturally leads us into a study of various efforts to maintain order in the community, going beyond the realm of public police forces and into the province of citizen action and private policing. Shearing maintains that conflicts over social order define the types of activities of interest to criminology. Struggles to define what is considered a disruption of social order, who will be defined as a troublemaker, and how they will be dealt with, are all issues of interest to the criminologist.

A concern with these issues takes the criminologist beyond officially defined crime and beyond the activities of official justice agencies. Criminologists who "follow their noses" and investigate disruptions of order, those who cause them, and those who try to restore order in the community often go well beyond those concerns which were traditionally defined as part of criminology. Criminology, he contends, has always been about ordering and the struggles over social order. Not everyone has recognized this fact, however, and this can limit the positive advance of the field of criminology in the future. Clifford Shearing is a faculty member and researcher at the Centre of Criminology, University of Toronto.

QUESTIONS

1. Does Shearing want to throw out or to incorporate the legalistic definition of criminology advocated by Tappan?
2. Would this definition of criminology include a study of the activities of the criminal justice system?
3. Would the conflicts and struggles over defining crime and criminality discussed by the Schwendingers and by Sutherland be included in Shearing's definition of criminology? Why or why not?

■ ■ ■

Is [criminology] a discipline in its own right? Is it a sub-field of another discipline, such as sociology or law? Should it be viewed as a field of inquiry to be tackled from the perspective of a variety of disciplines (sociology, law, history, political science, economics, psychology, etc.)?

These are questions of consequence as the answers to them have had a major influence on how criminology is studied and taught. . . .

My concern is with the very definition of this subject matter; with what it is that criminologists should be studying. Underlying the debate about the proper location of criminology within the social sciences is an implicit agreement about its subject matter. Criminology is about crime, the people who do it, the reasons why they do it, ways of stopping them from doing it and responses to it. Criminologists on both sides of the above divide [some arguing that criminology is a discipline and others viewing it as a focus of study for other disciplines] would agree that if one is studying one or other of the above phenomena then one is doing criminology and if one is not then one is doing something else. That criminology is a crime-ology is, most criminologists would agree, so obvious and elementary that it is not even worth discussing.

The conventional view of criminology's subject matter arises out of, and reflects two views of the social world, a Durkheimian view that sees the social reality as made up of objects, much like physical things, and an interactionist view which sees the social reality as essentially symbolic and made up of objects that are quite unlike physical things because they are constructed out of meanings. Both agree that social reality is fundamentally a reality of objects though they disagree about their ontological status. While this difference leads to conflicts at an epistemological level over how they should be studied they agree that criminology should study particular sorts of things, namely, crime related things.

In this view crime-ology is akin to something like apple-ology or perhaps fruit-ology and the argument about the place of crime-ology in the university may be compared to a debate over whether apple-ology is a sub-discipline of biology or should benefit from the insights of other disciplines as well, for instance, physics and chemistry.

The idea that there is an enterprise of crime-ology has become a bit of a thorn in my flesh. The problem is that as soon as I get involved in some issue within crime-ology my inquiry sooner or later leads me away from crime. I am not alone in this. It is not difficult, for example, to start thinking about crime, move to public policing, then find oneself examining private policing and end up studying the way the capital requirements of financial markets are established and regulated. All these topics share a family resemblance to one another but it is not at all clear to me, or to others, whether it makes much sense to call what is being studied crime-ology.

For the increasing number of us whose scholarship leads us away from crime-ology, this creates a few bureaucratic problems as people (most significantly university administrators and those who hold the research purse strings) begin to wonder why we are not doing crime-ology. These problems, unfortunately, are seldom very serious and inventive bureaucratic ploys can usually be developed to cope with them. However, this tendency does raise serious questions about the nature of criminology as a theoretically fruitful endeavor. If the pursuit of questions within a field constantly leads one beyond its boundaries, this suggests, to me at least, that something must be very wrong. Surely the boundaries of criminology should facilitate, not hamper, the development of ideas within it.

This problem is not solved by calling oneself a sociologist or a political scientist. The problem doesn't have to do with the perspective being used, or the lack thereof. The problem has to do with the way the topic of study is identified. The problem is that, whatever it is that unifies the topic, the family resemblance noted earlier, it is not crime.

One obvious response is that this is just a terminological problem about which it is not worth worrying. It is a terminological problem but it is also one well worth consideration. It is worth worrying about because the term "criminology," when read as crime-ology, focuses attention on an object "crime" that restricts rather than encourages inquiry.

When we think of ourselves as crime-ologists, we structure the way we see and approach the world and our study of it in a way that limits the theoretical potential of our enterprise. Crime is not a category that is theoretically central but rather one that is politically central. By defining ourselves as crime-ologists, we place ourselves squarely within a political, policy-oriented framework. Many people have made this point about criminology and one needs to look no further than at the conceptual debates that take place within criminology to see how true this is. In Britain, for example, a topical current debate is the self critique of the one-time "left idealists," now "left realists," who criticize the political naïveté of their former selves and use this as a stepping stone to develop a new political strategy for confronting the law and order politics of Margaret Thatcher. In the process, they heap scorn on the ends and motives of the conservative right realists who do "administrative criminology" which furthers bourgeois interests.

All scientific scholarship has its roots in practical matters, be it building bridges or deciding who to banish as undesirable and the knowledge it produces can be, and is, used to inform such questions. While scholarly endeavors are grounded in pragmatic concerns, and speak to them, if they are to grow and expand they should develop internally driven agendas and boundaries that lead them beyond the practical questions that gave rise to them. Without such autonomy they become stunted, their usefulness in practice is diminished, and they have difficulty reaching their potential either as theoretical systems or as problem solving devices. Scholarly autonomy permits a degree of inner directedness that is necessary for the paradigmatic leaps necessary for the growth that will give rise to new pragmatic implications. This piece of conventional scientific wisdom is central to the very idea of a university and is reflected in concepts like academic freedom, which promote scholarly independence from the pragmatic political concerns that govern most other spheres of social life.

Despite its commonplace character, this insight does not receive recognition amongst criminologists. In placing ourselves within institutional settings that assume we are engaged in crime-ology, we have remained very close to our pragmatic roots. So much so that much of the current research and thinking in criminology could just as well be done within think-tanks set up by political parties to develop policy and advance the interests of their constituents.

Nonetheless, there is evidence that the concern I have raised is widespread. "Criminologists" now publish in journals with titles such as "Law and Society" and work in Departments and Centres like Albany's School of Criminal Justice and Edinburgh's Centre for Criminology and the Social and Philosophical Study of Law. Such coping strategies, however, simply exchange one narrow set of boundaries for another. A focus on criminal justice directs attention away from a whole set of legitimate questions that are part of a crime focused criminology, while adding an *et cetera* clause to the term criminology does little to improve matters either.

So what can, and should, be done to broaden the scope of the field? If what we need to do is to make room for the actual research and thinking innovative scholarship requires, it makes sense to adopt an empirical approach and look at where scholarship, that started with crime, has in fact led.

In order to do so let me draw on my own experience. Like

many criminologists of my generation I began my scholarly life under the influence of labeling and subsequently the phenomenological perspective. One of the things this led me to do was to focus my research attention on the public police as an institution that responded to crime, or, more radically, constructed crime by responding to "trouble" of various sorts. While, at the time, this was not conventional criminology, the link to crime was quite apparent: police activity could be considered as either anti-crime or crime-making depending on how one viewed the relationship between crime and social reaction. Then I began to notice that there were a lot of people around who behaved like public police in all sorts of ways and responded to many of the same troubles but did not wear signs announcing themselves as POLICE and were not part of "the criminal justice system." As there were a lot of these people around I thought it would be silly for anyone interested in policing to ignore them. So I looked at these "private security" people. One of the first things I discovered was that not only were they not part of the criminal justice system but very often they had nothing whatsoever to do with it; they didn't constitute crime or criminals. They didn't even use the word "crime." But this wasn't the worst of it. The policing private security persons did was often done by non-specialists so that to examine it one had to look at accountants, clerks, parking attendants and the like. It was even difficult to see this policing as law related without adopting an expanded version of law in which nothing exists outside of law. By this time, policing looked like nothing that could reasonably be thought of as crime-ology. Of course, a little reflection makes clear that it is difficult to think of any policing as crime focused given what we know about what the public police spend their time doing.

What does this mean? Should we conclude that private policing is not a legitimate topic of criminology because it does not deal with crime, anti-crime or the making of crime in any traditional sense, because it is not part of the criminal justice system and because it is law related only in the most general sense? If we accept a crime focused definition of criminology the answer must be, yes. But to accept this would be to deny the very autonomy, I have argued, criminology requires.

By examining private policing we establish a broader framework for thinking about policing. The usefulness of such a framework becomes apparent immediately one studies the history of the public police. When one does so, one soon finds that one runs out of modern police as we know them and, not much later, out of criminal justice as well. However, one does not run out of policing.

What about a broader definition? Yes, but what would this be? How could we locate, and give unity to, an enterprise that included policing in this broad sense and would include the study of crime in a traditional sense?

The example I have chosen to make my point provides some help in pointing to the source of the problem and suggesting a new direction. What gets us into trouble is the way we go about carving up the criminological world. Despite our claims to have moved beyond Durkheim (labeling, phenomenology, Marxism, etc.), we still see our discipline in a fundamentally Durkheimian way. We see our field of inquiry as a terrain populated with things/objects. The question we ask when we look to establish boundaries is, "What things constitute the proper domain of criminology?" It is this question, and the way of seeing that generates it, that is the source of our trouble. Our fundamental phenomenon as the interactionists, and the phenomenologists, and the Marxists have been telling is the activity through which things are constituted. Our world is a constituted world at both the material and the symbolic level. As a constituted world it is constantly changing; what is constructed today can be deconstructed tomorrow; what was once constructive may no longer be constructed; and so on. By defining our field as a field of particular sorts of things, we accept an historically specific set of categories as the conceptual mainstays of our discipline. Consequently, as the social world changes around us or as we move back in time or examine other societies or categories, we become increasingly restrictive.

In a constituted world, as we now all should know, it is activity that is the fundamental phenomenon. If criminology is to identify a piece of this action as its special domain, then it must identify some segment of *activity* as its own, not one or more category of objects. This is precisely what many criminologists have done, and continue to do, when they follow their noses in the manner I have illustrated. What permits a move from public police to private security and beyond is a focus on policing, not police.

It is our failure to translate our theoretical insights and the practices they promote into a disciplinary definition that has produced the straight-jacket of crime-ology. It is because we have allowed ourselves, in our definition of our discipline, to remain so closely tied to the "natural attitude," that pervades practical, political and policy discourse, that we have created barriers, perhaps the appropriate metaphor would be a prison, that has stifled the development of our discipline. . . .

An examination of the things criminologists actually do makes clear that criminology is not about control but about social order, conceived of not simply as patterned activity but a guaranteed way of doing things, *and* the struggles that surround it. Ordering is not the same as controlling for order, is both more than and less than whatever it is that control accomplishes. I may control you and yet not be engaged in any sense in the production of order as both alternatives may be quite consistent with order. Similarly, you may resist me without undermining order.

The struggle over order, the activity that seeks to guarantee it and the activity that resists the realization of this guarantee, either in part or in whole, is the phenomenon that gives unity to criminological research and teaching. Ordering both includes crime-ology and goes beyond it in precisely the ways that work in our discipline in fact does; it thus provides exactly the elbow room necessary for theoretical development. A focus on the production and disruption of order identifies what is in every branch and school of social thought a central, perhaps even the definitive, social phenomenon as criminology's fundamental topic. In so doing, it at once recognizes why criminology is such a potentially fruitful field of inquiry and, at the same time, permits its realization by focusing attention on ordering as its central concern.

Does acceptance of the above mean that we have to find a new term that recognizes this focus? Do we have to adopt a strategy like that of a group within the Department of Criminology at the University of Ottawa in Canada who have called themselves a Group for the Study of the Production of Order? Fortunately, this is not necessary. Criminology can legitimately be read as more than crime-ology and indeed as having precisely the meaning the above argument requires. What is required is not a new term but an explicit and self-conscious recognized re-reading of the existing term so as to promote a broader enterprise that regards crime-ology as but one critical and historically important aspect of the whole.

There can be little doubt that criminology was initially intended to have a literal meaning. Its focus was clearly crime and this is what the term was meant to convey. This focus on crime was, however, simultaneously a focus on order and threats to it. Crime was relevant politically and theoretically because it was conceived of as the very embodiment of such a threat. One need only to read eighteenth century accounts of the state of urban order for evidence of this. Crime was a problem because order was a problem. Criminology was theoretically and politically relevant as a discipline because it studied this great threat to social order. As interest shifted from crime, and its sources, to the control of crime, it was still order that was the central topic; a topic that was approached through the study of the phenomenon most central to it—crime. Criminology, thus, has always been about ordering. What has changed, and what has created the definitional tension I have noted, has been the way order is conceived and the way it is resisted and supported. It is this change that necessitates a broadening of our conception to permit us to keep pace with the changing reality of ordering. . . .

What we forget, and what we need to forcefully remind ourselves of, is that it is not crime that is our central topic but the struggle around order and the products that it produces, among which are crime and criminal justice. Only then will criminology truly reflect its beginnings and the vision that inspired it. Without this vision, criminology will find the very phenomenon and changes it should be examining passing it by.

What Is the Purpose of Law and the Administration of Justice?

CHAPTER PREFACE

Criminologist Edwin Sutherland's definition of criminology is based on an analysis of how and why law is created and on research on the social functions of law and the administration of justice. Traditionally, criminologists have seen the law and the administration of justice as a form of institutionalized social control.

This idea led to the notion that law could be used to advance social reform and formed the basis for a movement in law called sociological jurisprudence. Reform-oriented legal scholars felt that lawmaking and the application of law should be studied from a sociological perspective. They hoped that once an objective social scientific understanding of law was developed, lawmaking, legal decision making, and the application of law to social issues could improve society and help solve social problems.

During the early part of this century, when the discipline of criminology began to take shape, criminologists began to ask how the law could be reformed to meet the demands of a changing society. Rather than study law to become aware of legal precedents and the evolution of the legal system, criminologists asked questions about what social interests were represented, protected, and influenced by the legal system.

A leading expert in this sociological approach to analyzing the functions of the law was Roscoe Pound, one of America's premiere jurists and legal scholars. According to Pound, various groups attempt to advance their interests through the process of lawmaking and law enforcement. Interest groups exerted pressure on governing bodies to recognize new social needs and new claims by making or changing the law. As these new claims are recognized in the law and the administration of justice, the legal system changes.

Criminologists began to analyze the law in a more scientific, objective manner. They postulated that law could be used to solidify and preserve the general interests of the community or, conversely, it could be used to serve certain class interests to the detriment of others. Law and the administration of justice can ensure a harmony of interests in society and maintain social order for the benefit of the majority or it can ensure the compliance of the masses to the interests of the few through the pomp and ritual of the court process. Criminologists have also analyzed law and justice as representing inherent social conflict in a society with class, race, cultural, and power differences that inevitably lead to discord and disagreement. For some criminologists, lawmaking and the justice system represent the will and power of the ruling class and are used to exert power over the underclass. For other criminologists, law and justice are necessary safeguards against the inevitable anarchy and disorder that prevail in a lawless society.

Many differences of opinion exist about the purposes of the legal system. These differences provide new and fascinating opportunities for criminologists to examine the law and the administration of justice as it copes with emerging areas of controversy. Perhaps criminology can offer some evidence that will resolve differences of opinion over what to expect of the law and the administration of justice. We need to know whether the legal system can help find solutions to new social problems in a changing society or whether it is more likely to drive us farther apart and create new conflicts in the future.

The Purpose of Law Is Social Control

ROSCOE POUND

Ideas about what the law and the administration of justice should accomplish for society have been formed by leading opinion makers working within the tradition of criminology. Roscoe Pound, one of the most influential, was a leader in establishing the approach to the study of law known as sociological jurisprudence. This approach maintained that the way to understand the law is to understand the interest groups involved in making and enforcing law. This understanding could be used to make the law a force for social good and social advancement. This was a view of law in society espoused by progressive reformers who wanted lawmaking and the administration of justice to have a positive impact on social change. This approach led to advances in criminology in understanding the social importance of law in society and the ways in which it is used to advance social interests. It also led to the development of a specialization in the sociology of law. Many scholars have since worked to build on the insights of Pound. Roscoe Pound was a leading American legal scholar and jurist from the early part of this century until his death in 1964. He was also dean of the Harvard Law School.

QUESTIONS

1. What does Pound mean by the term "social control"?
2. Why does Pound argue that the law replaced other forms of control as societies became more complex?
3. How does the law reinforce the power of the political state, according to the author?

■ ■ ■

In the modern world, law has become the paramount agency of social order. Our main reliance in the society of today is upon the force of politically organized society. We seek to adjust relations and order conduct through the orderly and systematic application of that force. At the moment this side of the law, its dependence upon force, is the one most insisted on. But it is well to remember that if law as a mode of social control has all the strength of force, it has also all the weakness of dependence on force. Moreover, that something very like law can exist and prove effective without any backing of force is shown by the achievements of international law from the seventeenth century to the last World War.

In a kin-organized society, a society in which the unit was not the individual human being but instead a group of kindred, the task of the law was a simple one of keeping the peace among warring groups. If one kinsman injured another, the internal discipline of the kin group took care of the matter. If a member of one kin group injured a member of another, there was no common superior to adjust the resulting controversy and the blood feud was a usual result. The first legal institutions were devised to regulate and ultimately to put an end to private war by requiring the vengeance of the injured kin to be bought off, and providing mechanical modes of trial in order to ascertain the facts. This idea of a regime of keeping the peace persists after many other functions have been added. It has but a limited field of social control for its province, leaving the greater part to the internal discipline of the kin group, the ethical custom of the community, and religious organization. But kin organization has substantially disappeared as a significant agency of social control. Organizations larger than the household exist today only for sentimental or historical or social purposes. Even the household has been losing its disciplinary effectiveness under the conditions of urban life. Juvenile Courts and Courts of Domestic Relations have taken over much of what was once the jurisdiction of the head of the family. A judge exercises authority to deal with truancy and incorrigibility, and proceedings in court replace the old-time interview between father and son in the family woodshed which formerly taught the truant to fear God and his father and the policeman.

Religion and Social Control

Religious organization was an effective agency of social control long after the kin group had ceased to be the social unit and even after politically organized society had attained not a little development. Often what we now call bodies of law in archaic societies were bodies of precepts declared by the priesthood and enforced by penances and exclusion from the society of the pious. In the beginnings of law much of this may be taken over by the state and given the sanction of force exercised by the officials of politically organized society. In England down to the Reformation and in parts of Continental Europe down to the era of the French Revolution, there was a system of church courts and church law which divided not unequally with the courts and law of the state the adjustment of relations and ordering of conduct. From the downfall of the Roman empire in the West to the twelfth century, the church bore the brunt of social control. From the beginning, the Christians were taught not to go to law with each other. They went with their controversies to the overseer of the local flock, the bishop, and he told them what the pious Christian would do in such a case. Out of this grew the bishop's court and a hierarchy of courts. Presently a body of law grew up for these courts, based on texts of Scripture, writings of the fathers of the church, canons of councils of the church, and decisions and rescripts of the popes, which has contributed much of the first significance to the law of today, and was in its time an agency of the highest importance toward maintaining and furthering civilization. But whatever hold religion may still have, religious organizations have lost their power over the mass of mankind. Social control has been all but completely secularized.

Morals have not had so effective an organization behind them. Yet the kin group disciplined the kinsman whose conduct brought reproach upon his kindred. At Rome, a power of censorship over morals, which first belonged to the king as patriarchal head of the Roman people, thought of as a society of kinsmen, passed to one of the magistrates of the republic and left remnants in the law which came down to the modern world. If such things no longer exist in politically organized society, trade and professional associations, trade-unions, social clubs, and fraternal organizations, with their codes of ethics, or their law or their standards of conduct or canons of what is done and what is not done, exercise, although in subordination to the law of the state, an increasing measure of control of individual conduct.

Social Control and Politics

But since the sixteenth century political organization of society has become paramount. It has, or claims to have and on the whole maintains, a monopoly of force. All other agencies of social control are held to exercise disciplinary authority subject to the law and within bounds fixed by law. The English courts will restore to membership one who has been wrongfully expelled from a social club. Courts have decided whether property left in trust for church purposes was being used according to the tenets of the church for which it was given. The household, the church, the associations which serve to some extent to organize morals in contemporary society, all operate within legally prescribed limits and subject to the scrutiny of the courts. Today social control is primarily the function of the state and is exercised through law. Its ultimate effectiveness depends upon the application of force exercised by bodies and agencies and officials set up or chosen for that purpose. It operates chiefly through law, that is, through the systematic and orderly application of force by the appointed agents.

It would be a mistake, however, to assume that politically organized society and the law by which it brings pressure to bear upon individuals are self-sufficient for the task of social control in the complex society of the time. The law must function on a background of other less direct but no less important agencies, the home and home training, religion, and education. If these have done their work properly and well much that otherwise would fall to the law will have been done in advance. Anti-social conduct calling for regulation and ill-adjusted relations with neighbors will have been obviated by bringing up and training and teaching, leading to life measured by reason. But conditions of urban life and of industry have seriously affected home training. It is much less effective in the metropolitan city than it was in the small, homogeneous neighborhood of the past. The general secularization of things, and distrust of creeds and dogmas, and hard-boiled realism, as it likes to think itself, of the present time have loosened the hold of religion. Education has become our main reliance for the background of social control. That too, however, is secularized and has not found itself equal to training in morals, if indeed that can be achieved by teaching. The problem of enforcing its precepts has become acute as law takes the whole field of social control for its province. . . .

The older positivism found laws of social development behind the evolution of politically organized society and so behind the law through which it operates. A newer positivism, however, looks at the legal ordering of society to see what it is, not as all it can be and as giving us a measure of what ought to be, but as showing what measures have been used, and what urged, and how the law has been able to use them; to see what men have taken to be the end of law, and whether there is some idea behind what they have assumed and acted on which does serve to do what they are trying to do, namely, to maintain, further, and transmit civilization.

I can imagine someone saying to me that it is unscientific to criticize the theories of skeptical realism with reference to the results to which they lead in action. Certainly it would be futile to criticize theories of physical nature in this way. But we are not dealing with physical nature, as to which opinions of good and bad and criticisms of its phenomena are irrelevant. We are dealing with phenomena in the domain and under the control of the human will and what is does not tell us the whole story. Here the ultimate question is always what ought to be. Unless governments exist for their own sake and judges and administrative officials judge and administer for the sake of exercising power, we cannot escape from the question: What is the end or purpose of the legal adjustment of relations and ordering of conduct? We cannot think of force as more than a means.

A rule of law without force behind it, says Jonas Jhering, is a contradiction in terms—"a light that lights not, a fire that burns not." Law involves force. Adjustment and ordering must rely ultimately on force even if they are possible chiefly because of habits of obedience on the part of all but an antisocial residuum which must be coerced. Indeed, the habit of obedience rests to no small extent upon the consciousness of intelligent persons that force will be applied to them if they persistently adhere to the antisocial residuum. The natural-law theory was not wrong in opposing law to force, meaning thereby force applied as such, upon no principle, on subjective opinions of what was expedient, or of the public good, or of personal advantage of the individual functionary. If it is not possible wholly to exclude the subjective personal element in the judicial and administrative processes, the history of law shows we can go very far toward doing it. Civilization rests upon the putting down of arbitrary, willful self-assertion and the substitution of reason. Even if we had not gone so far in achieving this as we believed we had done in the last century, one has only to compare the law of the last century and the administration of justice according to law in the last century with that of colonial America to see how much of what we now think of as the complacent self-flattery of the nineteenth century was after all justified.

We have been told that the acid test of theories of law is the attitude of the bad man—the man who cares nothing about justice or right or rights, but wants to know what will happen to him if he does or fails to do certain things. Is his attitude any more a test than that of the normal man, who objects to being subjected to the arbitrary will of another but is content to live a life measured by reason and takes part in the choosing of those who are to exercise the power of politically organized society in the expectation and to the end that they exercise it, as the medieval lawyer put it, under God and the law?

VIEWPOINT

2

The Purpose of the Law Is to Insure a Safe and Orderly Society

PATRICK R. ANDERSON AND DONALD J. NEWMAN

There are many differing expectations of law and justice in our society. Many different interest groups have attempted to make the administration of criminal justice meet their desires and needs. Patrick Anderson and Donald Newman analyze the different demands on the administration of justice in our society. They elaborate on the earlier statements of Roscoe Pound. They go into detail on the different ways that social institutions are expected to provide social control. This is to be achieved by the criminal law, law enforcement, and the administration of criminal justice pursuing the overall objectives of controlling and preventing crime. Detecting, arresting, convicting, incarcerating, and possibly rehabilitating criminals is accomplished to protect society, deter criminality, and control and prevent future crime. The picture they present is one of many competing demands on the administration of justice in our society. From their point of view, all of the activities of the criminal law and the justice system are intended to insure an ordered and safe society. Although these expectations may not always be met in practice, these are the goals that we expect these institutions to pursue. Patrick R. Anderson is a criminologist and professor at Florida Southern College. Donald J. Newman was a leading legal and criminal justice scholar and former dean of the School of Criminal Justice at the State University of New York, Albany.

QUESTIONS

1. How do the "crime control model" and the "due process model" relate to the goals of the administration of justice, according to the authors?
2. How do the authors believe that the "justice system" is related to the goal of creating an orderly society?
3. How are the expectations of the administration of justice related to the idea of social control, according to Anderson and Newman?

■ ■ ■

The current emphasis on crime data, as politicians and news commentators monitor the fluctuations of crime rates, arrests, prison populations, and other factors, has produced an increasing impatience with our failure to lower crime rates or increase arrests or lessen prison populations. People accustomed to looking to the bottom line, to the charts and graphs of industrial or economic progress, sometimes expect criminal justice agencies to demonstrate an ability to progress, to improve, to *win the war against crime.* If corporations were no more successful at improving statistical performance than criminal justice agencies are, it seems, they would go bankrupt.

One of the reasons comparisons of the criminal justice system with other large complex organizations, such as the armed forces or giant industrial corporations, are inappropriate is that the basic purposes of the criminal justice system are many and varied, and conflicts within and between the various agencies of criminal justice are not unusual. In corporate endeavors there usually is some agreement about objectives such as profits, growth, and perhaps public service. No such consensus exists about the specific purposes of the criminal justice system. Varied purposes are expressed, and there is often incongruity between both long-range and short-range objectives. For instance, police agencies want to lock offenders up; parole boards want to turn them loose. Police want to catch lawbreakers easily and quickly; courts demand the police carry out their duties in accordance with the cumbersome requirements of search warrants, warnings, and other due process procedures.

These multiple purposes compound the complexity of criminal justice processing. Although its principal objectives are to control crime and to maintain public order, the system rests on a set of multiple and occasionally conflicting beliefs and expectations as to how crime control and public order are best achieved. Some of these expectations, such as control through the punishment of violators, are ancient in origin, dating from the earliest conceptions of ordered society and drawing their philosophic justifications from ideas about human nature, sin, and repentance. Others, such as the rehabilitation of offenders, are latter-day products of social science, stemming from more modern concepts of behavior, personality, and change. Still others, such as the accurate and fair separation of the guilty from the innocent, come from our democratic political ideology, which stresses individual liberty, curbs on state power, and proper and humane treatment of even the worst among us.

In short, a variety of expectations about crime control affect the process of the criminal justice system. These expectations ebb and flow in their relative importance as times and philosophies change. All exist simultaneously, coloring every decision from the drafting and enacting of statutes to parole revocation. Several of these expectations are discussed below.

To Control and Prevent Crime

Whether short-range or long-range, the overall objectives of criminal justice fall into two general sets of purposes: the *control of crime* by solving crimes, arresting suspects, and processing and imprisoning offenders, and the *prevention of crime* through this processing or by other means. The crime control objective deals with the immediate situation and rests on the discovery of *past* criminal behavior, whereas crime prevention is *forward-looking*, forecasting and forestalling future crimes by present interventions. It is necessary to be aware of both control and prevention purposes, for only by such awareness can we explain certain legislative, court, and administrative agency activity.

It can be argued, of course, that control and prevention are so closely related as to be indistinguishable. For example, the purpose of the arrest, conviction, and correctional processing of an offender may be rehabilitation, with the aim of preventing future crimes. Or using marked police cars in high-crime neighborhoods may be designed to deter and therefore prevent criminal acts. Obviously, the two purposes become intertwined, though one or the other is usually given priority. *The use of force* by the police is primarily a control issue, but the *show of force* by police is future-directed and, in this respect, preventive in nature.

To Detect, Arrest, Convict, and Incarcerate Offenders

This is the most immediate, direct, and traditional purpose of criminal justice processing. The question of how best to do it, and to know when it has been done, is the source of many conflicts about criminal justice. In this respect, two major models can be applied, the crime control model and the due process model. Each generates disagreements about its worth and creates problems about how to achieve and measure success. The crime control model holds that the criminal justice process should be invoked often, vigorously, and fully against criminals in our society. Measures of effectiveness of this position include high arrest rates, the charging of the most serious crimes possible, the convicting of offenders as charged, and the sentencing of violators to maximum terms.

The due process model stance is that a better and more effective criminal justice system can be achieved when the system acts reluctantly and when its purpose is to divert as many suspects as possible from criminal justice processing or, if arrest and conviction must occur, to remove offenders from the system as rapidly as possible; when processing defendants to charge only according to what seems best for the individual; and after conviction to put the offender on probation or in a community correctional facility for a short period of time.

Which approach is better or more effective is open to debate and generates some strong conflicts about the basic nature of crime control in our society. For example, there is the question of whether a "good" police department is one that makes many arrests or is one that keeps the streets "cool" by adjusting conflicts, using arrest only as a last resort. There is also the question of whether the presumption under which the sentencing judge operates following conviction should be to imprison the offender unless he or she has a good record or to consider probation first, incarcerating only if the offender has a bad record.

To Punish Criminals

There is little doubt that punishment of violators is an important purpose of the criminal justice process. The *punitive ideal,* though among the most ancient approaches to crime control, is still a force of major significance. To some punishment is an end in itself, consistent with our moral support for an eye-for-an-eye concept of justice. But the punishment aspects of our crime control system are also designed to compel conformity by hurting violators, much as a dog is conditioned to obey or naughty children are spanked to teach them to be good. And punishment has a related though separate purpose: It is intended to *deter potential violators;* to frighten them off, by demonstrating that crime does not pay (see the next section).

The application of punishment to law violators *in proportion to the seriousness of their offenses* is the cornerstone of criminal codes and sentencing structures. Beyond this, however, the punitive theme runs through all the determinations of the criminal process, coloring the perceptions of all participants, including suspects and defendants as well as agency personnel, its influence reflected even in uniforms, accouterments and physical settings. At a minimum, the criminal justice process is designed to be stern and unpleasant; at its extreme, it is frankly punitive and indeed can put lawbreakers in cages for life or impose the death penalty on those who have wrongfully killed other people.

Though punitiveness may be muted by competing objectives, there is no pretense, official or otherwise, that the system is designed to further the best interests of those processed. This contrasts sharply with the underlying philosophies of other systems where state power is employed to compel conformity, as in public schooling, hospital commitment of the mentally ill, or the juvenile justice system. From start to finish, the criminal process is "the state *versus* John Doe," not as in delinquency processing, "the state *in the interest of* Johnny Doe."

Punishment is an aura pervasive throughout the process. It accounts in part for police behavior, which is typically far from friendly, even when correct, once the process starts. It is reflected in the prosecutor's need for convictions to maintain community support. It is visible in emotionally cool, stern, and formal court proceedings. It is epitomized by prisons. The punitive function of the criminal justice system not only has a long tradition, but even today it is never far from the surface at any decision point or in any program. Attempts to change criminal processing inevitably confront punishment requirements.

Early advocates of probation and parole achieved their objectives by demonstrating lower cost and greater effectiveness, but they also had to argue strongly that community sentences were indeed punishment. And modern correctional facilities, unwalled and without bars or cells, have been accepted slowly and grudgingly for fear they would diminish the punitive purposes of walled and turreted maximum-security prisons.

To Deter Criminals

Another goal of the criminal justice system is to effectively deter crime by stopping or frightening off potential lawbreakers. It is widely believed that permanent prevention of crime, if attainable at all, will require a basic modification of cultural values, the revision of opportunity structures, the reorganization of social class structures, and the elimination of economic imbalance. Personnel in criminal justice agencies generally see their preventive task in more modest terms. For the most part, *prevention* in the crime control context means short-range *deterrence* of potential violators.

Whether deterrence is actually possible is debatable, for inference about its effectiveness is essentially negative. How many people would commit crimes if they were not deterred is not known. There have been limited studies of certain offenses where a deterrent function has been observed. These tend to be planned, rational offenses where the chances of getting caught are immediate and certain. For example, in regard to more rational offenses like stealing, posting a police officer near an apple barrel is likely to reduce the number of apples stolen. But emotional crimes and crimes of passion, such as murder or child molestation, are difficult, perhaps impossible, to deter.

Two major approaches to deterrence are employed in the criminal justice system, and both generate controversies about their effectiveness and their appropriateness in our society. The first is based on creating a belief in the certainty of criminal justice processing and the hope that the severity of official reactions when offenders are caught will deter other people from initiating criminal activities. To this end there is a desire to make the criminal justice system appear *omnipresent*, its agents *visible*, arrest *certain*, and justice *swift*. At the police agency level, this involves such issues as the use of clearly marked prowl cars, uniformed officers with sidearms, techniques of frequent, random patrolling, and so on. It is expected that courts will be somber and dignified, with the raised bench and the black robes of the judges indicating seriousness of purpose in court proceedings—a posture critics feel is diminished by the more casual, juvenile court form of processing. It is expected that prisons too should look like prisons to those on the outside as well as to those incarcerated. The wall and the gun turrets of the maximum-security prison have dual functions: to control the inmates within and to demonstrate the severe price of crime to potential offenders on the outside.

A variation on this approach, though also designed to create an aura of certain arrest and stern punishment, maintains that the *system should be nearly invisible* while nurturing the belief that it is operating efficiently. Police should be primarily undercover, like narcotics officers who infiltrate the drug sub-culture to make arrests. Statistics on the effectiveness of law enforcement efforts should be kept confidential, and a sort of "crime does not pay" posture should be maintained.

The second approach to deterrence involves taking actions that *prevent opportunities for crime* to occur or that *assure quick discovery* of violators. Devices used range from television cameras in banks to exact-fare requirements on public transportation. In New York City a public announcement that many off-duty police officers were driving cabs markedly reduced the incidence of taxi holdups for a period of time. Airplane hijacking was once a serious problem that elicited a strong demand for prevention. In addition to using a con-structed "profile" of a skyjacker to screen passengers, airlines are required by federal law to subject passengers to luggage search and metal detection screening before boarding aircraft.

Experiments with other deterrence techniques range from the relatively simple and noncontroversial placing of "ghost" (unmanned) police cars distantly visible along superhighways to control traffic to the use of police dogs in surveillance and park patrol. But one problem with all deterrence techniques is the extent of the noncriminal population's willingness to tol-erate such inconveniences as exact-change rules, searches upon entering public transportation, or the saturation of neighborhoods with armed police.

The common desire to use the crime control system to deter potential wrong-doers from committing crimes is closely related to the punitive ideal. As might be expected, making examples of those caught and proved guilty is widely believed to be effective in achieving this purpose. This is the basic argu-ment of those favoring severe sentences, including the death penalty.

However, deterrence has a broader base. The *show of force* may accomplish conformity as well as or better than the *use of force*. Consequently, many practices in all agencies are influ-enced in some degree by deterrent objectives. The omnipresence of police on patrol, the secrecy of grand juries, the public nature of trials and sentencings by judges, and the visibility of prisons and other correctional agencies not only display the punitive nature of the system, but demonstrate its readiness to act.

While some attempts are made in practice to individualize justice by fitting the punishment to the characteristics and circumstances of the individual being processed, the action taken in a particular case is more routinely determined in part by its probable effect on others or, more abstractly, by how it may affect a general "respect for the law." An unobserved police officer may release a suspect with a reprimand; in similar situations but faced with an observing crowd, the officer may feel compelled to make an arrest. Sentences meted out in high-publicity cases tend to be more severe than otherwise. Wherever and whenever decisions about a suspect, defendant, or offender are partly based on considerations of the likely effects on others, including the "public," the deterrent function is being served.

To Protect the Community

There is a general expectation that the criminal justice process will protect the community from continued depredations of criminals. To accomplish this, authorities are permitted to take physical custody of suspects as well as of offenders and to restrain them, subject to legislative and court limitations and controls. The ultimate power of restraint is symbolized by the maximum security incarceration of convicted felons. In fact, a primary purpose of imprisonment is the *restraint* and *incapacitation* of offenders to protect the community, an objective that most prisons achieve very well indeed. This is often overlooked when prisons are labeled as failures because they do not successfully rehabilitate many prisoners.

Restraint for community protection is not limited to imprisonment and other postconviction processes. It is an important function from the very outset of the process. Police may arrest one suspect at gunpoint, handcuff him or her, and hold the individual in close detention until a bail hearing. Another suspect may be arrested without the use of any force or hardware, and experience little physical inhibition. Often high bail and always preventive detention reflect the community protection function. It may also be seen at the charging decision; certainly community protection is a consideration in plea negotiation. Sentencing alternatives directly reflect this function, and it is a major factor in determining probation conditions, prison program and housing assignments, selection for parole, and parole revocation. The entire correctional process rests always on a balance between the needs and desires of the offender and concerns for community protection, even in systems giving high priority to rehabilitative programs.

To Correct, or Rehabilitate, Criminals

It is generally expected that the criminal justice process will somehow reform or rehabilitate those caught up in it, or at least will not make them worse. It is recognized that virtually all persons who are processed, even those convicted and sentenced to life imprisonment, will eventually return to the community. Thus it behooves participants and agencies to take actions designed to enable their charges to live law-abiding lives once they are discharged from the process. Some argue that this may be accomplished by conditioning individuals through punishment to avoid the unpleasant consequences of criminal activity, much as animals can be conditioned to avoid painful stimuli. But more commonly today, agencies attempt to provide positive programs designed to rehabilitate prison inmates by changing their attitudes and teaching them new vocational skills; they also work to reintegrate offenders by assisting them to adjust to normal community living.

Although the corrective function has traditionally been assigned to postconviction agencies like prisons and probation and parole services, there is an increasing awareness that all stages of criminal justice have relevance to the corrective function. In this respect the police are seen as an intake agency, making a wide range of decisions within their discretion that have long-range effects on the fate of the persons with whom they have contact. The way an arrest is made, the amount of force used, the police behavior toward the suspect, and so on may influence the detainee's self-conception so as to harden his or her criminal attitudes or to have the opposite and more desirable effect of creating respect for the police and, more generally, for the legal process. Police diversion of suspects to community treatment resources rather than incarceration is seen as a corrective decision by many observers. The police rarely think of themselves as social workers, but the basic nature of their operations is increasingly seen—by the police as well as by others—to be critical to the overall objective of rehabilitation.

In the same manner, the discretion of the prosecutor to select among charges or to divert and not charge at all may be exercised with corrective purposes in mind. A basic motivation in plea negotiation is to individualize the consequences of conviction, rather than simply to avoid trial. And a trial itself may have corrective relevance. An opportunity to be heard, a day in court, a fair hearing have purposes beyond fact finding, perhaps acting to dispel cynicism and the belief in "railroading" not uncommonly expressed by offenders hurried through a guilty plea at a brief arraignment. Sentencing discretion is often delegated to courts in the expectation that the judge's choice will not only satisfy the punitive ideal but serve a corrective function as well.

The corrective function perhaps more than any other purpose of the criminal justice system ties together the discrete stages of the criminal justice process. From the perspective of this function it can be seen that decisions made at one point have relevance elsewhere, and that any overall function is ultimately served by the degree of congruence of all decisions.

Creation of an Ordered Society

It has been said that if criminals did not exist, they would have to be created, for they provide a necessary common enemy, a group of scapegoats, against whom we can measure our own righteousness. The efficiency and the vengeance elements of the criminal justice system are reinforced by other elements that are more symbolic and ceremonial.

The pomp and rituals of the criminal court, the starkness of prisons, and the presence of the police with sidearms are all visible embodiments of "justice" that serve to assure order and protection from disorder in our daily lives. Tradition and symbolism are not only important parts of the system, but occasionally they may be impediments to what appear to be rational and sensible reforms. There is a tendency, particularly among professional people within the criminal justice system, to attribute to the system a high degree of rationality and to assume that logic and research will bring about desired and needed changes. This is rarely the case. It can be demonstrated, for example, that small, modern prisons—rooms instead of cells, only a fence for perimeter security, inmates dressed in civilian clothing, free to move about the institution and eligible for work release and furloughs—are not only more effective but are much cheaper than warehousing inmates in walled maximum-security prisons. But whenever such correctional facilities have been proposed, there has been great opposition based on the widely held belief that prisons are not supposed to be this way, that such quarters are too pleasant to be prisons, and that they would weaken the deterrent function of imprisonment. Most of us have deeply ingrained opinions about the way prisons should be, the way police officers should dress, and the way judges should act when on the bench. The proponent of change may be frustrated by what appear to be illogical components of the criminal justice system if he or she fails to take into account the important symbolic value of those components.

The desire for an *ordered* and *safe society* implies more than the visible presence of agencies of justice, giving an appearance of law and order. There is also a demand that the system be effective, and that somehow the police, courts, and other agencies make our streets and neighborhoods safe and create an environment where both the business and the pleasure of our people can take place freely and safely. If, indeed, this is expected of our criminal justice system, it has failed ruefully in its task, particularly in the heart of our metropolitan areas.

VIEWPOINT

3

The Function of Law Must Go Beyond Crime Prevention and Control

DAVID E. DUFFEE

Much of the research conducted by criminologists on the structure and function of the law and the administration of justice has begun with assumptions about what the system of criminal justice is supposed to be or what it is supposed to do. According to David Duffee, it is not surprising that the realities of criminal justice in practice constantly fall short of public expectations. These public expectations have often been reinforced by self-serving administrators in criminal justice, by politicians, and by some criminologists and criminal justice researchers. However, much of criminology has been an exercise in debunking public expectations of criminal justice and discrediting self-serving rhetoric. Duffee argues that

Reprinted by permission of Waveland Press, Inc. from David E. Duffee, *Explaining Criminal Justice: Community Theory and Criminal Justice Reform* (Prospect Heights, IL: Waveland Press, 1980 [reissued 1990]). All rights reserved.

these battles between conservative and liberal expectations, between proponents of punishment and rehabilitation, and between control, due process, and prevention advocates may be beside the point. Maybe criminal justice is serving unappreciated and varied community needs while seemingly it is failing to live up to unrealistic expectations for doing justice. David Duffee, a criminologist and criminal justice researcher, is dean of the School of Criminal Justice at the State University of New York, Albany.

QUESTIONS

1. What does Duffee mean when he says that criminal justice has been treated as an "idealized system?"
2. What would it mean to view criminal justice as a part of an "interorganizational field," according to Duffee?
3. What does Duffee think of the possibilities of criminal justice actually providing crime deterrence and crime prevention?

■ ■ ■

Criminal justice is not constructed upon a narrow set of goals nor is it built to specifications established to increase the probability of a particular outcome or set of outcomes. Evaluating criminal justice against a set of goals to be accomplished and using empirical indicators to demonstrate outcomes fall short or wide of said goals is often merely an analytical exercise, valuable perhaps in establishing academic careers or in advancing a philosophy of punishment. But it is difficult to conceive of the findings of such analyses having the same relationship to criminal justice as such findings might have to an ad campaign, a television show, a new cosmetic, or a new gadget in the arsenal of the Strategic Air Command.

Criminal justice, unlike a project or an operation, is a basic social institution. It may wither away as the extended family has done, or it may reflower as some say formal religion in America has done. But it is stretching analogies to say that the extended family was "disassembled" because it did not achieve its goals or that formal religion has become popular because it has demonstrably brought its followers closer to God. As a social institution criminal justice is a minor one compared to the family, religion, or education. It involves far fewer people, costs less, and likely provides fewer social functions. It may be only a portion of the much larger political institution, but there is no doubt that it is a strongly embedded institutional social form. It has not been rationally constructed during a brief period of history as a means of accomplishing a few, clear-cut, specified goals. Asking that the criminal justice system achieve goals, such as deterring offenses or rehabilitating criminals, may seem logical, but it is unlikely that criminal justice has actually had to accomplish any particular goal to any particular degree in order to exist. Moreover, most of the goals against which outcomes of criminal justice are compared can and have been assigned to other social institutions as well. Familial, religious, and educational institutions might deter and deter with greater effectiveness than criminal justice. The same or other institutions may rehabilitate as well as or better than criminal justice.

Rather than ask what criminal justice hypothetically can do, we might gain more understanding about the system by asking what it does do, or why it exists within the American social system. Study upon study about what it specifically does not achieve does not enable us to cope with its endurance as a social institution. Since criminal justice is not a bounded organizational project, or even a set of endeavors geared to one set of specified objectives, the insistence of analyzing it as a unified system for the performance of specified objectives may inhibit our ability to understand how criminal justice operates in particular circumstances. Rather than idealize the system of "police-courts-corrections" and then expect real agencies to achieve some approximation of our ideal, it may be more productive, as a starting point, to examine criminal justice in the context of the milieu in which it is practiced.

Approaching criminal justice within a normative framework, or expecting the system to "do something," the analyst usually is forced to treat deviations from the ideal system as chance occurrences, or as evidence that certain actual systems need to be changed or upgraded in order to achieve expectations. We can approach the task of criminal justice analysis differently by examining criminal justice agencies in operation and by seeking to find the variables that explain the variation among agencies or constrain if not determine the operation of any single agency.

A wide variety of information is available that confirms that criminal justice is not a monolithic, commonly conceived, routine exercise. Criminal justice may well have different meanings in different places or behave differently under contrasting conditions. Before we attempt to change actual operating agencies to conform to a unitary conception of criminal justice, we may wish first to ask why such variations occur, whether these variations are functional equivalents, or whether the contrasting practices provide to the locality in which they are observed contributions to social order that might be lost if all criminal justice agencies everywhere behaved appropriately to the expectations of the analyst. . . .

Criminal Justice as a Unitary System

I have argued that the perception of the "criminal justice system" as a unitary, coherent set of interagency operations is more likely a belief or desire brought to the analysis by the analyst, rather than a characteristic of the agencies and operations observed. All criminal analysts acknowledge that no "criminal justice system" actually exists, but instead many separate systems in many different jurisdictions. But most criminal justice analysts gloss over the observed differences in order to stress the commonalities, or underscore variation across systems as dysfunctional to some conception of social order. The emphasis remains upon the unitary, idealized conception of criminal justice.

To conservatives and liberals alike, deviations from the unitary system of criminal justice are usually occasions for criticism. Conservatives tend to favor swiftness and surety of punishment and thus the expected increase in deterrence that might appear without deviations. Liberals tend to focus on the inhumaneness in some of the deviations observed and stress that in unitary systems such excesses could be controlled. Radicals decry the inhumaneness and injustice in coherent, unitary systems of criminal justice, but they take the existence of such a coherent monolith as fact, perhaps reflecting upon the reform agendas of conservatives and liberals, rather than on actual observation of criminal justice agencies.

Criminal justice operations vary widely across areas of the country. Contrary to the suppositions of the unified model, there is a wide variety of evidence that criminal justice agencies relate to each other not only as determined by their roles in the criminal process, but also as determined by their roles in a community political context. Indeed, there may be more variation between, say, the police and the prosecutor in towns A and B than between the production and sales forces in companies C and D. In systems that have output indicators to which quality can be assessed, variation will be less likely than in human systems that cannot specify the quality of the operation. Since there are few, if any, universal agreements about "good" police work, the non–criminal justice factors influencing the police may determine how police and prosecutor interact as much or more so than does the law. But if sales and production can be assessed separately and together in terms of their contribution to profit, it is *less* likely that factors extraneous to the system will predominate in structuring the linkages.

Frequent examples exist of rather significant variation in criminal justice practice and results across the myriad systems that actually exist. On a rather general level, Michael Banton's comparative observations of police in the United States and Scotland raises serious questions as to whether the police functions are the same in the two cultures. Banton argues that the Scottish officer is principally a symbol of community or social order and that beyond obeying and/or enjoying the ministerial quality of the police status, the Scottish officer has relatively little to do. In contrast, Banton finds the American policeman highly active and personal in the performance of his role. The American officer cannot defer to the general public regard for the police status. Instead, he needs to intervene actively in order to produce or maintain whatever semblance or level of order the officer personally feels to be appropriate to the instant situation. Stated in other terms, we might say that there is a higher, or more rigid, degree of institutionalization in Scottish interaction patterns than in American. The Scottish officer needs less often to call upon personal authority than his American counterpart because most people in the

Scottish village perceive the officer as a reminder or a reinforcement of norms that most of them hold in common. Banton constantly emphasizes that the Scottish officer defers to this consensus or common ground and usually obtains the expected result. In contrast, the American officer is likely to find less predictable the norms to which specific citizens adhere, and in addition is often confronted with a situation where citizens with different norms are in conflict. He cannot, in these situations, defer to a common, institutionalized understanding. Rather than function as a cultural reinforcement, a symbol of what is appropriate to all parties in a situation, the police officer in the United States more often functions as a means of resolving normative conflicts, or keeping such conflicts within bounds. . . .

The argument that police functions may differ between heterogeneous and homogeneous cultures is not limited to international comparisons. Banton, for example, is quick to comment on the marked variations among American police forces. He found much greater similarity across Great Britain than across the United States. At the same time, Banton, Wilkins, and others argue that the observed differences across nations can also be found *within* the United States. They suggest that the same high degree of density, interlocking roles, or institutionalization that accounts for the Scottish/American variation can account for many observed variations among different American communities. More specifically, the village policeman, or the officer in a small, homogeneous community is more likely to act as a symbol of consensual order than is a police officer in a complex urban environment. The officer in the urban setting is more likely to invoke the law as a means of obtaining or restoring order whereas the village officer is more likely to rely upon informal or cultural controls. Compared to the village officer, the urban officer less frequently has sufficient information about the norms operating in the situation at hand and less frequently has complete information about the participants in any disturbing situations. The urban police therefore are pressed more frequently toward treating one, or all, of the parties to a disturbance within the statuses and roles available within the criminal law.

While Banton's comments upon this possibility remain relatively anecdotal and Wilkins's are highly theoretical, an empirical validation is available in the work of James Q. Wilson. The major concern of Wilson's investigation was the extent to which community political and social variations constrained police department policy (written or unwritten) on the decisions of (1) when to intervene in a situation and (2) how to intervene. While Wilson's methodology was more appropriate to raising rather than testing hypotheses, his study examined police discretionary behavior in a large number of specific cities about which a wide variety of data were collected. Hence Wilson's work, while definitely requiring follow-up, provides a broader base for generalization than the more frequent two-culture or two-community comparisons.

Wilson's investigations led him to stipulate that in American cities, even in those of one legal code, there were at least three varieties of police behavior. Which type of behavior would emerge seemed highly dependent upon the local sociopolitical context. He found in Syracuse, New York, a "legalistic style" of policing, meaning that the police, on the average, tended to invoke a rule or enforce a law as the "solution" (or appropriate response) in a large number of disturbance situations. This style, which also appeared in Oakland, California, seemed contingent upon the emergence of a reform government in a relatively large city. Hence there had been recent political promises for greater activity on the part of public service organizations as well as promises that services would not be provided on politically discriminatory bases, but to all citizens equally.

In other cities, generally somewhat smaller in size, Wilson's investigations often encountered a "watchman style" police force. This type of organization, which was found in Albany, Amsterdam, and Newburg, New York, tended to stem from machine politics and patronage, low pay and low respect for public workers, and city governments that were dominated by one party, one ethnic group, or some other force that had collapsed or simplified the standards applicable to public behavior. "Watchman" police departments were unlikely to intervene frequently and unlikely to utilize the criminal sanction as the solution to disturbing situations. Instead, most discretionary police matters were handled informally, the object being to maintain order or contain the situation rather than arrest an offender.

Finally, Wilson observed a "service style" police department in other communities, usually those that were fairly homogeneous, fairly small, and relatively middle-class. In such communities Wilson observed that city government officials belonged to the same class as the majority of their constituents and that relatively high agreement existed that government was a civic duty and policing a public service. Hence, police were very often engaged in a variety of service efforts unrelated to law enforcement and were likely to respond to disturbing situations as occasions for counseling or rendering help rather than enforcing rules. Compared to legalistic departments, service departments did not intervene in a formal fashion, but compared to watchman departments they intervened fairly frequently.

Wilson tends to treat these three different patterns of policing as functional equivalents. That is, they are analyzed as three distinct means or processes for achieving the same end, the maintenance of public order. But an application of the Banton/Wilkins theory to the Wilson data would suggest that the ends achieved as well as the means used may have differed. That is, different functional domains were established for the police organization in the various cities. The function to be performed seemed dependent both upon the linkages between the police and the local political structure and upon the extent to which normative consensus existed in the community. In those instances when the police operated as a control, there was often little resort to the criminal sanction, as well as wide agreement across the community upon standards by which to judge behavior. In instances where there was low consensus, and the police acted "professionally," or within the confines of enforcing the law, there was often much less agreement about public order, higher crime rates, and greater intergroup conflict. These data would tend to support Theodore Mills's contention . . . that criminal justice as a social control to deviance operates in simple rather than complex social systems, because the criteria of order that are prerequisites to the application of negative feedback are lacking in highly complex, urban systems. If deterrence/retribution or social welfare assumptions hold at all, they would seem most likely to hold in smaller, homogeneous communities. These communities usually do not provide us with the impetus to reform the criminal justice system because the type and level of deviance recorded therein is not troublesome.

At the same time that we note significant differences in what the police and other agencies of justice do, relative to the type of community in which they operate, more specific linkages among justice and non-justice agencies also seem important. The emphasis on the control function of the justice system, and upon the coherent superordinate goals of the system, has resulted in downplay of the interorganizational linkages both across justice agencies and among any particular set of justice and non-justice agencies. Consequently there is too great a tendency to perceive the criminal justice system as a single organization rather than as a loosely coupled string of agencies that are components in many other community systems as well.

Roland Warren and his colleagues argue that the functions performed by social service agencies are incomplete and inaccurately understood if we examine only the goals and internal operations of a single agency or even the exchanges between agency diads. More important to the analysis of community structure and process is the ability of the analyst to examine the consequences of "the interorganizational field," or the interactions among multiple agency sets.

Jerome Skolnick and J. Richard Woodworth take a step in this direction in their analysis of a morals detail in two western police departments. Their goal was to highlight the impact of bureaucratic linkages between organizations upon both the reported crime rate in an area and the means of response. Their choice of crimes, statutory rape, was chosen because it is a crime to which the police universally pay little attention and the community norms are ambivalent at best. In examining rates of arrest in two contiguous cities the investigators discovered marked variation, regardless of the fact that neither police department gave high priority to enforcement and individual officers detested the assignment. The explanation of the differences in reported rape and arrest, then, had little to do with community value differences, incidence of the behavior, or police attitude toward the crime. In one city, the police department and the department of welfare pooled information, the welfare department refusing to pay support unless a paternity complaint was filed by the mother with the police department. In the other city, the police and welfare organizations operated separately. The first department made far more arrests and successful prosecutions. . . .

Criminal Justice as an Integrated System

Variations across communities and jurisdictions may allow us to ask whether the criminal justice system has the same functions in all places. Variations across separate agencies within the same criminal justice system may allow us to ask whether the control model of the system is anywhere appropriate as a description. The presentation of criminal justice as a societal control would suggest that the system operates toward planned goals with planned methods.

But it is frequently observed that the interaction among the agencies of criminal justice is cumbersome and slow, and takes place without many rules: "Nowhere within the legal system is there formal provision for organizational subordination of one subsystem to the other so that decisions in any one subsystem can be directly and effectively enforced in others by administrative or other organizational sanctions. The law itself, rather than organizational implementation generally governs such relationships." But to see this interagency characteristic as negative or deficient is not necessary, nor is it inherent in the nature of the processes involved. Homans writes, for example, that "much legal behavior is ritual" and that the criminal justice agencies are not structured to "have much effect on the law breaker."

VIEWPOINT

4

The Law Serves the Interests of the Power Elite

RICHARD QUINNEY

Richard Quinney's theory of the "social reality of crime"
presented here is based on the observation that definitions
of crime are created through law and the administration of
justice. The agents of the law represent the interests of the
"ruling classes" or "elites" in our society. The dominant
interest groups who wield the most power in our society
incorporate their interests into the criminal law. Criminal law
and the definitions of criminal behavior incorporated in the
law represent conflicts between class interests in our society.
Those who have power use the law and the administration of
justice to regulate the behavior of those with conflicting interests and less power. Quinney makes the point that crime is a
judgment that those with power make about the behavior
and characteristics of others. The powerful can use the
machinery of criminal justice and the power of the communications media to enforce and publicize their judgments about

From Richard Quinney, *The Social Reality of Crime.* Boston: Little, Brown, 1970.
Reprinted with permission of the author.

others, based on their interests. Once this is institutionalized in the law and the administration of justice, it becomes natural to view crime from the elite perspective. Thus, some acts that may be objectively harmful to the interests of most people in society can be ignored by the law and the justice system. On the other hand, acts that do less overall harm to society and are engaged in by the powerless segments of society are defined as crime. From Quinney's point of view, crime is what the power elite decides is against its own interests. Richard Quinney is the author of many articles and books in criminology, including *The Social Reality of Crime*, from which this viewpoint is excerpted. His latest book on criminology is *Criminology as Peacemaking*. He is a professor in the department of sociology at Northern Illinois University.

QUESTIONS

1. How does Quinney propose to change our focus from the idea of criminal behavior as individual pathology to an understanding of the formation and administration of criminal law?
2. What ramifications does the above shift in focus have for criminology and criminal justice, according to Quinney?
3. What does it mean to view law, crime, and crime control as examples of social conflict?

■ ■ ■

The history of contemporary sociology is characterized by a progressive loss in faith—faith that anything exists beyond man's imagination. We are consequently being led to new assumptions about our craft and the substance of our labors. New ways of attacking old problems are making this a dynamic period for sociology.

Perhaps in no other sociological realm is intellectual revisionism more apparent than in the study of crime. In these pages I will indicate how current thoughts and trends in the sociological study of crime can culminate in a theory of crime. The theory that I will present—*the theory of the social reality of crime*—rests upon theoretical and methodological assumptions that reflect the happenings of our time; it is meant to provide an understanding of crime that is relevant to our contemporary experiences.

Assumptions: Explanation in the Study of Crime

Until fairly recent times studies and writings in criminology were shaped almost entirely by the criminologist's interest in "the criminal." In the last few years, however, those who study crime have realized that crime is relative to different legal systems, that an absolute conception of crime—outside of legal definitions—had to be replaced by a relativistic (that is, legalistic) conception. Many criminologists have therefore turned to studying how criminal definitions are constructed and applied in a society.

Two schools of thought have developed. Some argue that crime is properly studied by examining the offender and his behavior. Others are convinced that the criminal law is the correct object: how it is formulated, enforced, and administered. The two need not become deadlocked in polemics. The long overdue interest in criminal definitions happily corrects the absurdities brought about by studying the offender alone; the two approaches actually complement one another. A synthesis of the criminal behavior and criminal definition approaches can provide a new theoretical framework for the study of crime. . . .

Theory: The Social Reality of Crime

The theory contains six propositions and a number of statements within the propositions. With the first proposition I define crime. The next four are the explanatory units. In the final proposition the other five are collected to form a composite describing the social reality of crime. The propositions and their integration into a theory of crime reflect assumptions about explanation and about man and society. . . .

PROPOSITION 1 (DEFINITION OF CRIME): *Crime is a definition of human conduct that is created by authorized agents in a politically organized society.*

This is the essential starting point in the theory—a definition of crime—which itself is based on the concept of definition. Crime is a *definition* of behavior that is conferred on some persons by others. Agents of the law (legislators, police, prosecutors, and judges), representing segments of a politically organized society, are responsible for formulating and administering criminal law. Persons and behaviors, therefore, become criminal because of the *formulation* and *application* of criminal definitions. Thus, *crime is created.*

By viewing crime as a definition, we are able to avoid the commonly used "clinical perspective," which leads one to concentrate on the quality of the act and to assume that criminal behavior is an individual pathology. Crime is not inherent in behavior, but is a judgment made by some about the actions and characteristics of others. This proposition allows us to focus on the formulation and administration of the criminal law as it touches upon the behaviors that become defined as criminal. Crime is seen as a result of a process which culminates in the defining of persons and behaviors as criminal. It follows, then, that *the greater the number of criminal definitions formulated and applied, the greater the amount of crime.*

PROPOSITION 2 (FORMULATION OF CRIMINAL DEFINITIONS): *Criminal definitions describe behaviors that conflict with the interests of the segments of society that have the power to shape public policy.*

Criminal definitions are formulated according to the interests of those *segments* (types of social groupings) of society which have the *power* to translate their interests into *public policy*. The interests—based on desires, values, and norms—which are ultimately incorporated into the criminal law are those which are treasured by the dominant interest groups in the society. In other words, those who have the ability to have their interests represented in public policy regulate the formulation of criminal definitions.

That criminal definitions are formulated is one of the most obvious manifestations of *conflict* in society. By formulating criminal law (including legislative statutes, administrative rulings, and judicial decisions), some segments of society protect and perpetuate their own interests. Criminal definitions exist, therefore, because some segments of society are in conflict with others. By formulating criminal definitions these segments are able to control the behavior of persons in other segments. It follows that *the greater the conflict in interests between the segments of a society, the greater the probability that the power segments will formulate criminal definitions.*

The interests of the power segments of society are reflected not only in the content of criminal definitions and the kinds of penal sanctions attached to them, but also in the *legal policies* stipulating how those who come to be defined as "criminal" are to be handled. Hence, procedural rules are created for enforcing and administering the criminal law. Policies are also established on programs for treating and punishing the criminally defined and for controlling and preventing crime. In the initial criminal definitions or the subsequent procedures, and in correctional and penal programs or policies of crime control and prevention, the segments of society that have power and interests to protect are instrumental in regulating the behavior of those who have conflicting interests and less power. Finally, law changes with modifications in the interest structure. When the interests that underlie a criminal law are no longer relevant to groups in power, the law will be reinterpreted or altered to incorporate the dominant interests. Hence, *the probability that criminal definitions will be formulated is increased by such factors as (1) changing social conditions, (2) emerging interests, (3) increasing demands that political, economic, and religious interests be protected, and (4) changing conceptions of the public interest.* The social history of law reflects changes in the interest structure of society.

PROPOSITION 3 (APPLICATION OF CRIMINAL DEFINITIONS): *Criminal definitions are applied by the segments of society that have the power to shape the enforcement and administration of criminal law.*

The powerful interests intervene in all stages in which criminal definitions are created. Since interests cannot be effectively protected by merely formulating criminal law, enforcement and administration of the law are required. The interests of the powerful, therefore, operate in *applying* criminal definitions. Consequently, crime is "political behavior and the criminal becomes in fact a member of a 'minority group' without sufficient public support to dominate the control of the police power of the state" [, according to George B. Vold]. Those whose interests conflict with the interests represented in the law must either change their behavior or possibly find it defined as "criminal."

The probability that criminal definitions will be applied varies according to the extent to which the behaviors of the powerless conflict with the interests of the power segments. Law enforcement efforts and judicial activity are likely to be increased when the interests of the powerful are threatened by the opposition's behavior. Fluctuations and variations in the application of criminal definitions reflect shifts in the relations of the various segments in the power structure of society.

Obviously, the criminal law is not applied directly by the powerful segments. They delegate enforcement and administration of the law to authorized *legal agents*, who, nevertheless, represent their interests. In fact, the security in office of legal agents depends on their ability to represent the society's dominant interests.

Because the interest groups responsible for creating criminal definitions are physically separated from the groups to which the authority to enforce and administer law is delegated, local conditions affect the manner in which criminal definitions are applied. In particular, communities vary in the law enforcement and administration of justice they expect. Application is also affected by the visibility of acts in a community and by its norms about reporting possible offenses. Especially important are the occupational organization and ideology of the legal agents. Thus, *the probability that criminal definitions will be applied is influenced by such community and organizational factors as (1) community expectations of law enforcement and administration, (2) the visibility and public reporting of offenses, and (3) the occupational organization, ideology, and actions of the legal agents to whom the authority to enforce and administer criminal law is delegated.* Such factors determine how the dominant interests of society are implemented in the application of criminal definitions.

The probability that criminal definitions will be applied in *specific situations* depends on the actions of the legal agents. In the final analysis, a criminal definition is applied according to an *evaluation* by someone charged with the authority to enforce and administer the law. In the course of "criminalization," a criminal label may be affixed to a person because of real or fancied attributes: [Austin T. Turk writes,] "Indeed, a person is evaluated, either favorably or unfavorably, not because he *does* something, or even because he *is* something, but because others react to their perceptions of him as offensive or inoffensive." Evaluation by the definers is affected by the way in which the suspect handles the situation, but ultimately their evaluations and subsequent decisions determine the criminality of human acts. Hence, *the more legal agents evaluate behaviors and persons as worthy of criminal definition, the greater the probability that criminal definitions will be applied.*

PROPOSITION 4 (DEVELOPMENT OF BEHAVIOR PATTERNS IN RELATION TO CRIMINAL DEFINITIONS): *Behavior patterns are structured in segmentally organized society in relation to criminal definitions, and within this context persons engage in actions that have relative probabilities of being defined as criminal.*

Although behavior varies, all behaviors are similar in that they represent the *behavior patterns* of segments of society. Therefore, all persons—whether they create criminal definitions or are the objects of criminal definitions—act according to *normative systems* learned in relative social and cultural settings. Since it is not the quality of the behavior but the action taken against the behavior that makes it criminal, that which is defined as criminal in any society is relative to the behavior patterns of the segments of society that formulate and apply criminal definitions. Consequently, *persons in the segments of society whose behavior patterns are not represented in formulating and applying criminal definitions are more likely to act in ways that will be defined as criminal than those in the segments that formulate and apply criminal definitions.*

Once behavior patterns are established with some regularity within the respective segments of society, individuals are provided with a framework for developing *personal action patterns*. These patterns continually develop for each person as he moves from one experience to another. It is the development of these patterns that gives his behavior its own substance in relation to criminal definitions.

Man constructs his own patterns of action in participating with others. It follows, then, that *the probability that a person will develop action patterns that have a high potential of being defined as criminal depends on the relative substance of (1) structured opportunities, (2) learning experiences, (3) interpersonal associations and identifications, and (4) self-conceptions.* Throughout his experiences, each person creates a conception of himself as a social being. Thus prepared, he behaves according to the anticipated consequences of his actions.

During experiences shared by the criminal definers and the criminally defined, personal action patterns develop among the criminally defined because they are so defined. After such persons have had continued experience in being criminally defined, they learn to manipulate the application of criminal definitions.

Furthermore, those who have been defined as criminal begin to conceive of themselves as criminal; as they adjust to the definitions imposed upon them, they learn to play the role of the criminal. Because of others' reactions, therefore, persons may develop personal action patterns that increase the likelihood of their being defined as criminal in the future. That is, *increased experience with criminal definitions increases the probability of developing actions that may be subsequently defined as criminal.*

Thus, both the criminal definers and the criminally defined are involved in reciprocal action patterns. The patterns of both the definers and the defined are shaped by their common, continued, and related experiences. The fate of each is bound to that of the other.

PROPOSITION 5 (CONSTRUCTION OF CRIMINAL CONCEPTIONS): *Conceptions of crime are constructed and diffused in the segments of society by various means of communication.*

The "real world" is a social construction: man with the help of others creates the world in which he lives. Social reality is thus the world a group of people create and believe in as their own. This reality is constructed according to the kind of "knowledge" they develop, the ideas they are exposed to, the manner in which they select information to fit the world they are shaping, and the manner in which they interpret these conceptions. Man behaves in reference to the *social meanings* he attaches to his experiences.

Among the constructions that develop in a society are those which determine what man regards as crime. Wherever we find the concept of crime, there we will find conceptions about the relevance of crime, the offender's characteristics, and the relation of crime to the social order. These conceptions are constructed by communication. In fact, *the construction of criminal conceptions depends on the portrayal of crime in all personal and mass communications.* By such means, criminal conceptions are constructed and diffused in the segments of a society. The most critical conceptions are those held by the power segments of society. These are the conceptions that are certain of becoming incorporated into the social reality of crime. In general, then, *the more the power segments are concerned about crime, the greater the probability that criminal definitions will be created and that behavior patterns will develop in opposition to criminal definitions.* The formulation and application of criminal definitions and the development of behavior patterns related to criminal definitions are thus joined in full circle by the construction of criminal conceptions.

PROPOSITION 6 (THE SOCIAL REALITY OF CRIME): *The social reality of crime is constructed by the formulation and application of criminal definitions, the development of behavior patterns related to criminal definitions, and the construction of criminal conceptions.*

These five propositions can be collected into a composite. The theory, accordingly, describes and explains phenomena that increase the probability of crime in society, resulting in the social reality of crime.

Since the first proposition is a definition and the sixth is a composite, the body of the theory consists of the four middle propositions. These form a model, as diagrammed in Figure 1, which relates the propositions into a theoretical system. Each proposition is related to the others forming a theoretical system of developmental propositions interacting with one another. The phenomena denoted in the propositions and their relationships culminate in what is regarded as the amount and character of crime in a society at any given time, that is, in the social reality of crime.

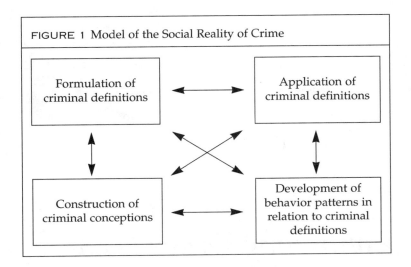

FIGURE 1 Model of the Social Reality of Crime

Formulation of criminal definitions

Application of criminal definitions

Construction of criminal conceptions

Development of behavior patterns in relation to criminal definitions

A Theoretical Perspective for Studying Crime

The theory as I have formulated it is inspired by a change currently altering our view of the world. This change, found at all levels of society, has to do with the world that we all construct and, at the same time, pretend to separate ourselves from in assessing our experiences. Sociologists, sensing the problematic nature of existence, have begun to revise their theoretical orientation, as well as their methods and subjects of investigation.

For the study of crime, a revision in thought is directing attention to the process by which criminal definitions are formulated and applied. In the theory of the social reality of crime I have attempted to show how a theory of crime can be consistent with some revisionist assumptions about theoretical explanation and about man and society. The theory is cumulative in that the framework incorporates the diverse findings from criminology.

The synthesis has been brought about by conceiving of crime as a constructive process and by formulating a theory according to a system of propositions. The theory is integrative in that all relevant phenomena contribute to the process of creating criminal definitions, the development of the behaviors of those who are involved in criminal defining situations, and the construction of criminal conceptions. The result is the social reality of crime that is constantly being constructed in society.

Controlling Drugs Is an Appropriate Use of Criminal Law

JAMES Q. WILSON

As criminal justice agencies have invested increasing amounts of resources and personnel in the "war on drugs," many questions have been raised about the law enforcement approach to drug control. James Q. Wilson is a criminologist and criminal justice researcher who has remained steadfast in his belief that our present policy of relying on legislation and criminal justice enforcement to control drugs and to deter drug use is good policy. He argues that we are not losing the war on drugs. The present policy of interdiction and enforcement combined with education and enforced treatment is the best approach to this problem, according to Wilson. James Q. Wilson, unlike many other contemporary criminologists, is a firm believer in deterrence through legal enforcement and

From James Q. Wilson, "Against the Legalization of Drugs." Reprinted from *Commentary*, February 1990, by permission; all rights reserved.

punishment. In his view, laws against drug importation, sales, and use have a definite part to play in controlling drugs in our society.

James Q. Wilson is Collins Professor of Management and Public Policy at UCLA. He has served on numerous national commissions related to crime policy and is the author of *Thinking About Crime* and *Crime and Human Nature*.

QUESTIONS

1. What evidence does Wilson present for his argument that without our present "war on drugs" our drug problem would be worse?
2. What evidence does Wilson use to refute the argument that we have lost the "war on drugs?"
3. Do you find Wilson's arguments persuasive? Why or why not?

■ ■ ■

The notion that abusing drugs such as cocaine is a 'victimless crime' is not only absurd but dangerous. Even ignoring the fetal drug syndrome, crack-dependent people are, like heroin addicts, individuals who regularly victimize their children by neglect, their spouses by improvidence, their employers by lethargy, and their co-workers by carelessness. Society is not and could never be a collection of autonomous individuals. We all have a stake in ensuring that each of us displays a minimal level of dignity, responsibility, and empathy. We cannot, of course, coerce people into goodness, but we can and should insist that some standards must be met if society itself—on which the very existence of the human personality depends—is to persist. Drawing the line that defines those standards is difficult and contentious, but if crack and heroin use do not fall below it, what does?

The advocates of legalization will respond by suggesting that my picture is overdrawn. Ethan Nadelmann of Princeton argues that the risk of legalization is less than most people suppose. Over 20 million Americans between the ages of 18 and 25 have tried cocaine (according to a government survey), but only a quarter of a million use it daily. From this Nadelmann concludes that at most 3 percent of all young people who try cocaine develop a problem with it. The implication is clear: make the drug legal and we only have to worry about 3 percent of our youth.

The implication rests on a logical fallacy and a factual error. The fallacy is this: the percentage of occasional cocaine users who become binge users *when the drug is illegal* (and thus expensive and hard to find) tells us nothing about the percentage who will become dependent when the drug is legal (and thus cheap and abundant). Drs. Frank Gawin and Everett Ellinwood report, in common with several other researchers, that controlled or occasional use of cocaine changes to compulsive and frequent use "when access to the drug increases" or when the user switches from snorting to smoking. More cocaine more potently administered alters, perhaps sharply, the proportion of "controlled" users who become heavy users.

The factual error is this: the federal survey Nadelmann quotes was done in 1985, *before* crack had become common. Thus the probability of becoming dependent on cocaine was derived from the responses of users who snorted the drug. The speed and potency of cocaine's action increases dramatically when it is smoked. We do not yet know how greatly the advent of crack increases the risk of dependency, but all the clinical evidence suggests that the increase is likely to be large.

It is possible that some people will not become heavy users even when the drug is readily available in its most potent form. So far there are no scientific grounds for predicting who will and who will not become dependent. Neither socio-economic background nor personality traits differentiate between casual and intensive users. Thus, the only way to settle the question of who is correct about the effect of easy availability on drug use, Nadelmann or Gawin and Ellinwood, is to try it and see. But that social experiment is so risky as to be no experiment at all, for if cocaine is legalized and if the rate of its abusive use increases dramatically, there is no way to put the genie back in the bottle, and it is not a kindly genie.

Have We Lost?

Many people who agree that there are risks in legalizing cocaine or heroin still favor it because, they think, we have lost the war on drugs. 'Nothing we have done has worked' and the current federal policy is just 'more of the same.' Whatever the costs of greater drug use, surely they would be less than the costs of our present, failed efforts.

That is exactly what I was told in 1972—and heroin is not quite as bad a drug as cocaine. We did not surrender and we did not lose. We did not win, either. What the nation accomplished then was what most efforts to save people from themselves accomplish: the problem was contained and the number of victims minimized, all at a considerable cost in law enforcement and increased crime. Was the cost worth it? I think so, but others may disagree. What are the lives of would-be addicts worth? I recall some people saying to me then, "Let them kill themselves." I was appalled. Happily, such views did not prevail.

Have we lost today? Not at all. High-rate cocaine use is not commonplace. The National Institute on Drug Abuse (NIDA) reports that less than 5 percent of high-school seniors had used cocaine within the last 30 days. Of course this survey misses young people who have dropped out of school and miscounts those who lie on the questionnaire, but even if we inflate the NIDA estimate by some plausible percentage, it is still not much above 5 percent. Medical examiners reported in 1987 that about 1,500 died from cocaine use; hospital emergency rooms reported about 30,000 admissions related to cocaine abuse.

These are not small numbers, but neither are they evidence of a nationwide plague that threatens to engulf us all. Moreover, cities vary greatly in the proportion of people who are involved with cocaine. To get city-level data we need to turn to drug tests carried out on arrested persons, who obviously are more likely to be drug users than the average citizen. The National Institute of Justice, through its Drug Use Forecasting (DUF) project, collects urinalysis data on arrestees in 22 cities. As we have already seen, opiate (chiefly heroin) use has been flat or declining in most of these cities over the last decade. Cocaine use has gone up sharply, but with great variation among cities. New York, Philadelphia, and Washington, D.C., all report that two-thirds or more of their arrestees tested positive for cocaine, but in Portland, San Antonio, and Indianapolis the percentage was one-third or less.

In some neighborhoods, of course, matters have reached crisis proportions. Gangs control the streets, shootings terrorize residents, and drug-dealing occurs in plain view. The police seem barely able to contain matters. But in these neighborhoods—unlike at Palo Alto cocktail parties—the people are not calling for legalization, they are calling for help. And often not much help has come. Many cities are willing to do almost anything about the drug problem except spend more money on it. The federal government cannot change that; only local voters and politicians can. It is not clear that they will.

It took about ten years to contain heroin. We have had experience with crack for only about three or four years. Each year we spend perhaps $11 billion on law enforcement (and some of that goes to deal with marijuana) and perhaps $2 million on treatment. Large sums, but not sums that should lead anyone to say, 'We just can't afford this anymore.'

The illegality of drugs increases crime, partly because some users turn to crime to pay for their habits, partly because some users are stimulated by certain drugs (such as crack or PCP) to act more violently or ruthlessly than they otherwise would, and partly because criminal organizations seeking to control drug supplies use force to manage their markets. These also are serious costs, but no one knows how much they would be reduced if drugs were legalized. Addicts would no longer steal to pay black-market prices for drugs, a real gain. But some, perhaps a great deal, of that gain would be offset by the great increase in the number of addicts. These people, nodding on heroin or living in the delusion-ridden high of cocaine, would hardly be ideal employees. Many would steal simply to support themselves, since snatch-and-grab, opportunistic crime can be managed even by people unable to hold a regular job or plan an elaborate crime. Those British addicts who get their supplies from government clinics are not models of law-abiding decency. Most are in crime, and though their per-capita rate of criminality may be lower thanks to the cheapness of their drugs, the total volume of crime they produce may be quite large. Of course, society could decide to support all unemployable addicts on welfare, but that would mean that gains from lowered rates of crime would have to be offset by large increases in welfare budgets.

Proponents of legalization claim that the costs of having more addicts around would be largely if not entirely offset by having more money available with which to treat and care for them. The money would come from taxes levied on the sale of heroin and cocaine.

To obtain this fiscal dividend, however, legalization's supporters must first solve an economic dilemma. If they want to raise a lot of money to pay for welfare and treatment, the tax rate on the drugs will have to be quite high. Even if they themselves do not want a high rate, the politicians' love of 'sin taxes' would probably guarantee that it would be high anyway. But the higher the tax, the higher the price of the drug, and the higher the price the greater the likelihood that addicts will turn to crime to find the money for it and that criminal organizations will be formed to sell tax-free drugs at below-market rates. If we managed to keep taxes (and thus prices) low, we would get that much less money to pay for welfare and treatment and more people could afford to become addicts. There may be an optimal tax rate for drugs that maximizes revenue while minimizing crime, bootlegging, and the recruitment of new addicts, but our experience with alcohol does not suggest that we know how to find it.

The Benefits of Illegality

The advocates of legalization find nothing to be said in favor of the current system except, possibly, that it keeps the number of addicts smaller than it would otherwise be. In fact, the benefits are more substantial than that.

First, treatment. All the talk about providing 'treatment on demand' implies that there is a demand for treatment. That is not quite right. There are some drug-dependent people who genuinely want treatment and will remain in it if offered; they should receive it. But there are far more who want only short-term help after a bad crash; once stabilized and bathed, they are back on the street again, hustling. And even many of the addicts who enroll in a program honestly wanting help drop out after a short while when they discover that help takes time and commitment. Drug-dependent people have very short time horizons and a weak capacity for commitment.

These two groups—those looking for a quick fix and those unable to stick with a long-term fix—are not easily helped. Even if we increase the number of treatment slots—as we should—we would have to do something to make treatment more effective.

One thing that can often make it more effective is compulsion. Douglas Anglin of UCLA, in common with many other researchers, has found that the longer one stays in a treatment program, the better the chances of a reduction in drug dependency. But he, again like most other researchers, has found that drop-out rates are high. He has also found, however, that patients who enter treatment under legal compulsion stay in the program longer than those not subject to such pressure. His research on the California civil-commitment program, for example, found that heroin users involved with its required drug-testing program had over the long term a lower rate of heroin use than similar addicts who were free of such constraints. If for many addicts compulsion is a useful component of treatment, it is not clear how compulsion could be achieved in a society in which purchasing, possessing, and using the drug were legal. It could be managed, I suppose, but I would not want to have to answer the challenge from the American Civil Liberties Union that it is wrong to compel a person to undergo treatment for consuming a legal commodity.

Next, education. We are now investing substantially in drug-education programs in the schools. Though we do not yet know for certain what will work, there are some promising leads. But I wonder how credible such programs would be if they were aimed at dissuading children from doing something perfectly legal. We could, of course, treat drug education like smoking education: inhaling crack and inhaling tobacco are both legal, but you should not do it because it is bad for you. That tobacco is bad for you is easily shown; the Surgeon General has seen to that. But what do we say about crack? It is pleasurable, but devoting yourself to so much pleasure is not a good idea (though perfectly legal)? Unlike tobacco, cocaine will not give you cancer or emphysema, but it will lead you to neglect your duties to family, job, and neighborhood? Everybody is doing cocaine, but you should not?

Again, it might be possible under a legalized regime to have effective drug-prevention programs, but their effectiveness would depend heavily, I think, on first having decided that cocaine use, like tobacco use, is purely a matter of practical consequences; no fundamental moral significance attaches to either. But if we believe—as I do—that dependency on certain mind-altering drugs *is* a moral issue and that their illegality rests in part on their immorality, then legalizing them undercuts, if it does not eliminate altogether, the moral message.

That message is at the root of the distinction we now make between nicotine and cocaine. Both are highly addictive; both have harmful physical effects. But we treat the two drugs differently, not simply because nicotine is so widely used as to be beyond the reach of effective prohibition, but because its use does not destroy the user's essential humanity. Tobacco shortens one's life, cocaine debases it. Nicotine alters one's habits, cocaine alters one's soul. The heavy use of crack, unlike the heavy use of tobacco, corrodes those natural sentiments of sympathy and duty that constitute our human nature and make possible our social life. To say, as does Nadelmann, that distinguishing morally between tobacco and cocaine is "little more than a transient prejudice" is close to saying that morality itself is but a prejudice. . . .

If I Am Wrong . . .

No one can know what our society would be like if we changed the law to make access to cocaine, heroin, and PCP easier. I believe, for reasons given, that the result would be a sharp increase in use, a more widespread degradation of the human personality, and a greater rate of accidents and violence.

I may be wrong. If I am, then we will needlessly have incurred heavy costs in enforcement and some forms of criminality. But if I am right, and legalizers prevail anyway, then we will have consigned millions of people, hundreds of thousands of infants, and hundreds of neighborhoods to a life of oblivion and disease. To the lives and families destroyed by alcohol we will have added countless more destroyed by cocaine, heroin, PCP, and whatever else a basement scientist can invent.

Controlling Drugs Is Not an Appropriate Use of Criminal Law and the Administration of Justice

TODD AUSTIN BRENNER

There has been much debate within criminology about the wisdom of using the criminal law to regulate drugs in our society. Drug legislation, arrests, prosecutions, and incarceration take up a great deal of the time and resources of lawmakers and criminal justice agencies. A growing number of prominent and legitimate voices have been heard in recent years advocating drug legalization. These spokespersons for the idea of legalization view our present efforts to control drugs as a waste of valuable resources. They claim that the "war on drugs" is a monumental fraud perpetrated on the public by unknowing or unscrupulous politicians and

From Todd Austin Brenner, "The Legalization of Drugs: Why Prolong the Inevitable?" This article was originally published in the *Capital University Law Review* 18 (1989):171-79.

enforcement agencies to serve their own interests. In this viewpoint, Todd Austin Brenner reviews the economic impact of drug enforcement and argues that our present policies do not deter illegal drug use. Todd Austin Brenner is an attorney in private practice. He received his J.D. in 1990 from Capital University Law School in Washington, D.C.

QUESTIONS

1. What evidence does Brenner present to prove that our policies of drug interdiction and arrest for illegal drug sale and use have been failures?
2. What evidence does Brenner present that policies of deterrence have not worked?
3. Does this argument persuade you that drug criminalization is bad policy? Why or why not?

■ ■ ■

Even if society cannot accept the human rights arguments of personal autonomy and anti-paternalism, surely society must realize, in a utilitarian sense, how criminalization of drug use is adversely affecting, at the very least, the economic and criminal justice systems.

Economic Concerns

The effects on the economy caused by drug criminalization are inarguably devastating. Americans spend at least $100 billion a year, or twice as much as is spent for oil, to purchase illegal drugs. This money is untaxed, of course, and is reputed to fall into the hands of organized crime, which is lured into the business by the incredible profit margin inherent to the industry.

Hurting the economy much worse than untaxed revenues are the government's attempts to limit the supply of drugs entering the country and to seize this supply once it has crossed the borders. Since 1981, the U.S. government has spent over $10 billion to stop the importation of drugs, with little or no success. There are as many drugs in the country now as there ever have been, and the continual decline in price of most drugs suggests that competition is building year by year. The truth of the matter is that sealing America's borders is a futile, unintelligent attempt at controlling supply. The United States has a 5,400 mile border with Canada and a 1,900 mile border with Mexico. To 'seal' these borders, $14 billion for airplanes and another $6 billion for operations is necessary, a recent study revealed. Such a proposal is not economically feasible. As it now stands, only 10% of all illegal narcotics are prevented from entering the country, while it is estimated that only another 10% would be blocked if further draconian, military measures are undertaken.

Another sobering fact with regard to interdiction is that "hard drugs" such as cocaine are easy to conceal. In fact, one fully loaded cargo plane could supply the entire U.S. market for one year. It is no surprise, then, that the estimated price per 'drug bust' in 1987 was between $350,000 and $400,000. Yet, these 'busts' have little impact on buyers because of the voluminous supply; consequently, demand remains unaffected.

A major benefit arising from legalization of drugs would be the revenues generated from the taxation of these drugs. The societal view of taxing "sinful" activities is not a favorable one, but the government nevertheless taxes cigarettes, alcohol and even *Hustler* magazine. Perhaps if society were educated about the pragmatic results of taxation, views could change. For instance, taxing marijuana alone would produce $20 billion at the current rate of consumption. Currently, $1.2 billion is spent annually on drug treatment, or one-eighteenth of the amount taxing marijuana would generate. The problem, of course, is convincing the public that taxing drugs is no more sinful than taxing pornography.

Criminal Law Concerns

Deterrence Proponents of drug criminalization insist that the threat of arrest acts as a valuable deterrent. Simple logic refutes such a conclusion, however, in that the chances of getting caught with drugs are so slight that anyone taking the least of precautions will avoid arrest. In fact, the drug most easily detected, marijuana, is nearly undetectable. In 1987, there were 378,709 marijuana arrests and 25 million people who used the drug. Thus the chance of getting caught for these users was about 1 in 63. For more potent drugs which are harder to detect, the risk is even smaller.

Criminalization does not provide a valuable deterrent because it doesn't take into account that choices people make are intrinsically determined; what people decide to do with their bodies is the result of individual choice. Therefore, deterrence of drug use should be achieved through education rather than the law. Once this process is in gear, other forces such as peer pressure and socially felt stigmas attached to drug use will produce a domino educational effect, a force much more powerful than the law. Furthermore, the thrill of illegality will be removed from those who cherish it.

Criminalization proponents counter with the suggestion that if tougher, draconian measures were invoked, deterrence of drug use would be more effectively achieved. While this may be true, the costs would simply be too high. Prisons and courtrooms would be excessively crowded, enforcement costs would increase, and subsequently taxes would be raised to fund such measures. Moreover, if prison sentences were inflated or capital punishment imposed on drug dealers, killing policemen would be worth it. Sentencing drug users, furthermore, to jail or prison would not only expose them to 'real' criminals, but also crowd the prisons to the point where neither the drug user nor the hard criminal would have a realistic chance of reform.

Drug-Related Crime Another concern of anti-legalizers is the level of crime that would result due to legalization. An initial consequence would be a reduction in junkie-related robberies and deaths. The significantly reduced prices of drugs would alleviate the temptation to steal or rob for drug money and also curb the desire to attack drug dealers or gangs. Gang warfare would be reduced as would incidental murders.

Drug-related crime, though, would increase if drug users were permitted access to inexpensive drugs, criminalization proponents maintain. This criminogenetic philosophy, on the surface, seems logical. However, what advocates of this reasoning fail to realize is that criminalization forces drug users to steal for money and brings them into contact with 'real' criminals, resulting in the commission of incidental crime. Furthermore, the stigma attached to engaging in an illegal activity may encourage chemical dependence because of the fear of coming forward for help, thus causing the temptation of incidental crime necessary to support the dependency. Also, the use of depressant drugs, such as heroin and marijuana, is thought to suppress violent behavior, whereas alcohol, the most popular drug, heightens violent tendencies.

Where the criminogenesis argument is most weak, though, is in its underlying rationale: to prevent drug-related crime, society forbids the use of drugs themselves. Crimes are punishable because of the harm caused to society; culpability is assessed only upon the discovery of the intentional will of the actor. The intake of drugs may lead to temptation, but temptation is only a factor in a person's will. Therefore, punishing a person for drug use to stop him from committing a crime is to punish factors for the will, not the direct causes.

Other Concerns

Children Perhaps the greatest concern of those opposing legalization of drugs is its possible effects on children. Undoubtedly a wave of confusion will be felt by children if drugs are legalized. Confusion, though, may be a favorable alternative to what children are feeling today.

Children today are bombarded with news about the drug problem. They hear repeatedly about the 'Just Say No' campaign. They hear from adults about the evil of drugs. They hear about classmates who may happen to indulge in drugs. The problem with all this communication is that at the same time children hear it, they also know that drugs are illegal. The result is that children begin to feel a sense of disrespect for law and authority.

Additionally, children already have the ability to obtain drugs, but in a very dangerous manner. They have to deal with drug dealers, who may very well manipulate these children into taking harder drugs or 'dealing' drugs to friends. Furthermore, the contents of the drugs these children buy are dangerously questionable. In the worst-case scenario, upon legalization only those persons who would be over the majority age would be permitted to purchase drugs and these drugs would be in pure form, free from dangerous substances.

In the final analysis, it is parents who must exercise

responsibility in educating and disciplining their offspring. Parents should give their children an honest description of the effects of drugs and help them understand that this is a society in which freedom of choice is considered extremely important and that wisdom and responsibility are vital.

Pronouncing Benediction   Another gargantuan roadblock for legalization advocates is society's view that to legalize is to advocate. This attitude is a fatal misconception. Society surely does not advocate watching pornography nor does it advocate riding a motorcycle without wearing a helmet, but those activities are not criminalized. One way to overcome the benediction concern is to use some of the enormous tax money for negative, or at the very least educational, advertising, while at the same time forbidding any form of promotional advertising. Such an approach would run contrary to the alcohol industry, which spends enormous amounts of money for promotional advertising, and would run nearly parallel to the cigarette industry, where warnings are now placed on every pack of cigarettes. The nicotine warnings have had positive effects, such as lowering the rate of use.

Increased Addiction   The possibility of increased addiction to drugs has been another argument against legalization. The simple rebuttal to this conjecture is that there is no evidence to support it. A popular belief is that drug use itself leads to addiction, a belief totally unfounded. Studies have shown that psychological factors are more directly attributable to drug addiction than physical factors. Hence, a person's desire to become addicted, whether obscure or overt, dictates whether or not he will indeed become addicted.

Another misconception about addiction is that productivity is sure to take a 'nosedive' once a person becomes dependent or that an addict cannot live a normal life. Interestingly, doctors have the highest addiction rate of any group, without leading abnormal or unproductive lives.

Criminalizing drug use discourages addicts from coming forward with their problem. In the first place, addicts are afraid to come forward because of the criminal label associated with such an action. Secondly, in areas of the country where drug addiction is widespread, insufficient funding for treatment programs has created waiting lists up to several months long. Legalization would cure both defects, taking the fear out of coming for help while also generating tax dollars to support treatment programs.

A Realistic Proposal

Step One   Criminalizing the use of marijuana amounts to what can be described as a half-law—it is on the 'books' but not enforced. Several states have realized the futility of enforcement as well as the exorbitant demand for the drug and, as a result, have decriminalized marijuana on that basis. The time has come for federal recognition of those facts. A law which labels 18 million users as criminals is absurd.

Step Two   Following the inevitable success of the decriminalization experiment should be the complete legalization of marijuana. This stage would act as the real test. Distribution and taxation of the drug would be handled the same way alcohol is dispensed—through licensed sellers. Restrictions on time, place, and manner of sale would also apply, just as with alcohol. Public ingestion would be strictly prohibited, as would the sale of marijuana in places of public accommodation. Furthermore, stiff penalties for driving while under the influence of marijuana would be strictly enforced.

Step Three   The final step in the enactment, assuming that marijuana legalization proves successful, is the complete legalization of all narcotics. Legalization, however, does not mean commercial sale. Drugs causing permanent addiction, such as heroin and 'crack', would be banned from sale. Instead, these drugs would be offered free of charge at clinics where addicts have been registered. Simultaneously, these addicts would be helped in trying to overcome their illness and would hopefully be cured.

The initial results of this proposal will undoubtedly be disturbing. Confusion over national morality will certainly mount. It is vitally important that legalization be accompanied by education. The reasons why legalization of drugs has occurred should be communicated to all citizens. Everyone must know that as individuals, people ought to be afforded a choice to define their personal well-being and ultimate aspirations. Revenues from the taxes imposed on the drugs will be used in massive education of this type along with non-promotional advertisements. In the long run, not only will drug use decrease, but national strength will be re-established as a result of a country proud of individual freedom.

Drug-Testing The compromise to such a proposal takes the form of drug-testing. The right to use drugs is absolute only to the extent that no direct harm is felt by others. Therefore, persons on whom many lives depend, such as airline pilots, must recognize the fact that their conduct has the potential to injure many persons. Thus the airline pilot is still afforded a freedom of choice: he can use drugs and not be an airline pilot or not use them and perform his assigned duty.

However, in jobs where lives do not depend on the assigned performance of the worker, testing would probably not be necessary because if the employee is unable to perform at the acceptable level, the employee is likely to lose his job anyway. In any event, employers should be given more discretion upon the legalization of drugs when deciding whether a drug test is in order.

Conclusion

America is becoming more and more health conscious. Americans are eating and sleeping better and exercising more. In this country's shifting attitude toward improved health, there has never been a legislative enactment requiring people to stay fit. Paternalism did not act as the guide; rather, individual instincts and personal pride were responsible. Drugs will not stand in the way of this fitness evolution. The citizenry simply knows better.

The drug problem has largely been caused by unnecessary over-criminalization. Since almost all damage caused by drugs is felt by the user himself, legislating moral behavior is no longer necessary. The problem cannot be effectively curtailed by the government's new 'shotgun' approach of 'zero tolerances' and massive federal spending. The time has come for the government to look for the individual for help, not vice versa.

What Causes Criminal Behavior?

Chapter Preface

At the time criminology was established in the United States in the early part of this century, the positivistic approach based on research through observation and experience had a major impact on all of the emerging social sciences. Criminologists began to apply this approach to the study of questions such as what causes crime.

An emphasis on positivism to answer such questions led to a reliance on the scientific method of gathering and analyzing data. Before this, those who studied crime emphasized legal reform and changes in sentencing procedures. This emphasis on legal reform was characteristic of "classical criminology." It did not involve scientific data gathering but attempted to base reform of criminal justice on philosophical principles of justice. Classical criminology emphasized free will and deterring crime through punishment. In contrast to this, positivistic criminologists have generally assumed that crime is produced by forces beyond the control of the offender. Thus, from an approach to understanding crime that is consistent with the basis of criminal law and criminal justice, criminologists moved to an approach that de-emphasized free will and sought causes outside the control of the criminal.

The person who is generally acknowledged to be the founder of positivistic criminology is Italian criminologist Cesare Lombroso. He observed convicted criminals in an attempt to determine the special characteristics of the "criminal man" or the "born criminal." He claimed to find physical and mental differences distinguishing many criminal offenders. According to Lombroso, these distinguishing characteristics also influenced criminals' morality. He postulated that many criminals exhibit physical, mental, and moral characteristics of savage, uncivilized groups.

Lombroso's theories of the born criminal were used in the United States to justify eugenics programs in which prisoners were castrated so they could not reproduce. These theories and programs fell into disrepute when testing programs used on prisoners and delinquent youth indicated few differences between these groups and the general population. However, attempts have been revived throughout this century to prove that genetic and brain abnormalities account for criminal behavior and violence. These approaches to understanding criminal behavior are resisted by those who argue that they will be used to justify special incarceration, suspension of civil liberties, and abusive treatment intervention for minority populations.

As criminology evolved in the United States in the twentieth century, it was dominated by sociologists. Sociologists downplayed biology and psychology and focused on class, race, cultural and social background, environment, and peer influences. This allowed criminologists to recommend programs for social change and the rehabilitation of offenders as remedies for crime. These theories gained acceptance because they assume that criminals and delinquents are sociologically distinct from law-abiding citizens. If social conditions produce criminals, rehabilitation programs can be useful and should be politically supported.

By placing a focus on environmental causes of crime, criminologists concluded that criminal attitudes and behavior are learned. This idea was first articulated by Edwin Sutherland and other sociologists who were part of the Chicago school of sociology.

Those criminologists associated with the Chicago school focused the study of criminology on the socialization process, group conflicts over values, and areas of the city in which criminal and deviant lifestyles and associations develop. This approach still dominates modern American criminological research and theory. Adherents to this theory argue that crime prevention must be achieved through identification of and modification of social conditions that encourage criminality.

An extension of this approach to criminology became the "labeling" perspective on deviance. The labeling perspective blames causes of crime and delinquency on the criminal justice system which labels criminals. One of the earliest and most influential sociologists to articulate this perspective was Howard S. Becker. He argued that the authorities and agencies who react to deviant behavior, such as schools, police, prosecutors, and correctional authorities create crime. Institutions, not individuals, should be studied by criminologists. This encouraged criminologists to study the attitudes, values, procedures, and goals of authority figures who processed delinquents and criminals.

Other criminologists influenced by sociological theory began to look at group attachments (such as attachments to family, school, peers, and adult authority figures) that influence law-abiding and illegal behavior. Their focus was not on what makes the criminal distinct but on why most people do not engage in criminal behavior. They emphasized social bonds that contain and control behavior to maintain social order. This approach to understanding the differences between the criminal and the law-abiding members of society is called containment, control, or social bond theory. Advocates of this theory claim that law-abiding citizens have forged bonds with those who would be harmed by our criminal behavior. We do not wish to hurt those we care about so we sometimes defer our short-term interest to get what we want when we want it in favor of long-term commitment to those whose support we value and whose positive opinion of us matters in the long run. From this point of view, the attention lavished on the criminal and the money spent on studying criminal behavior could better be used to understand how to maintain social order and encourage crime prevention.

All of these approaches to understanding and alleviating crime have influenced the development of criminology in this country during this century. The viewpoints in this chapter attempt to present the main arguments.

Primitive Physiological Characteristics Cause Criminal Behavior

GINA LOMBROSO-FERRERO

The basic premise of positivistic criminology was that criminal offenders share characteristics that make them different from law-abiding citizens. Factors beyond their control lead them to commit crime. Therefore, the task of positivistic criminology is to discover these special characteristics so that crime can be prevented in the future by treating the biological and psychological pathologies of criminals. The first criminologist to base research on these ideas was Cesare Lombroso. He studied convicted criminals in Italy and claimed to have discovered special physical and psychological "anomalies" that characterize the criminal type or the "born criminal." Although later sociologically oriented criminologists discredited this type of

Excerpted from Gina Lombroso-Ferrero, *Criminal Man, According to the Classification of Cesare Lombroso.* New York: G.P. Putnam's Sons, 1911.

research and theorizing, it continues in some forms today. It has become common in criminology for violent and repeat offenders to be characterized as predators. This implies that they are similar to skulking beasts or savages waiting to pounce on unsuspecting citizens. As we will see in the viewpoint by C. Ray Jeffery, some criminologists still pursue this approach that attempts to set the criminal apart from the normal human being in their genetic makeup, biological development, and mental capabilities. Gina Lombroso-Ferrero is the daughter of Cesare Lombroso and has also engaged in criminological research.

QUESTIONS

1. How does the author characterize the "Positive School of Penal Jurisprudence"?
2. What sets that school apart from the previous "Classical School of Penal Jurisprudence"?
3. What does it mean to say that criminals share certain "anomalies"? What are the examples cited?

■ ■ ■

The Development of Positivistic Criminology

The Classical School of Penal Jurisprudence, of which Cesare Beccaria was the founder and Francesco Carrara the greatest and most glorious disciple, aimed only at establishing sound judgments and fixed laws to guide capricious and often undiscerning judges in the application of penalties. In writing his great work, the founder of this School was inspired by the highest of all human sentiments—pity; but although the criminal incidentally receives notice, the writings of this School treat only of the application of the law, not of offenders themselves.

This is the difference between the Classical and the Modern School of Penal Jurisprudence. The Classical School based its doctrines on the assumption that all criminals, except in a few extreme cases, are endowed with intelligence and feelings like normal individuals, and that they commit misdeeds consciously, being prompted thereto by their unrestrained desire for evil. The offence alone was considered, and on it the whole existing penal system has been founded, the severity of the sentence meted out to the offender being regulated by the gravity of his misdeed.

The Modern, or Positive, School of Penal Jurisprudence, on the contrary, maintains that the antisocial tendencies of criminals are the result of their physical and psychic organization, which differs essentially from that of normal individuals; and it aims at studying the morphology and various functional phenomena of the criminal with the object of curing, instead of punishing, him. The Modern School is therefore founded on a new science, Criminal Anthropology, which may be defined as the Natural History of the Criminal, because it embraces his organic and psychic constitution and social life, just as anthropology does in the case of normal human beings and the different races.

If we examine a number of criminals, we shall find that they exhibit numerous anomalies in the face, skeleton, and various psychic and sensitive functions, so that they strongly resemble primitive races. It was these anomalies that first drew my father's attention to the close relationship between the criminal and the savage and made him suspect that criminal tendencies are of atavistic origin.

When a young doctor at the Asylum in Pavia, he was requested to make a post-mortem examination on a criminal named Vilella, an Italian Jack the Ripper, who by atrocious crimes had spread terror in the Province of Lombardy. Scarcely had he laid open the skull, when he perceived at the base, on the spot where the internal occipital crest or ridge is found in normal individuals, a small hollow, which he called *median occipital fossa*. . . . This abnormal character was correlated to a still greater anomaly in the cerebellum, the hypertrophy of the vermis, *i.e.*, the spinal cord which separates the cerebellar lobes lying underneath the cerebral hemispheres. This vermis was so enlarged in the case of Vilella, that it almost formed a small, intermediate cerebellum like that found in the lower types of apes, rodents, and birds. This anomaly is very rare among inferior races, with the exception of the South America Indian tribe of the Aymaras of Bolivia and Peru, in whom it is not infrequently found (40%). It is seldom met within the insane or other degenerates, but later investigations have shown it to be prevalent in criminals.

This discovery was like a flash of light. "At the sight of that skull," says my father, "I seemed to see all at once, standing out clearly illumined as in a vast plain under a flaming sky, the problem of the nature of the criminal, who reproduces in civilized times characteristics, not only of primitive savages, but of still lower types as far back as the carnivora."

Thus was explained the origin of the enormous jaws, strong canines, prominent zygomae and strongly developed orbital arches which he had so frequently remarked in criminals, for these peculiarities are common to carnivores and savages, who tear and devour raw flesh. Thus also it was easy to understand why the span of the arms in criminals so often exceeds the height, for this is a characteristic of apes, whose fore-limbs are used in walking and climbing. The other anomalies exhibited by criminals—the scanty beard as opposed to the general hairiness of the body, prehensile foot, diminished number of lines in the palm of the hand, cheek-pouches, enormous development of the middle incisors and frequent absence of the lateral ones, flattened nose and angular or sugar-loaf form of the skull, common to criminals and apes; the excessive size of the orbits, which, combined with the hooked nose, so often imparts to criminals the aspect of birds of prey, the projection of the lower part of the face and jaws (prognathism) found in negroes and animals, and supernumerary teeth (amounting in some cases to a double row as in snakes) and cranial bones (epactal bone as in the Peruvian Indians): all these characteristics pointed to one conclusion, the atavistic origin of the criminal, who reproduces physical, psychic, and functional qualities of remote ancestors.

Subsequent research on the part of my father and his disciples showed that other factors besides atavism come into play in determining the criminal type. These are: disease and environment. Later on, the study of innumerable offenders led them to the conclusion that all law-breakers cannot be classed in a single species, for their ranks include very diversified types, who differ not only in their bent towards a particular form of crime, but also in the degree of tenacity and intensity displayed by them in their perverse propensities, so that, in reality, they form a graduated scale leading from the born criminal to the normal individual.

Born criminals form about one third of the mass of offenders, but, though inferior in numbers, they constitute the most important part of the whole criminal army, partly because they are constantly appearing before the public and also because the crimes committed by them are of a peculiarly monstrous character; the other two thirds are composed of criminaloids (minor offenders), occasional and habitual criminals, etc., who do not show such a marked degree of diversity from normal persons.

Let us commence with the born criminal, who as the principal nucleus of the wretched army of law-breakers, naturally manifests the most numerous and salient anomalies.

The median occipital fossa and other abnormal features just enumerated are not the only peculiarities exhibited by this aggravated type of offender. By careful research, my father and others of his School have brought to light many anomalies in bodily organs, and functions both physical and mental, all of which serve to indicate the atavistic and pathological origin of the instinctive criminal.

It would be incompatible with the scope of this summary, were I to give a minute description of the innumerable anomalies discovered in criminals by the Modern School, to attempt to trace such abnormal traits back to their source, or to demonstrate their effect on the organism. This has been done in a very minute fashion in the three volumes of my father's work *Criminal Man* and his subsequent writings on the same subject, *Modern Forms of Crime*, *Recent Research in Criminal Anthropology*, *Prison Palimpsests*, etc., etc., to which readers desirous of obtaining a more thorough knowledge of the subject should refer.

The present volume will only touch briefly on the principal characteristics of criminals, with the object of presenting a general outline of the studies of criminologists.

Physical Anomalies of the Born Criminal

The Head

As the seat of all the greatest disturbances, this part naturally manifests the greatest number of anomalies, which extend from the external conformation of the brain-case to the composition of its contents.

The criminal skull does not exhibit any marked characteristics of size and shape. Generally speaking, it tends to be larger or smaller than the average skull common to the region or country from which the criminal hails. It varies between 1,200 and 1,600 c.c.: *i.e.*, between 73 and 100 cubic inches, the normal average being 92. This applies also to the cephalic index; that is, the ratio of the maximum width to the maximum length of the skull multiplied by 100, which serves to give a concrete idea of the form of the skull, because the higher the index, the nearer the skull approaches a spherical form, and the lower the index, the more elongated it becomes. The skulls of criminals have no characteristic cephalic index, but tend to an exaggeration of the ethnical type prevalent in their native countries. In regions where dolichocephaly (index less than 80) abounds, the skulls of criminals show a very low index; if, on the contrary, they are natives of districts where brachycephaly (index 80 or more) prevails, they exhibit a very high index.

In 15.5% we find trochocephalous or abnormally round heads (index 91). A very high percentage (nearly double that of normal individuals) have submicrocephalous or small skulls. In other cases the skull is excessively large (macrocephaly) or abnormally small and ill shaped with a narrow, receding forehead (microcephaly, 0.2%). More rarely the skull is of normal size, but shaped like the keel of a boat (scaphocephaly, 0.1% and subscaphocephaly, 6%). Sometimes the anomalies are still more serious and we find wholly asymmetrical skulls with protuberances on either side (plagiocephaly, 10.9%), or terminating in a peak on the bregma or anterior fontanel (acrocephaly, . . .), or depressed in the middle (cymbocephaly, sphenocephaly). At times, there are crests or grooves along the sutures (11.9%) or the cranial bones are abnormally thick, a characteristic of savage peoples (36.6%) or abnormally thin (8.10%). Other anomalies of importance are the presence of Wormian bones in the sutures of the skull (21.22%), the bone of the Incas already alluded to (4%), and above all, the median occipital fossa. Of great importance also are the prominent frontal sinuses found in 25% (double that of normal individuals), the semicircular line of the temples, which is sometimes so exaggerated that it forms a ridge and is correlated to an excessive development of the temporal muscles, a common characteristic of primates and carnivores. Sometimes the forehead is receding, as in apes (19%), or low and narrow (10%).

The Face

In striking contrast to the narrow forehead and low vault of the skull, the face of the criminal, like those of most animals, is of disproportionate size, a phenomenon intimately connected with the greater development of the senses as compared with that of the nervous centres. Prognathism, the projection of the lower portion of the face beyond the forehead, is found in 45.7% of criminals. Progeneismus, the projection of the lower teeth and jaw beyond the upper, is found in 38%, whereas among normal persons the proportion is barely 28%. As a natural consequence of this predominance of the lower portion of the face, the orbital arches and zygomae show a corresponding development (35%) and the size of the jaws is naturally increased, the mean diameter being 103.9 mm. (4.09 inches) as against 93 mm. (3.66 inches) in normal persons. Among criminals 29% have voluminous jaws.

The excessive dimensions of the jaws and cheek-bones admit of other explanations besides the atavistic one of a greater development of the masticatory system. They may have been influenced by the habit of certain gestures, the setting of the teeth or tension of the muscles of the mouth, which accompany violent muscular efforts and are natural to men who form energetic or violent resolves and meditate plans of revenge.

Asymmetry is a common characteristic of the criminal physiognomy. The eyes and ears are frequently situated at different levels and are of unequal size, the nose slants towards one side, etc. This asymmetry, as we shall see later, is connected with marked irregularities in the senses and functions.

Sensory and Functional Peculiarities of the Born Criminal

The above-mentioned physiognomical and skeletal anomalies are further supplemented by functional peculiarities, and all these abnormal characteristics converge, as mountain streams to the hollow in the plain, towards a central idea—the atavistic nature of the born criminal.

An examination of the senses and sensibility of criminals gives the following results:

General Sensibility

Tested simply by touching with the finger, a certain degree of obtuseness is noted. By using an apparatus invented by DuBois-Reymond and adopted by my father, the degree of sensibility obtained was 49.6 mm in criminals as against 64.2 mm in normal individuals. Criminals are more sensitive on the left side, contrary to normal persons, in whom greater sensibility prevails on the right.

Sensibility to Pain

Compared with ordinary individuals, the criminal shows greater insensibility to pain as well as to touch. This obtuseness sometimes reaches complete analgesia or total absence of feeling (16%), a phenomenon never encountered in normal persons. The mean degree of dolorific sensibility in criminals is 34.1 mm. whereas it is rarely lower than 40 mm. in normal individuals. Here again the left-handedness of criminals becomes apparent, 39% showing greater sensibility on the left.

Tactile Sensibility

The distance at which two points applied to the finger-tips are felt separately is more than 4 mm. in 30% of criminals, a degree of obtuseness only found in 4% of normal individuals. Criminals exhibit greater tactile sensibility on the left. Tactile obtuseness varies with the class of crime practised by the individual. While in burglars, swindlers, and assaulters, it is double that of normal persons, in murderers, violators, and incendiaries it is often four or five times as great.

Sensibility to the Magnet, which scarcely exists in normal persons, is common to a marked degree in criminals (48%).

Meteoric Sensibility

This is far more apparent in criminals and the insane than in normal individuals. With variations of temperature and atmospheric pressure, both criminals and lunatics become agitated and manifest changes of disposition and sensations of various kinds, which are rarely experienced by normal persons.

Sight is generally acute, perhaps more so than in ordinary individuals, and in this the criminal resembles the savage. Chromatic sensibility, on the contrary, is decidedly defective, the percentage of colour-blindness being twice that of normal persons. The field of vision is frequently limited by the white and exhibits much stranger anomalies, a special irregularity of outline with deep peripheral scotoma, which is a special characteristic of the epileptic.

Hearing, Smell, Taste are generally of less than average acuteness in criminals. Cases of complete anosmia and qualitative obtuseness are not uncommon.

Agility

Criminals are generally agile and preserve this quality even at an advanced age. When over seventy, Vilella sprang like a goat up the steep rocks of his native Calabria, and the celebrated thief "La Vecchia," when quite an old man, escaped from his captors by leaping from a high rampart at Pavia.

Strength

Contrary to what might be expected, tests by means of the dynamometer show that criminals do not usually possess an extraordinary degree of strength. There is frequently a slight difference between the strength of the right and left limbs, but more often ambidexterity, as in children, and a greater degree of strength in the left limbs.

Psychology of the Born Criminal

The physical type of the criminal is completed and intensified by his moral and intellectual physiognomy, which furnishes a further proof of his relationship to the savage and epileptic.

Natural Affections

These play an important part in the life of a normally constituted individual and are in fact the *raison d´être* of his existence, but the criminal rarely, if ever, experiences emotions of this kind and least of all regarding his own kin. On the other hand, he shows exaggerated and abnormal fondness for animals and strangers. La Sola, a female criminal, manifested about as much affection for her children as if they had been kittens and induced her accomplice to murder a former paramour, who was deeply attached to her; yet she tended the sick and dying with the utmost devotion.

In the place of domestic and social affections, the criminal is dominated by a few absorbing passions: vanity, impulsiveness, desire for revenge, licentiousness.

Moral Sense

The ability to discriminate between right and wrong, which is the highest attribute of civilized humanity, is notably lacking in physically and psychically stunted organisms. Many criminals do not realize the immorality of their actions. In French criminal jargon conscience is called "la muette," the thief "l´ami," and "travailler" and "servir" signify to steal. A Milanese thief once remarked to my father: "I don't steal. I only relieve the rich of their superfluous wealth." Lacenaire, speaking of his accomplice Avril, remarked, "I realized at once that we should be able to work together." A thief asked by Ferri what he did when he found the purse stolen by him contained no money, replied, "I call them rogues." The notions of right and wrong appear to be completely inverted in such minds. They seem to think they have a right to rob and murder and that those who hinder them are acting unfairly. Murderers, especially when actuated by motives of revenge, consider their actions righteous in the extreme.

Repentance and Remorse

We hear a great deal about the remorse of criminals, but those who come into contact with these degenerates realize that they are rarely, if ever, tormented by such feelings. Very few confess their crimes: the greater number deny all guilt in a most strenuous manner and are fond of protesting that they are victims of injustice, calumny, and jealousy. As Despine once remarked with much insight, nothing resembles the sleep of the just more closely than the slumbers of an assassin.

Many criminals, indeed, allege repentance, but generally from hypocritical motives; either because they hope to gain some advantage by working on the feelings of philanthropists, or with a view to escaping, or, at any rate, improving their condition while in prison. . . .

The Criminal Type

All the physical and psychic peculiarities of which we have spoken are found singly in many normal individuals. Moreover, crime is not always the result of degeneration and atavism; and, on the other hand, many persons who are considered perfectly normal are not so in reality. However, in normal individuals, we never find that accumulation of physical, psychic, functional, and skeletal anomalies in one and the same person, that we do in the case of criminals, among whom also entire freedom from abnormal characteristics is more rare than among ordinary individuals.

Just as a musical theme is the result of a sum of notes, and not of any single note, the criminal type results from the aggregate of these anomalies, which render him strange and terrible, not only to the scientific observer, but to ordinary persons who are capable of an impartial judgment.

VIEWPOINT

2

Society Creates Criminal Behavior

RANDALL COLLINS

In this viewpoint Randall Collins points out the influence of
Emile Durkheim, a French sociologist, on criminology.
Durkheim insisted that social problems such as crime must be
seen as social facts rather than as cases of individual
pathology. Durkheim insisted that society manufactures
crime, creates criminals, and engages in ritualized punishment to ensure social solidarity. In identifying with the
authorities responsible for crime control against our internal
criminal enemies, we feel a sense of belonging to a larger
whole. We reinforce the values and ideals that maintain the
social status quo. Collins adds that crime is a political issue.
Issues of crime and crime control are designed to solidify
political power in our society. From this point of view, the
interesting thing about crime is not discovering what is peculiar about those who commit it but analyzing its symbolic
significance for maintaining a particular social order. The

Excerpted from *Sociological Insight: An Introduction to Nonobvious Sociology* by
Randall Collins. Copyright © 1982 by Oxford University Press, Inc. Reprinted
by permission of Oxford University Press, Inc.

insight that crime is a creation of those who hold power in society has influenced American criminology, as we saw in the last chapter. Criminologists have sought the causes of crime in group associations and group conflicts. They have asked how crime, justice, and punishment serve the interests of those in positions of power. Randall Collins is a professor of sociology at the University of California at Riverside. He is the author of many texts and articles on sociology and social problems, including *Sociological Insight: An Introduction to Nonobvious Sociology*, from which this excerpt is taken.

QUESTIONS

1. According to Durkheim, what is the importance of the ritual of crime and punishment to our society?
2. From this point of view, why are efforts at crime prevention and deterrence seemingly ineffective in our society?
3. According to Collins, why is there so much emphasis by politicians and the mass media in our society on the most atypical crimes?

■ ■ ■

Crimes divide into quite different sorts. There are victimless crimes, very much created by social movements that define them as criminal; people who become labeled as criminal because of these sorts of offenses usually become involved in networks of other sorts of criminality as a result of the law-enforcement process. There are also property crimes, which have some relevance to the way in which individuals make their careers as criminals, but which would by no means disappear if laws stopped being enforced. And there are crimes of passion, which seem to be of a much more personal nature, and which do not seem to be related to any of the factors we have considered here.

Is there any perspective that encompasses all of this? Yes, I believe there is. But it is the most nonobvious of all, and one which does not resonate any too well in the hearts of either conservatives, liberals, or radicals. It is a perspective that declares that crime is a normal, and even necessary, feature of all societies.

The Social Necessity of Crime

This perspective, like so many of the nonobvious ideas in sociology, traces back to Emile Durkheim. In this view, crime and its punishment are a basic part of the rituals that uphold any social structure. Suppose it is true that the process of punishing or reforming criminals is not very effective. The courts, the police, the parole system—none of these very effectively deter criminals from going on to a further life of crime. This would not surprise Durkheim very much. It can be argued that the social purpose of these punishments is not to have a real effect upon the criminal, but to enact a ritual for the benefit of society.

Recall that a ritual is a standardized, ceremonial behavior, carried out by a group of people. It involves a common emotion, and it creates a symbolic belief that binds people closer to the group. Carrying out rituals over and over again is what serves to keep the group tied together. Now in the case of punishing criminals, the group that is held together is not the criminals' group. It is the rest of society, the people who punish the criminals. The criminal is neither the beneficiary of the ritual, nor a member of the group that enacts the ritual, but only the raw material out of which the ritual is made.

The Crime-Punishment Ritual

Picture a courtroom scene. A man is being charged with murder. The scene is theatrical in a stiffly traditional way. The judge sits up behind a high wooden desk, cloaked in a black robe, an aloof and authoritative figure symbolizing the law. The wood-paneled walls are lined with volumes of statutes and cases: the history of the law is there in gilt bindings. A railing marks off the area in front of the judge's bench, a kind of sacred space guarded by an armed bailiff, into which no one may enter without the judge's consent. To one side, the jury is cordoned off in another special space, the jury box. The accused prisoner is in another special place in the room, flanked by his defense lawyers and by more armed guards: the negative space of the prisoner's box into which no one would willingly tread.

The whole scene, in short, is ritualized, a tableau displaying the various parties to the enactment of justice.

Witnesses are brought forward and sworn to take the proceedings in an especially solemn manner, incurring the risk of punishment upon themselves if they fail to do so. The attorneys for each side argue the case, following an elaborate etiquette, and attempting to stir up a collective sentiment among the jury members that will sway the verdict in their favor. And back behind the railing sits the public, both in person and in the intermediaries of the press.

It is this last group—the public—who are the true object of the ritual. The trial, ultimately, is staged for their benefit. A murderer is found guilty, or not; in either case, the law is personified, acted out, made into a living being. The public is impressed, once again, that the laws do exist, and that they are not to be violated. Especially when someone is found guilty of a serious crime, above all a spectacular murder, which draws the attention of the whole community, the ritual has a powerful emotional effect. That is when there is a maximal public focus on this ceremonial event and the widest participation in the collective emotion. For the dynamics of the ritual, it does not matter just what kind of emotion this is; it could be revulsion and disgust against a heinous act, or anger and the desire to punish, or on the contrary, sympathy for the accused in the awareness of mitigating circumstances. The important thing is that the emotion be a strong one, and that it be widely shared. It is this common emotional participation that draws the group together, and reestablishes it as a community.

The main object of a crime-punishment ritual, then, is not the criminal but the society at large. The trial reaffirms belief in the laws, and it creates the emotional bonds that tie the members of society together again. From this point of view, exactly how the criminal reacts to all this is irrelevant. The criminal is an outsider, an object of the ritual, not a member of it. He or she is the necessary material for this solidarity-producing machine, not the recipient of its benefits. It is the dramatics of the trial that counts, the moments when it is before the public eye. Afterwards, it may all come unravelled. The conviction may be reversed on appeal for some technical error. Criminals may go to an overcrowded prison where they make new criminal contacts and acquire a deeper commitment to the criminal role. Sooner than expected, the parole board may decide to relieve crowding in the prison by releasing them, and they are back out on parole and into the routine of police checks and parole officers and all the rest of an ongoing criminal career. If we look at the criminal justice system from the point of view of somehow doing something to deter the criminal, it appears ineffective, even absurd. It makes more sense once we realize that all the social pressure falls upon dramatizing the initiation of punishment, and that this is done to convince society at large of the validity of the rules, not necessarily to convince the criminal.

An even more paradoxical conclusion follows from this. Society needs crime, says Durkheim, if it is to survive; without crimes, there would be no punishment rituals. The rules could not be ceremonially acted out and would decay in the public consciousness. The moral sentiments that are aroused when the members of society feel a common outrage against some heinous violation would no longer be felt. If a society went too long without crimes and punishments, its own bonds would fade away and the group would fall apart.

For this reason, Durkheim explained, society is in the business of manufacturing crimes, if they do not already exist in sufficient abundance. Just what would count as a crime may vary a great deal, relative to what type of society it is. Even a society of saints would find things to make crimes out of: any little matters of falling off into less saintliness than the others would do. To put it another way, the saints, too, would have their central, especially sacred rules, and those who did not respect them as intensely as the others would be singled out for punishment rituals that served to dramatize and elevate the rules all the more.

How much of Durkheim's theory can we accept? Some of the way it is phrased, I would say, is inaccurate. Durkheim presents us with a functional argument: *if* society is to survive, *then* it must have crime. But there is no necessity that any particular kind of society must survive; hence there is no necessity that crime should exist for this purpose. Durkheim is better looked at as explaining a mechanism that *sometimes* is used: if certain rituals are carried out (in this case, punishment rituals), then social integration increases; if not, then there is less integration. Whether or not the mechanism will be used is another matter.

But if we shift our viewpoint slightly, we can see that there will be plenty of occasions when the mechanism will in fact be invoked. Society as a whole is only a concept, and hence "society" does not actually *do* anything. The real actors on the stage are various individuals and groups. It is these groups that use ritual punishments in order to increase their own feelings of solidarity and their own power to dominate other groups.

So we can say that concern about punishing criminals is an aspect of the struggle among groups. It is a symbolic form of politics. If you think about it, there is no strictly rational reason why people should be concerned about crimes against other people. Why should I care if someone else is robbed, murdered, or raped? That is not a very moral or public-spirited thing to say, but that is precisely the point: people have to feel some moral involvement with a group for them to care about "the crime problem." You could reply, of course, that everyone should be worried about crimes against other people because it could happen to you, too. Well, yes and no: about 1 percent of the U.S. population is the victim of some sort of crime every year. Objectively, your reasons for identifying with crime victims are not very strong if your chance of being victimized is so low.

Some groups, it is true, have much higher victimization rates: the poor, blacks, and the young. Teenagers, who commit the most crimes, are also the most frequent victims: whereas well below 1 percent of people over age fifty are subject to a crime of theft or violence, as high as 15 percent of all teenagers have something stolen from them each year, and about 6 percent are subject to violence. Paradoxically, *it is precisely those people who are least subject to crime who are most upset about the crime problem.* Concern about crime, then, is largely a symbolic issue. Those people who are most subject to it are the ones least likely to raise an outcry about it.

The process, I suggest, is a political one; crime is a political issue. Some politicians talk about it a great deal. Why should they want to do so? Because the very idea of crime arouses many people, especially if it can be invoked in an imaginative way so that people identify with the victims of crime. The newspapers and mass media aid in this by vividly publishing those particular crimes that have the most "human interest." But these are the crimes in which the victim is the most *untypical*, i.e., a senior citizen, or from the upper class or white population. This kind of selective dramatization of crime and its punishment (the courtroom scene) works as a Durkheimian ritual to mobilize the population—and incidentally, to help get certain politicians elected because of their strong leadership on the crime problem.

These rituals appeal the most to people who are already tightly integrated into dominant groups. The key audience consists of prosperous middle-aged or elderly people in suburbs and small towns, for example, who get a moral charge out of reading about the crime problem in the newspaper while sitting back in their easy chairs. These are the people whose own communities are organized with the greatest amount of ritual solidarity, and hence they are most susceptible to the moral appeal of punishing criminals who have victimized someone else. They are also the people who are most concerned to punish offenders on purely symbolic issues, such as drugs, gambling, or prostitution. These "crimes without victims" do not actually affect the people who are outraged by them at all. They are rather symbolic offenses against the ideals that the highly integrated, and hence highly moralistic, dominant groups consider to be the essence of righteousness. It is by getting upset about victimless crimes that these groups reassert their own status and their own feelings of righteousness. The very act of being outraged makes them feel their own membership in "respectable" society.

Punishment rituals hold society together in a certain sense: they hold together the structure of domination. They do this partly by mobilizing emotional support for politicians and the police. Above all, they increase the feelings of solidarity within the privileged classes and enable them to feel superior to those who do not follow their own ideals. Outrage about crime legitimates the social hierarchy. The society that is held together by the ritual punishment of crime is the stratified society.

In this sense, crime is built into the social structure. Whatever resources the dominant group uses for control will have corresponding crimes attached to them. Since there is an ongoing struggle among groups over domination, some groups will violate other groups' standards. And those individuals who are least integrated into any groups will pursue their own individual aims without regard for the morality held by others. Therefore, there is usually no shortage of actions that are offensive to many groups in a society. And these violations are to a certain extent welcome by the dominant groups. Crime gives them an occasion for putting on ceremonies of punishment that dramatize the moral feelings of the community, which bolsters their group domination.

This means that every type of society will have its own special crimes. What is constant in all societies is that somehow the laws will be set in such a way that crimes and punishments do occur. A tribal society has its taboos, the violation of which calls down ferocious punishment. The Puritans of the New England colonies, with all their intense moral pressures, believed in the crime of witchcraft. Capitalist societies have endless definitions of criminality relating to property. Socialist societies have their crimes as well, especially political crimes of disloyalty to the state, as well as the individualistic crimes of failing to participate whole-heartedly in the collective. The ritual perspective finds that all societies manufacture their own types of crime. It may be possible to shift from one type of crime to another, but not to do away with crime altogether.

Crime is not simply a matter of poverty and social disorganization, nor of particularly evil or biologically defective individuals. The labeling theory is closer to the truth, but the processes are much wider than merely social-psychological occurrences within the minds of offenders. Criminals are only part of a larger system, which encompasses the whole society.

The Limits of Crime

If the whole social structure is producing crime, we might wonder if there is any limit to how much crime it produces. If crime helps hold society together, doesn't it follow, paradoxically, that the more crime there is the better integrated the society will be? Obviously, there must come a point at which the amount of crime is too great. There would be no one left to enforce the laws, and society would fall apart.

Nevertheless, this does not usually happen. If we look further into the matter, the reasons turn out to be not so much that the law-enforcement side effectively controls crime, but that crime tends to limit itself. Look at what happens when crime becomes more and more successful. Individual criminals can do only so much. They are much more effective at stealing, embezzling, or whatever if they are organized. Individual thieves give way to gangs, and gangs to organized crime syndicates. But notice, organized crime now becomes a little society of its own. It creates its own hierarchy, its own rules, and it attempts to enforce these rules upon its own members. Organized crime tends toward regularity and normalcy. It begins to deplore unnecessary violence and strife. The more successful it is, the more it approximates an ordinary business. The very success of crime, then, tends to make it more law-abiding and less criminal. The same thing can be seen historically.

At some points in history, political power consisted of little more than marauding gangs of warriors or robber barons that plundered whoever came their way. The very success of some of these well-armed criminals, if we may call them that, meant that they had to take more responsibility for maintaining social order around them. At a minimum, the violent gang of warriors had to maintain discipline among themselves if it was to operate effectively in plundering others. The more successful a robber-baron became, the more he turned into an enforcer of laws. The state arose from a type of criminality but was forced to create a morality just to survive.

If social life creates crime, then crime also tends to create its own antithesis. Crime tends to drive out crime. It is not so easy, after all, to be a successful criminal. If you start out today to be a thief, let us say, how do you go about it? In many ways it is like learning any other occupation. You need to learn the tricks of the trade: how to break into a house, how to open a locked car. You need to know where to acquire the proper tools: where to get guns, if you want to be an armed robber. And you need to learn how to dispose of the loot once you have stolen it; it doesn't do you much good to steal a lot of television sets and stereos if you have no way of selling them for cash. And the more expensive the stolen goods, the more difficult it is to dispose of them profitably. To realize very much when stealing jewelry or artwork, for example, one needs both special training in how to recognize objects of value and special connections for getting rid of them. Stolen cars, too, because of the elaborate regulations of licensing and serial numbers, can only be profitably gotten rid of by tying in with a smoothly functioning criminal organization.

Any new criminal starting out on a life of crime has a lot to learn and many connections to make. Most novice criminals cannot make it very far in the crime world for exactly the same sort of reasons that most people in legitimate business never make it to the level of corporation executive. The average robbery nets less than $100, which is not exactly a fast way to get rich. Crime is a competitive world, too, as soon as one goes into it seriously in order to make a good living from it. Part of this is a kind of market effect, a process of sheer supply and demand. The more stolen goods show up at the fence, the less will be paid for them. The more criminals involved in any particular racket, the less take there will be for any one of them. Established criminals have no reason to want to help just anyone who wants to learn the trade and acquire the necessary connections. Hence, many novice criminals are simply "flunked out"; there isn't enough room for them in the world of crime.

Perhaps it is for this reason that crime rates peak for the youth population between ages fifteen and eighteen, and drop off rapidly thereafter. Youths at this age are not seriously committed to crime; they do not know much about the criminal world. They don't have much money of their own, or very much sense of what one can do with money. Small robberies may seem like an easy way to get a few luxuries. Auto theft, for example, is especially high at this age. But teenagers have little sense of how to market a stolen car; they are more likely to joy-ride around in it for a while and then abandon it. Obviously one can't make much of a living out of this sort of thing. If the crime rate starts dropping off in the late teens, and reaches a fairly low level by the age of thirty, it is not so much because of the effectiveness of the law enforcement system but simply because most youthful criminals wash out of a career in crime. (Again, as I mentioned, most crimes are committed by males, and that is the occupational pattern to pay attention to here.) Crime simply doesn't bring in enough income for them, and they are forced to turn to something else to make their way in the adult world.

In the final analysis, the problem of crime, and its solution as well, is built much more deeply into the social structure than common sense would lead us to believe. Crime is so difficult to control because it is produced by large-scale social processes.

VIEWPOINT

3

Criminal Behavior Is Caused by Biological and Neuropsychiatric Differences

C. RAY JEFFERY

This viewpoint traces the history of attempts to identify biological, psychological, and neuropsychiatric factors that differentiate the criminal from the law-abiding population. This quest to identify what characteristics make the criminal different and account for criminal behavior began with Lombroso. C. Ray Jeffery also discusses the more modern attempts to uncover factors that account for criminal behavior and make the criminal special. This kind of approach to understanding criminal behavior has not been a popular one in American criminology. As Jeffery indicates, in the United States a sociological approach dominated criminology. Jeffery argues that the kinds of research he reviews here could lead to better crime prevention as childhood developmental problems

Excerpted from *Varieties of Criminology*, Gregg Barak, ed. Reprinted with permission of Greenwood Publishing Group, Inc., Westport, CT. Copyright © 1994 by Gregg Barak.

could be anticipated and, possibly, corrected. He views the "high risk" group of offenders as treatable if the proper technologies, based on the research he discusses, could be applied early. C. Ray Jeffery is a criminologist on the faculty of Florida State University. He has published widely on criminology, environmental design and crime, and biological and neuropsychiatric factors as applied to crime.

QUESTIONS

1. What has been the history and impact of biological criminology?
2. According to Jeffery, what are the differences between the sociological approach and the biological approach to understanding crime and criminality?
3. What distinction does Jeffery make between a theory of crime and a theory of criminal behavior?

■ ■ ■

The Early Years

Biology and Criminology in the Nineteenth Century

The history of criminology does not reflect the early beginnings as found in medicine and biology because in the 1920s the term "criminology" was used to apply to sociology. Criminology started with the positive school of Lombroso and others in an attempt to apply science to the study of human behavior. The main figures in this movement were Charles Darwin, Cesare Lombroso, Gregor Mendel, and Sigmund Freud.

However, before Lombroso's time there were a number of prominent figures who were developing the study of the brain in relationship to human behavior. In 1806 P. Pinel published his *Treatise on Insanity*, Francis Gall had published his work on phrenology and behavior in 1826, J. Pritchard had published *A Treatise on Insanity* in 1835, Darwin published the *Origin of Species* in 1859, and Paul Broca's work on the brain was emerging at the same time. Mendel's original work on genetics appeared in 1866. Herbert Spencer's *First Principles* appeared in 1862 using a bioevolutionary model for the study of society, and his *Principles of Psychology*, published in 1896, was naturalistic, evolutionary, biological, and positivistic. Thus, the influence of biology on the study of man was very great in the nineteenth century, and Lombroso's work was only a small part of the movement.

The works of Rush, Maudsley, and Ellis in particular are a background to the study of biological criminology. Benjamin Rush was a physician who was prominent in colonial history, having signed the Declaration of Independence. He is also known as the father of American psychiatry. His book, *Medical Inquires and Observations Upon the Diseases of the Mind*, was published in 1812. Rush was instrumental in focusing on the physical causes of mental disorders—in other words, the relationship between brain and behavior. He ended his treatise with a plea to physicians to understand the role of the human brain in behavioral problems.

The work of Henry Maudsley, M.D., was critical to the development of a neuropsychiatric approach. His book, *The Physiology and Pathology of the Mind*, was published in 1867 and it still stands as a classic in neuropsychiatry. Maudsley worked to integrate physiology and the pathologies of the mind by focusing on the structure and function of the brain. He viewed mental illnesses as a result of brain pathologies.

Maudsley identified the several parts of the brain and nervous system according to the neurology of his time, and he discussed free will as a problem in nervous energy. He related mental illness to the "chemical changes in the nerves," which is identical with the current concept of the neurotransmitter system. He dealt with the problems of classification and treatment of mental disorders but without the benefit of Computerized Axial Tomography (CAT), Magnetic Resonance Imaging (MRI), and Positron Emission Tomography (PET) scans. He also mentioned diet and nutrition as aspects of mental health, another contemporary idea.

Other works cited by Robinson as contributions to the history of psychology include Alexander Bain's *The Senses and the Intellect*, published in 1855; Alfred Binet's *Alterations of Personality*, published in 1896; Binet's *The Mind and the Brain*, published in 1907; and David Ferrier's *The Functions of the Brain*, published in 1886. In the late nineteenth and early twentieth centuries, Ramon Y. Cajal and Charles Sherrington introduced the idea of the synapse as a gap between neurons, a major stepping stone in the development of modern neurology. In 1881 Moriz Benedikt published a landmark book entitled *Anatomical Studies Upon Brains of Criminals* in which he found major differences between normal brains and the brains of criminals. This book contains a wealth of information that has never been made a part of criminology. It can be said that by 1920 many significant works had emerged in biological criminology.

A major landmark in biological criminology was the publication of *The Criminal*. Havelock Ellis is better known for his later work on human sexuality, but his book on criminality established the biological approach firmly within European thought. Ellis followed Lombroso in discussions of criminal types from biological to social, and he found the causes of crime to range from genetics to brain structure to diet, geography, and social environment. He observed that many criminals had childhood problems such as behavioral problems, fire setting, cruelty to animals and to other children, epilepsy, left-handedness, and poor sexual adjustment. He cited many current studies of criminals, including a Scottish study of 5,000 criminals that found major physiological defects in this population. Ellis also cited insensitivity to pain, moral insensibility, and a desire for strong sensory stimulation as characteristics of criminals, and all of these are today considered important indicators of criminality and psychopathic behavior. He noted that female criminals are more like males than their noncriminal female counterparts.

Ellis argued for a treatment and prevention approach to behavioral problems in place of the prison/punishment approach. He noted that executions were used sparingly and that prisons were improving. He also supported the positivistic notion of indefinite sentences in place of fixed sentences, since the purpose of the criminal justice system is to reform and prevent, not to punish. I can only imagine that Dr. Ellis would be horrified to wake up to the criminal justice system of the early 1990s, which is dependent upon executions and long, fixed prison sentences.

It is worth noting that Ellis placed great emphasis on nutrition, which is still a novel approach today. . . . In his concluding chapter he emphasized a scientific approach to criminal behavior and the resolution of the conflict between legal and scientific criminology.

At the turn of the century, three books appeared in the United States devoted to criminology and a Darwinian/Lombrosian perspective. Arthur MacDonald's (1893) *Criminology* had an introduction by Lombroso, as did *The Criminal* by August Drahms (1900). Drahms' book presented a Lombrosian interpretation of criminality for an American audience, including detailed discussions of heredity, instincts, and brain organization. Philip Parsons (1909) in his *Responsibility for Crime* cited Ellis, Lombroso, Drahms, and Maudsley as the great figures in criminology. Parsons classified criminals according to the Lombrosian system, and he noted that crime is the normal functioning of an abnormal mind. His formula for crime was *Criminal Personality* × *Stimulus* = *Crime*, or *Organism* × *Environment* = *Crime*. In his work, Parsons discussed the environment but only in interaction with the individual or *Heredity* × *Environment* = *Individual*. He noted the high rate of alcoholism and insanity among criminals, a factor still important in contemporary criminology.

The focus of most criticism of biology came from sociologists and was directed at Lombroso. Wolfgang responded to these criticisms, saying "Lombroso illuminated the scientific study of criminal behavior with many provocative ideas and deserves a place of honor in his own field." Such ideas as brain damage, alcoholism, and epilepsy, which were present in this early work, have assumed new importance in recent years, owing to the emergence of a new neurology and scientific knowledge that was not present at the time Lombroso was writing.

The Early Sociological Years

In 1829 A. M. Guerry and Adolphe Quetelet published separate but nearly identical works on the social statistics of crime. They looked at such factors as age, sex, poverty, geography, education, race, and crime. Quetelet referred to his work as "Social Physics," whereas Guerry labeled his "Moral Statistics." With these two statisticians we observe a shift from the individual offender to statistical correlates of crime as found in official government data banks. Interest moved from the structure of the criminal's brain to the number of criminals who were male or in poverty. This research methodology has characterized much of sociological criminology to this day.

These works were followed by the appearance of Emile Durkheim in 1895 with the argument that all facts were social to the exclusion of biology and psychology. For Durkheim crime was a social fact that helped to maintain the social order by upholding the common values of society that the criminal had violated.

The sociological work of Durkheim and Karl Marx ignored the work of Auguste Comte as the father of sociological positivism. Comte argued that sociology must be based on biology and must be scientific in nature following the model of physics. Sociology followed the model of statistical analysis and aggregate data rather than scientific observations of individual events, as well as the concept of the socialized individual.

The social approach was strengthened by the appearance of Marx's *Das Capital* in 1859, the same year Darwin's *Origin of Species* appeared. Marx argued for a class-conflict interpretation of social evolution. He borrowed the ideas of conflict and evolution from Darwin but placed them in a social rather than biological form. Other writings followed Marx in the class conflict approach to crime, a movement that reemerged in the 1960s and 1970s as part of the conflict/critical/radical approach to crime analysis. This approach totally ignores the biological basis for conflict as found in studies of brain structure, neuroendocrine systems, and male/female differences.

The conflict between biology and sociology came to a head at the 1889 second Congress of International Criminology held in Paris. This meeting was sponsored by the faculty of the Medical School of Paris, a point worth noting as to the interest of medicine in criminology at that time in history. Lombroso, Raffaele Garofalo, Enrico Ferri, and Gabriel Tarde were present along with a distinguished gathering of biologists, physicians, and sociologists. Rennie has labeled this the great debate between biology and socialism. At this conference Tarde presented his ideas of social environmental determinism and set the stage for the theory of imitation and differential association.

The sociological image of humankind is one of a socialized individual who committed crime only because of defective socialization. This view is in stark contrast to the psychobiological image of man as a dangerous animal, or as Desmond Morris (1967) expressed it in *The Naked Ape*, an ape in a gray flannel suit with a veneer of culture.

The Early Psychological Years

Three types of psychology have emerged over the years. Psychology has always reflected the division between mind and body, or mentalism and physicalism. Psychology reflects the philosophical divisions between mind-body dualism as found in Plato, René Descartes, Immanuel Kant, and others, and the physicalism of science and positivism as found in Isaac Newton, John Locke, Thomas Hobbes, David Hume, J. S. Mill, and others. We have already reviewed some major works in nineteenth-century psychology that showed the attempt of some writers to overcome the dualism of mind and body and to regard the brain/body system as a monistic one. The concept of a mind or "psyche" is well ingrained in psychology as found in introspective psychology, which is based on data from the mind as reported to the psychologist through written tests and verbal comments. Mentalistic psychology has been challenged by both behavioral and biological psychology in the twentieth century. Early psychology was founded in physiological psychology, as illustrated by *Elements of Physiological Psychology* by Ladd (1887). Experimental psychology received a major boost from the work of Wilhelm Wundt who was an M.D. trained in physiology. His *Principles of Physiological Psychology* (1873) set a standard for the development of psychology as a laboratory science, and his laboratory in Leipzig became a model for laboratories in England and the United States. The International Congress of Physiological Psychology was founded during 1889 in Paris and it was devoted to biology and genetics. This occurred before the founding of the American Psychological Association in 1897.

Another major interpretation of the human behavior perspective was that of Sigmund Freud. Freud was a physician and neurologist who engaged in psychotherapy with neurotic patients in his practice in Vienna. He introduced conflict, psychosexual development, unconscious processes, dream analysis, and free association as major concepts within clinical psychology. Psychoanalytic psychology depended on interpretations of dreams, thought processes, verbal statements, the Rorschach inkblot test, the Thematic Apperception Test, and other indirect measures of internal mental/physical processes.

Freud did not have the neurological knowledge needed to put forth an integrated theory of behavior, so he used mentalistic concepts such as Id, Ego, and Superego to explain the human personality. The basic biological instincts of food, sex, thirst, and survival are to be found in the Id, whereas the Ego and Superego develop from experiences with the social environment. When the three are in conflict personality disorders appear, such as psychoses or neuroses or character disorders.

Freud in his *Project for Scientific Psychology* (1895) attempted to find a neurological basis for his system, and he argued that ultimately psychiatry and medicine would be joined. Freud is considered by some as the father of psychobiological psychology. Freud would be very happy and comfortable with the new neuropsychiatry that has emerged in the past twenty years.

The behavioral school of psychology emerged with I. P. Pavlov, J. B. Watson, and B. F. Skinner. Behaviorism is based on a denial of introspectionism and mentalism as approaches to the study of human behavior, and in their places the behaviorist used the direct observation of behavior within a controlled laboratory setting. Behavior was studied as a response to a stimulus or environmental condition—that is, the environment determined behavior. This psychological environmentalism totally denied the role of human genetics and brain functioning in the study of behavior. The behaviorist ignored or minimized these topics. According to this psychology, the environment impacted upon behavior without an organism, or the organism was an "empty organism." Environmental determinism as found in behaviorism ignored the role of the brain in learning theory, even though Pavlov had emphasized the unconditioned or biological relationship between stimulus and response.

The third model of behavior to emerge was that of biological psychology and neuropsychiatry. This is the model now used in psychology and psychiatry as a basic model of human behavior.

Three Models of Behavior

To summarize, we are dealing with three models of behavior:

1. Introspective psychology or mentalism, which assumes that the environment changes the mental processes, which in turn control behavior or *Environment→Mind→Behavior*. The mental processes are never directly observed but are inferred from behavior. This theory of behavior is found in introspective psychology and in sociology, where it is assumed that attitudes and values determine behavior. These are often referred to as self-concepts or role models.

2. Behavioral psychology, where the environment or stimulus produces the behavior, or *Environment→Behavior*, usually treated as Stimulus-Response relationships.

3. Biological psychology, where the environment interacts with the individual by means of the brain, and in turn the brain controls behavior. This is an *Environment→Brain→Behavior* model of behavior, sometimes referred to as an *Environment→ Organism→Behavior* approach. Only in this model is there an integration of biology and psychology, and this type of psychology recaptures the movement of the nineteenth century as found in Rush, Maudsley, and Havelock Ellis to make the brain sciences a basic foundation for psychiatry and psychology.

The New Era

Interdisciplinary Criminology

The compartmentalization of knowledge as it occurs in universities means that the biologists never talk to the economists or criminologists, whereas the problems each is involved with call for knowledge from other fields. Criminology must integrate the knowledge from biology, psychology, sociology, and law, as well as other fields. The major components of such an approach to criminology include genetics and brain functioning within biology; learning theory and personality development within psychology; the social environment within sociology; and the legal aspects of crime and criminal behavior within the law. Each level of analysis is based on the other levels.

153

Criminology must begin with a basic theory of behavior, not of criminal behavior. Criminal behavior is a subcategory of behavior based on the legal/criminal justice system. We need a theory of behavior to explain the behavior of judges, jurors, police officers, prosecutors, and the like. This is a *theory of crime*, or why certain acts are reacted to by society as criminal acts. We also need a theory of behavior to explain the behavior of those individuals whom we classify as criminals. This is a *theory of criminal behavior*. In turn, we must develop an interdisciplinary theory of behavior and then apply it to the explanations of crime and criminal behavior. . . .

Implications for Crime Prevention

New Prevention Strategies

Crime prevention means preventing the crime *before* it occurs rather than waiting for it to occur. This usually takes the shape of crime prevention through environmental design, but the discussion in this viewpoint suggests that some heavy attention be paid to the biological variables involved in criminal behavior. This would include early pre- and postnatal care for pregnant women and infants. Such care would be concerned with alcohol and drug use by pregnant women, the nutritional status of the mother, low birth weight of the infant, hyperactivity or brain damage of the infant, and other medical problems that could lead to later behavioral problems.

As the child develops, the early symptoms of behavioral disorders such as enuresis, child abuse, violence by the child against other children or animals, fire-setting, running away from home, inadequate family care , truancy from school, and school disciplinary problems must be dealt with at an early age. The cooperation of parents, teachers, pediatricians, and social counselors must be secured. Neurological examinations including CAT, MRI, and PET scans must be provided when the medical examination indicates that they are needed.

Attention must be paid to the 5 percent of the delinquent population that commits 50 percent of the serious offenses, and especially the core group of violent offenders who are drug addicts. This effort must identify the "high risk" group at an early age and move them into treatment programs before they have committed ten or twenty major felonies. We must look for individual differences rather than at statistical categories of offenders. In short, the question is not "what disease does the person have?" but "what person has the disease?" We should not ask "how many men are criminals?" but rather "what men are criminals?"

The Politics of Crime Prevention

The current U.S. policy is to control crime through the criminal justice system, waiting for the crime to occur before taking action retroactively. We spend millions of dollars on the police-courts-prison system, whereas we spend virtually nothing on research and prevention. In order to put a crime-prevention program into place we need to totally change our approach to crime, and the politicians are not willing to do this. The political system must move from a punitive to a preventive framework. There must be major changes in the legal system, which would relate criminal law much more to science and technology and much less to prisons and executions; otherwise, our high crime rate will continue in the future.

Criminal Behavior Is Learned

RONALD L. BOOSTROM
AND JOEL H. HENDERSON

Theoretical criminology in the United States has been largely
developed by those who approached the study of crime and
criminality from a sociological perspective. Causes of crime
were sought in group associations, cultural values and norms,
and group conflicts. No one has been more responsible for this
approach to the study of crime than Edwin Sutherland. He
helped to establish a way of studying crime and criminal
behavior that was characteristic of the Chicago school of sociology. This approach has defined the study of crime for many
generations of criminologists and their students. Sutherland
developed the idea that criminals learn the skills, knowledge,
and motivations for criminal behavior in a socialization process
and in associations with others. Thus, crime and criminal

Ronald L. Boostrom and Joel H. Henderson, "A Scientific Research Program
for Criminology: The Chicago School and Sociological Criminology." In
Structures of Knowing, Richard C. Monk, ed. Lanham, MD: University Press of
America, 1986. Reprinted by permission of the authors.

behavior are developed over time in a normal learning process just as law-abiding behavior is learned. Sutherland elaborated this idea in his theory of "differential association." In this viewpoint Ronald Boostrom and Joel Henderson discuss the importance of Sutherland's insights. They also review the impact of others working within the tradition of the Chicago school. This approach revolutionized the study of crime in the United States, moving it away from the former dominance by biological and psychological positivism. Ronald Boostrom and Joel Henderson are professors of criminal justice administration in the School of Public Administration and Urban Studies at San Diego State University.

QUESTIONS

1. According to the authors, what does the theory of differential association tell us about the causes of crime?
2. How does this theory contrast with the idea that the criminal is biologically or psychologically abnormal, according to Boostrom and Henderson?
3. According to the authors, how did the ecological approach to criminology relate to the theory of differential association?

■ ■ ■

Early biological, anthropological, and psychological theories mirrored standard folk images of crime and reinforced political repression in the name of law and order. . . .

The Development of Sociological Criminology

By the 1920's in the United States, during the period of ascendancy of the Chicago school of sociology, an ecological and environmental approach to the study of crime was taking hold and becoming more palatable. The multiple-factor approach, like all positivistic approaches, based the search for the causes of crime on the peculiarities of the offender. As a sociological approach to the study of crime gained legitimacy, individual peculiarities were no longer seen as the source of crime. It was believed that the causes of crime could be shown to be the result of normal societal processes operating on normal human beings. The community and the culture were analyzed to discover their criminogenic qualities which were conducive to the emergence of criminality. The idea that criminal behavior is similar to any other social behavior became the basic conceptual underpinning of the Chicago school, as well as later sociological approaches to the study of crime. . . .

No student of the Chicago school pushed the sociological frame of reference in the study of crime harder or further than Edwin Sutherland. Sutherland was one of the early Ph.D. products of the University of Chicago sociology department, receiving his doctorate in 1913. Because of his dissatisfaction with the positivistic multiple-factor approach to criminology prevalent when he was a student and a young professor assigned to teach criminology classes, he decided to write a text of his own. His *Criminology,* published in 1924, became a classic text. It has gone through ten editions and still exerts an influence on the field. Four editions of the book were published prior to Sutherland's death in the 1950's and the last six editions were revised by Donald Cressey, the last student to receive a Ph.D. degree under Sutherland.

Sutherland's *Criminology* provided the first coherent statement of a sociological approach to criminology as well as devastating critiques of other prevailing non-sociological perspectives on crime. Sutherland intended to extend the scientific research program of the Chicago school to the study of crime. He wanted to socialize his students to the same theoretical perspectives, the same research methods, and the same norms and values being worked out by other members of the Chicago school.

Like other members of the Chicago school, Sutherland was cognizant of the differential ecological distribution of crime rates, crime trends, and criminal areas. He incorporated this structural level of analysis into his theorizing about the nature of crime. He was also concerned about understanding the social psychological process by which an individual is socialized to adapt to a criminal lifestyle. The key for Sutherland to integrate these two levels of analysis was the discovery that differential distribution of criminal areas leads to differential networks of interaction and association. Working out the linkages between the statistical distribution of crime, differential social organization, differential socialization, and the impact of all of these factors on individual behavior was the basis for Sutherland's extension of the Chicago scientific approach to the study of criminology.

Sutherland's extension of the scientific research program of the Chicago school stands the test of time very well. His approach to the study of criminology had the effect of coopting the field for sociologists. After reviewing the original 1924 edition of Sutherland's *Criminology*, Gilbert Geis concluded "if it were used as a text today, the 1924 edition still would provide an undergraduate with an excellent understanding of important modes of reasoning about key matters involved in criminal behavior and responses to it."

The distinctly sociological view that crime is acquired through a normal learning process in a social and cultural setting was a lasting contribution made to criminology by Sutherland and other members of the Chicago school. Sutherland began a type of analysis which is today characteristic of the conflict and labeling perspectives on crime and criminality. In an early article he analyzed the relation of crime to culture conflict. He stated that criminal behavior is itself "a part of the process of conflict, of which law and punishment are the other parts." He went on to say:

> This process begins in the community before the law is enacted, and continues in the community and in the behavior of particular offenders after punishment is inflicted. This process seems to go on somewhat as follows: A certain group of people feel that one of their values—life, property, beauty of landscape, theological doctrine—is endangered by the behavior of others. If the group is politically influential, the value important, and the danger serious, they secure the enactment of law and thus win the cooperation of the State in the effort to protect their value. . . .

The Theory of Differential Association

At the heart of Sutherland's effort to apply the scientific research program of the Chicago school to criminology was his theory of "differential association." By extension, the development and application of this theory to criminological studies can also be seen as an effort to extend the scientific research program of the Durkheimian school. This concept involved the specification of a set of interrelated propositions designed to explain the occurrence of criminal behavior.

Prior to the specification of this theory, Sutherland had engaged in a life history study of a professional thief (1937). He presented the view that criminals gradually learn the skills, the knowledge, and the motivation for engaging in criminal behavior. Two years later, in a revision of his criminology textbook, he specified his theory of differential association. He offered this theory as an explanation which would replace simplistic multiple-factor and enculturation explanations of crime.

The elements of this theory of differential association had been fully developed by 1947 and have been presented in subsequent editions of the Sutherland and Cressey criminology text as follows:

1. Criminal behavior is learned.
2. Criminal behavior is learned in interaction with other persons in a process of communication.
3. The principal part of the learning of criminal behavior occurs within intimate personal groups.
4. When criminal behavior is learned, the learning includes (a) techniques of committing the crime, which are sometimes very complicated, sometimes very simple; (b) the specific direction of motives, drives, rationalizations, and attitudes.
5. The specific direction of motives and drives is learned from definitions of the legal codes as favorable or unfavorable.
6. A person becomes delinquent because of an excess of definitions favorable to violation of law over definitions unfavorable to violation of law.
7. Differential associations may vary in frequency, duration, priority, and intensity.
8. The process of learning criminal behavior by association with criminal and anti-criminal patterns involves all of the mechanisms that are involved in any other learning.
9. While criminal behavior is an expression of general needs and values, it is not explained by those needs and values since non-criminal behavior is an expression of the same needs and values.

The above propositions, and the theory of differential association incorporating them, provided an integrative theory for criminology focusing on the individual's associations and learning experiences. It provided a social psychological focus and a focus on the etiology of criminal behavior. It continues to be relevant to one of the major concerns specified for criminology by Sutherland—the understanding of criminal behavior. It continues to serve as one of the major theoretical perspectives in contemporary criminology. Cressey has contended that any major theoretical advance in criminology is obligated to build upon the framework provided by Sutherland. Cressey argues that the theory survives today and should provide a basis for future research because it organizes all research and research findings, and provides a solid basis for neutralizing competitive theories. . . .

It guaranteed the dominance of sociological theory in criminology. It also represented the spearhead of a revolution against biological positivism. The idea that crime is learned in the same way that other non-deviant forms of behavior are was a revolutionary concept at the time Sutherland began to articulate it.

The Criminal Justice System Creates Crime

HOWARD S. BECKER

In this viewpoint Howard S. Becker contends that deviant behavior, such as criminal behavior, can best be understood by analyzing the actions and motivations of those who make and enforce rules of behavior. Whether a particular act is considered a crime depends on how authorities react to it. Therefore, the activities of criminal justice authorities should be studied to understand the causes of criminality. Becker views those who create and enforce laws, as well as other types of rules, as "moral entrepreneurs." These moral entrepreneurs are interested in crusading for the enforcement of their own view of reality and their own values. "Outsiders" are created through this process as their views and behavior are discredited and outlawed. This view of crime as rulemaking, rule breaking, and rule enforcement extended some of the earlier sociological perspectives on the causes of crime. It is a view that has had a major impact on American criminology. It justified a concern with studying the process of lawmaking and the activities of agencies and agents of criminal justice. It also led to a cynical view of the claims made by the law and law enforcers. The view that the law is made and enforced to justify and reinforce the values of the powerful, sometimes at the expense of the powerless, was also expanded by this "labeling theory" approach to criminology. Howard S. Becker is a professor of sociology at Northwestern University in Evanston, Illinois. He was an originator and leader of the labeling approach to the study of deviance. He is author of a classic of criminology, *Outsiders*, from which this excerpt is taken.

QUESTIONS

1. What does Becker mean when he states that "deviance is not a quality of the act the person commits?"
2. What persons or groups can you think of who are examples of "moral entrepreneurs?"
3. According to Becker, how do "moral crusades" become institutionalized?

■ ■ ■

O ne] sociological view . . . defines deviance as the infraction of some agreed-upon rule. It then goes on to ask who breaks rules, and to search for the factors in their personalities and life situations that might account for the infractions. This assumes that those who have broken a rule constitute a homogeneous category, because they have committed the same deviant act.

Such an assumption seems to me to ignore the central fact about deviance: it is created by society. I do not mean this in the way it is ordinarily understood, in which the causes of deviance are located in the social situation of the deviant or in "social factors" which prompt his action. I mean, rather, that *social groups create deviance by making the rules whose infraction constitutes deviance,* and by applying those rules to particular people and labeling them as outsiders. From this point of view, deviance is not a quality of the act the person commits, but rather a consequence of the application by others of rules and sanctions to an "offender." The deviant is one to whom that label has successfully been applied; deviant behavior is behavior that people so label.

Since deviance is, among other things, a consequence of the responses of others to a person's act, students of deviance cannot assume that they are dealing with a homogeneous category when they study people who have been labeled deviant. That is, they cannot assume that these people have actually committed a deviant act or broken some rule, because the process of labeling may not be infallible; some people may be labeled deviant who in fact have not broken a rule. Furthermore, they cannot assume that the category of those labeled deviant will contain all those who actually have broken a rule, for many offenders may escape apprehension and thus fail to be included in the population of "deviants" they study. Insofar as the category lacks homogeneity and fails to include all the cases that belong in it, one cannot reasonably expect to find common factors of personality or life situation that will account for the supposed deviance.

What, then, do people who have been labeled deviant have in common? At the least, they share the label and the experience of being labeled as outsiders. I will begin my analysis with this basic similarity and view deviance as the product of a transaction that takes place between some social group and one who is viewed by that group as a rule-breaker. . . .

Whether an act is deviant, then, depends on how other people react to it. You can commit clan incest and suffer from no more than gossip as long as no one makes a public accusation; but you will be driven to your death if the accusation is made. The point is that the response of other people has to be regarded as problematic. Just because one has committed an infraction of a rule does not mean that others will respond as though this had happened. (Conversely, just because one has not violated a rule does not mean that he may not be treated, in some circumstances, as though he had.)

The degree to which other people will respond to a given act as deviant varies greatly. Several kinds of variation seem worth noting. First of all, there is variation over time. A person believed to have committed a given "deviant" act may at one time be responded to much more leniently than he would be at some other time. . . .

The degree to which an act will be treated as deviant depends also on who commits the act and who feels he has been harmed by it. Rules tend to be applied more to some persons than others. Studies of juvenile delinquency make the point clearly. Boys from middle-class areas do not get as far in the legal process when they are apprehended as do boys from slum areas. The middle-class boy is less likely, when picked up by the police, to be taken to the station; less likely when taken to the station to be booked; and it is extremely unlikely that he will be convicted and sentenced. This variation occurs even though the original infraction of the rule is the same in the two cases. Similarly, the law is differentially applied to Negroes and whites. It is well known that a Negro believed to have attacked a white woman is much more likely to be punished than a white man who commits the same offense; it is only slightly less well known that a Negro who murders another Negro is much less likely to be punished than a white man who commits murder. This, of course, is one of the main points of Sutherland's analysis of white-collar crime: crimes committed by corporations are almost always prosecuted as civil cases, but the same crime committed by an individual is ordinarily treated as a criminal offense.

Some rules are enforced only when they result in certain consequences. The unmarried mother furnishes a clear example. Vincent points out that illicit sexual relations seldom result in severe punishment or social censure for the offenders. If, however, a girl becomes pregnant as a result of such activities the reaction of others is likely to be severe. (The illicit pregnancy is also an interesting example of the differential enforcement of rules on different categories of people. Vincent notes that unmarried fathers escape the severe censure visited on the mother.)

Why repeat these commonplace observations? Because, taken together, they support the proposition that deviance is not a simple quality, present in some kinds of behavior and absent in others. Rather, it is the product of a process which involves responses of other people to the behavior. The same behavior may be an infraction of the rules at one time and not at another; may be an infraction when committed by one person, but not when committed by another; some rules are broken with impunity, others are not. In short, whether a given

165

act is deviant or not depends in part on the nature of the act (that is, whether or not it violates some rule) and in part on what other people do about it.

Some people may object that this is merely a terminological quibble, that one can, after all, define terms any way he wants to and that if some people want to speak of rule-breaking behavior as deviant without reference to the reactions of others they are free to do so. This, of course, is true. Yet it might be worthwhile to refer to such behavior as *rule-breaking* behavior and reserve the term deviant for those labeled as deviant by some segment of society. I do not insist that this usage be followed. But it should be clear that insofar as a scientist uses "deviant" to refer to any rule-breaking behavior and takes as his subject of study only those who have been *labeled* deviant, he will be hampered by the disparities between the two categories.

If we take as the object of our attention behavior which comes to be labeled as deviant, we must recognize that we cannot know whether a given act will be categorized as deviant until the response of others has occurred. Deviance is not a quality that lies in behavior itself, but in the interaction between the person who commits an act and those who respond to it.

Rules and Their Enforcement

The question here is simply: when are rules made and enforced? I noted earlier that the existence of a rule does not automatically guarantee that it will be enforced. There are many variations in rule enforcement. We cannot account for rule enforcement by invoking some abstract group that is ever vigilant; we cannot say that "society" is harmed by every infraction and acts to restore the balance. We might posit, as one extreme, a group in which this was the case, in which all rules were absolutely and automatically enforced. But imagining such an extreme case only serves to make more clear the fact that social groups are ordinarily not like this. It is more typical for rules to be enforced only when something provokes enforcement. Enforcement, then, requires explanation.

The explanation rests on several premises. First, enforcement of a rule is an enterprising act. Someone—an entrepreneur—

must take the initiative in punishing the culprit. Second, enforcement occurs when those who want the rule enforced publicly bring the infraction to the attention of others; an infraction cannot be ignored once it is made public. Put another way, enforcement occurs when someone blows the whistle. Third, people blow the whistle, making enforcement necessary, when they see some advantage in doing so. Personal interest prods them to take the initiative. Finally, the kind of personal interest that prompts enforcement varies with the complexity of the situation in which enforcement takes place. . . .

Moral Entrepreneurs

Rules are the products of someone's initiative and we can think of the people who exhibit such enterprise as *moral entrepreneurs*. Two related species—rule creators and rule enforcers—will occupy our attention.

Rule Creators

The prototype of the rule creator, but not the only variety as we shall see, is the crusading reformer. He is interested in the content of rules. The existing rules do not satisfy him because there is some evil which profoundly disturbs him. He feels that nothing can be right in the world until rules are made to correct it. He operates with an absolute ethic, what he sees is truly and totally evil with no qualification. Any means is justified to do away with it. The crusader is fervent and righteous, often self-righteous.

It is appropriate to think of reformers as crusaders because they typically believe that their mission is a holy one. The prohibitionist serves as an excellent example, as does the person who wants to suppress vice and sexual delinquency or the person who wants to do away with gambling. . . .

. . . Moral crusaders typically want to help those beneath them to achieve a better status. That those beneath them do not always like the means proposed for their salvation is another matter. But this fact—that moral crusades are typically dominated by those in the upper levels of the social structure—means that they add to the power they derive from the legitimacy of their moral position, the power they derive from their superior position in society. . . .

The moral crusader, however, is more concerned with ends than with means. When it comes to drawing up specific rules (typically in the form of legislation to be proposed to a state legislature or the federal Congress), he frequently relies on the advice of experts. Lawyers, expert in the drawing of acceptable legislation, often play this role. Government bureaus in whose jurisdiction the problem falls may also have the necessary expertise, as did the Federal Bureau of Narcotics in the case of the marihuana problem.

As psychiatric ideology, however, becomes increasingly acceptable, a new expert has appeared—the psychiatrist. . . .

. . . The influence of psychiatrists in other realms of the criminal law has increased in recent years.

In any case, what is important about this example is not that psychiatrists are becoming increasingly influential, but that the moral crusader, at some point in the development of his crusade, often requires the services of a professional who can draw up the appropriate rules in an appropriate form. The crusader himself is often not concerned with such details. Enough for him that the main point has been won; he leaves its implementation to others.

By leaving the drafting of the specific rule in the hands of others, the crusader opens the door for many unforeseen influences. For those who draft legislation for crusaders have their own interests which may affect the legislation they prepare. It is likely that the sexual psychopath laws drawn by psychiatrists contain many features never intended by the citizens who spearheaded the drives to "do something about sex crimes," features which do however reflect the professional interests of organized psychiatry.

The Fate of Moral Crusades

A crusade may achieve striking success, as did the Prohibition movement with the passage of the Eighteenth Amendment. It may fail completely, as has the drive to do away with the use of tobacco or the anti-vivisection movement.

It may achieve great success, only to find its gains whittled away by shifts in public morality and increasing restrictions imposed on it by judicial interpretations, such has been the case with the crusade against obscene literature.

One major consequence of a successful crusade, of course, is the establishment of a new rule or set of rules, usually with the appropriate enforcement machinery being provided at the same time. . . .

Only some crusaders, then, are successful in their mission and create, by creating a new rule, a new group of outsiders. Of the successful, some find they have a taste for crusades and seek new problems to attack. Other crusaders fail in their attempt and either support the organization they have created by dropping their distinctive mission and focusing on the problem of organizational maintenance itself or become outsiders themselves, continuing to espouse and preach a doctrine which sounds increasingly queer as time goes on.

Rule Enforcers

The most obvious consequence of a successful crusade is the creation of a new set of rules. With the creation of a new set of rules we often find that a new set of enforcement agencies and officials is established. Sometimes, of course, existing agencies take over the administration of the new rule, but more frequently a new set of rule enforcers is created. The passage of the Harrison Act presaged the creation of the Federal Narcotics Bureau, just as the passage of the Eighteenth Amendment led to the creation of police agencies charged with enforcing the Prohibition Laws.

With the establishment of organizations of rule enforcers, the crusade becomes institutionalized. What started out as a drive to convince the world of the moral necessity of a new rule finally becomes an organization devoted to the enforcement of the rule. Just as radical political movements turn into organized political parties and lusty evangelical sects become staid religious denominations, the final outcome of the moral crusade is a police force. To understand, therefore, how the rules creating a new class of outsiders are applied to particular people we must understand the motives and interests of police, the rule enforcers.

Although some policemen undoubtedly have a kind of crusading interest in stamping out evil, it is probably much more typical for the policeman to have a certain detached and objective view of his job. He is not so much concerned with the content of any particular rule as he is with the fact that it is his job to enforce the rule. When the rules are changed, he punishes what was once acceptable behavior just as he ceases to punish behavior that has been made legitimate by a change in the rules. The enforcer, then, may not be interested in the content of the rule as such, but only in the fact that the existence of the rule provides him with a job, a profession, and a raison d'être.

Since the enforcement of certain rules provides justification for his way of life, the enforcer has two interests which condition his enforcement activity: first, he must justify the existence of his position and, second, he must win the respect of those he deals with. . . .

Enforcers, then, responding to the pressures of their own work situation, enforce rules and create outsiders in a selective way. Whether a person who commits a deviant act is in fact labeled a deviant depends on many things extraneous to his actual behavior: whether the enforcement official feels that at this time he must make some show of doing his job in order to justify his position, whether the misbehaver shows proper deference to the enforcer, whether the "fix" has been put in, and where the kind of act he has committed stands on the enforcer's list of priorities.

The professional enforcer's lack of fervor and routine approach to dealing with evil may get him into trouble with the rule creator. The rule creator, as we have said, is concerned with the content of the rules that interest him. He sees them as the means by which evil can be stamped out. He does not understand the enforcer's long-range approach to the same problems and cannot see why all the evil that is apparent cannot be stamped out at once.

When the person interested in the content of a rule realizes or has called to his attention the fact that enforcers are dealing selectively with the evil that concerns him, his righteous wrath may be aroused. The professional is denounced for viewing the evil too lightly, for failing to do his duty. The moral entrepreneur, at whose instance the rule was made, arises again to say that the outcome of the last crusade has not been satisfactory or that the gains once made have been whittled away and lost.

Deviance and Enterprise: A Summary

Deviance—in the sense I have been using it, of publicly labeled wrongdoing—is always the result of enterprise. Before any act can be viewed as deviant, and before any class of people can be labeled and treated as outsiders for committing the act, someone must have made the rule which defines the act as deviant. Rules are not made automatically. Even though a practice may be harmful in an objective sense to the group in which it occurs, the harm needs to be discovered and pointed out. People must be made to feel that something ought to be done about it. Someone must call the public's attention to these matters, supply the push necessary to get things done, and direct such energies as are aroused in the proper direction to get a rule created. Deviance is the product of enterprise in the largest sense; without the enterprise required to get rules made, the deviance which consists of breaking the rule could not exist.

Deviance is the product of enterprise in the smaller and more particular sense as well. Once a rule has come into existence, it must be applied to particular people before the abstract class of outsiders created by the rule can be peopled. Offenders must be discovered, identified, apprehended and convicted (or noted as "different" and stigmatized for their nonconformity, as in the case of legal deviant groups such as dance musicians). This job ordinarily falls to the lot of professional enforcers who, by enforcing already existing rules, create the particular deviants society views as outsiders.

It is an interesting fact that most scientific research and speculation on deviance concerns itself with the people who break rules rather than those who make and enforce them. If we are to achieve a full understanding of deviant behavior, we must get these two possible foci of inquiry into balance. We must see deviance, and the outsiders who personify the abstract conception, as a consequence of a process of interaction between people, some of whom in the service of their own interests make and enforce rules which catch others who, in the service of their own interests, have committed acts which are labeled deviant.

Lack of Self-Control Causes Crime

MICHAEL R. GOTTFREDSON
AND TRAVIS HIRSCHI

Another approach to the study of crime that had a major
impact on American criminology is called containment, control, or social bond theory. This perspective assumes that
most people have a natural tendency to take what they want
when they want it but are restrained from doing so because
of ties to the conventional social order. Most people feel that
they have too much to lose by breaking the law. If our ties to
conventional order or our social bonds are weakened, we are
free to commit delinquent or criminal acts. This approach
changes the focus of traditional criminology. Criminologists
operating from a positivistic perspective on crime traditionally looked for the special characteristics of the criminal or
delinquent offender in order to explain criminal behavior.
Social bond theory asks why most people do not violate the

law. The answer is that the stake in conformity and in the existing social order prevent us from taking the risk. Attachments to others and involvement in legitimate social activities prevent most people from breaking the law. In this viewpoint, Gottfredson and Hirschi contend that low levels of self-control and an orientation toward immediate gratification rather than long-term rewards are characteristic of those who get involved in criminal behavior. Michael R. Gottfredson and Travis Hirschi are criminologists on the faculty of the University of Arizona. They are the authors of many books and articles on criminal and delinquent behavior, including *A General Theory of Crime,* from which this viewpoint is excerpted.

QUESTIONS

1. Why does the theory presented by the authors assume that no special explanations of crime and delinquency are required to understand the causes of crime?
2. What reasons do the authors cite to explain why criminal acts are more likely to be committed by those with low self-control?
3. From the point of view of this theory, what kinds of crime prevention efforts would be most likely to work?

■ ■ ■

Classical theory is a theory of social or external control, a theory based on the idea that the costs of crime depend on the individual's current location in or bond to society. What classical theory lacks is an explicit idea of self-control, the idea that people also differ in the extent to which they are vulnerable to the temptations of the moment. Combining the two ideas thus merely recognizes the simultaneous existence of social and individual restraints on behavior.

An obvious alternative is the concept of criminality. The disadvantages of that concept, however, are numerous. First, it connotes causation or determinism, a positive tendency to crime that is contrary to the classical model and, in our view, contrary to the facts. Whereas self-control suggests that people differ in the extent to which they are restrained from criminal acts, criminality suggests that people differ in the extent to which they are compelled to crime. The concept of self-control is thus consistent with the observation that criminals do not require or need crime, and the concept of criminality is inconsistent with this observation. By the same token, the idea of low self-control is compatible with the observation that criminal acts require no special capabilities, needs, or motivation; they are, in this sense, available to everyone. In contrast, the idea of criminality as a special tendency suggests that criminal acts require special people for their performance and enjoyment. Finally, lack of restraint or low self-control allows almost any deviant, criminal, exciting, or dangerous act; in contrast, the idea of criminality covers only a narrow portion of the apparently diverse acts engaged in by people at one end of the dimension we are now discussing. . . .

The Elements of Self-Control

Criminal acts provide *immediate* gratification of desires. A major characteristic of people with low self-control is therefore a tendency to respond to tangible stimuli in the immediate environment, to have a concrete "here and now" orientation. People with high self-control, in contrast, tend to defer gratification.

Criminal acts provide *easy or simple* gratification of desires. They provide money without work, sex without courtship, revenge without court delays. People lacking self-control also tend to lack diligence, tenacity, or persistence in a course of action.

Criminal acts are *exciting, risky, or thrilling.* They involve stealth, danger, speed, agility, deception, or power. People lacking self-control therefore tend to be adventuresome, active, and physical. Those with high levels of self-control tend to be cautious, cognitive, and verbal.

Crimes provide *few or meager long-term benefits.* They are not equivalent to a job or a career. On the contrary, crimes interfere with long-term commitments to jobs, marriages, family, or friends. People with low self-control thus tend to have unstable marriages, friendships, and job profiles. They tend to be little interested in and unprepared for long-term occupational pursuits.

Crimes require *little skill or planning*. The cognitive requirements for most crimes are minimal. It follows that people lacking self-control need not possess or value cognitive or academic skills. The manual skills required for most crimes are minimal. It follows that people lacking self-control need not possess manual skills that require training or apprenticeship.

Crimes often result in *pain or discomfort for the victim*. Property is lost, bodies are injured, privacy is violated, trust is broken. It follows that people with low self-control tend to be self-centered, indifferent, or insensitive to the suffering and needs of others. It does not follow, however, that people with low self-control are routinely unkind or antisocial. On the contrary, they may discover the immediate and easy rewards of charm and generosity.

Recall that crime involves the pursuit of immediate pleasure. It follows that people lacking self-control will also tend to pursue immediate pleasures that are *not* criminal: they will tend to smoke, drink, use drugs, gamble, have children out of wedlock, and engage in illicit sex.

Crimes require the interaction of an offender with people or their property. It does not follow that people lacking self-control will tend to be gregarious or social. However, it does follow that, other things being equal, gregarious or social people are more likely to be involved in criminal acts.

The major benefit of many crimes is not pleasure but relief from momentary irritation. The irritation caused by a crying child is often the stimulus for physical abuse. That caused by a taunting stranger in a bar is often the stimulus for aggravated assault. It follows that people with low self-control tend to have minimal tolerance for frustration and little ability to respond to conflict through verbal rather than physical means.

Crimes involve the risk of violence and physical injury, of pain and suffering on the part of the offender. It does not follow that people with low self-control will tend to be tolerant of physical pain or to be indifferent to physical discomfort. It does follow that people tolerant of physical pain or indifferent to physical discomfort will be more likely to engage in criminal acts whatever their level of self-control.

The risk of criminal penalty for any given criminal act is small, but this depends in part on the circumstances of the offense. Thus, for example, not all joyrides by teenagers are equally likely to result in arrest. A car stolen from a neighbor and returned unharmed before he notices its absence is less likely to result in official notice than is a car stolen from a shopping center parking lot and abandoned at the convenience of the offender. Drinking alcohol stolen from parents and consumed in the family garage is less likely to receive official notice than drinking in the parking lot outside a concert hall. It follows that offenses differ in their validity as measures of self-control: those offenses with large risk of public awareness are better measures than those with little risk.

In sum, people who lack self-control will tend to be impulsive, insensitive, physical (as opposed to mental), risk-taking, shortsighted, and nonverbal, and they will tend therefore to engage in criminal and analogous acts. Since these traits can be identified prior to the age of responsibility for crime, since there is considerable tendency for these traits to come together in the same people, and since the traits tend to persist through life, it seems reasonable to consider them as comprising a stable construct useful in the explanation of crime.

The Many Manifestations of Low Self-Control

Our image of the "offender" suggests that crime is not an automatic or necessary consequence of low self-control. It suggests that many noncriminal acts analogous to crime (such as accidents, smoking, and alcohol use) are also manifestations of low self-control. Our image therefore implies that no specific act, type of crime, or form of deviance is uniquely required by the absence of self-control.

Because both crime and analogous behaviors stem from low self-control (that is, both are manifestations of low self-control), they will all be engaged in at a relatively high rate by people with low self-control. Within the domain of crime, then, there will be much versatility among offenders in the criminal acts in which they engage.

Research on the versatility of deviant acts supports these predictions in the strongest possible way. The variety of manifestations of low self-control is immense. In spite of years of tireless research motivated by a belief in specialization, no credible evidence of specialization has been reported. In fact, the evidence of offender versatility is overwhelming.

By versatility we mean that offenders commit a wide variety of criminal acts, with no strong inclination to pursue a specific criminal act or a pattern of criminal acts to the exclusion of others. Most theories suggest that offenders tend to specialize, whereby such terms as robber, burglar, drug dealer, rapist, and murderer have predictive or descriptive import. In fact, some theories create offender specialization as part of their explanation of crime. For example, Cloward and Ohlin create distinctive subcultures of delinquency around particular forms of criminal behavior, identifying subcultures specializing in theft, violence, or drugs. In a related way, books are written about white-collar crime as though it were a clearly distinct specialty requiring a unique explanation. Research projects are undertaken for the study of drug use, or vandalism, or teen pregnancy (as though every study of delinquency were not a study of drug use and vandalism and teenage sexual behavior). Entire schools of criminology emerge to pursue patterning, sequencing, progression, escalation, onset, persistence, and desistance in the career of offenses or offenders. These efforts survive largely because their proponents fail to consider or acknowledge the clear evidence to the contrary. Other reasons for survival of such ideas may be found in the interest of politicians and members of the law enforcement community who see policy potential in criminal careers or "career criminals."

Occasional reports of specialization seem to contradict this point, as do everyday observations of repetitive misbehavior by particular offenders. Some offenders rob the same store repeatedly over a period of years, or an offender commits several rapes over a (brief) period of time. Such offenders may be called "robbers" or "rapists." However, it should be noted that such labels are retrospective rather than predictive and that they typically ignore a large amount of delinquent or criminal behavior by the same offenders that is inconsistent with their alleged specialty. Thus, for example, the "rapist" will tend also to use drugs, to commit robberies and burglaries (often in concert with the rape) to have a record for violent offenses other than rape. There is a perhaps natural tendency on the part of observers (and in official accounts) to focus on the most serious crimes in a series of events, but this tendency should not be confused with a tendency on the part of the offender to specialize in one kind of crime.

Recall that one of the defining features of crime is that it is simple and easy. Some apparent specialization will therefore occur because obvious opportunities for an easy score will tend to repeat themselves. An offender who lives next to a shopping area that is approached by pedestrians will have repeat opportunities for purse snatching, and this may show in his arrest record. But even here the specific "criminal career" will tend to quickly run its course and to be followed by offenses whose content and character is likewise determined by convenience and opportunity (which is the reason why some form of theft is always the best bet about what a person is likely to do next).

The evidence that offenders are likely to engage in noncriminal acts psychologically or theoretically equivalent to crime is, because of the relatively high rates of these "noncriminal" acts, even easier to document. Thieves are likely to smoke, drink, and skip school at considerably higher rates than nonthieves. Offenders are considerably more likely than nonoffenders to be involved in most types of accidents, including household fires, auto crashes, and unwanted pregnancies. They are also considerably more likely to die at an early age. . . .

The Causes of Self-Control

We know better what deficiencies in self-control lead to than where they come from. One thing is, however, clear: low self-control is not produced by training, tutelage, or socialization. As a matter of fact, all of the characteristics associated with low self-control tend to show themselves in the absence of nurturance, discipline, or training. Given the classical appreciation of the causes of human behavior, the implications of this fact are straightforward: the causes of low self-control are negative rather than positive; self-control is unlikely in the absence of effort, intended or unintended, to create it. (This assumption separates the present theory from most modern theories of crime, where the offender is automatically seen as a product of positive forces, a creature of learning, particular pressures, or specific defect. We will return to this comparison once our theory has been fully explicated.)

At this point it would be easy to construct a theory of crime causation, according to which characteristics of potential offenders lead them ineluctably to the commission of criminal acts. Our task at this point would simply be to identify the likely sources of impulsiveness, intelligence, risk-taking, and the like. But to do so would be to follow the path that has proven so unproductive in the past, the path according to which criminals commit crimes irrespective of the characteristics of the setting or situation.

We can avoid this pitfall by recalling the elements inherent in the decision to commit a criminal act. The object of the offense is clearly pleasurable, and universally so. Engaging in the act, however, entails some risk of social, legal, and/or natural sanctions. Whereas the pleasure attained by the act is direct, obvious, and immediate, the pains risked by it are not obvious, or direct, and are in any event at greater remove from it. It follows that, though there will be little variability among people in their ability to see the pleasures of crime, there will be considerable variability in their ability to calculate potential pains. But the problem goes further than this: whereas the pleasures of crime are reasonably equally distributed over the population, this is not true for the pains. Everyone appreciates money; not everyone dreads parental anger or disappointment upon learning that the money was stolen.

So, the dimensions of self-control are, in our view, factors affecting calculation of the consequences of one's acts. The impulsive or shortsighted person fails to consider the negative or painful consequences of his acts; the insensitive person has fewer negative consequences to consider; the less intelligent person also has fewer negative consequences to consider (has less to lose). . . .

There is good evidence that some of the traits predicting subsequent involvement in crime appear as early as they can be reliably measured, including low intelligence, high activity level, physical strength, and adventuresomeness. The evidence suggests that the connection between these traits and commission of criminal acts ranges from weak to moderate. Obviously, we do not suggest that people are born criminals, inherit a scale for criminality, or anything of the sort. In fact, we explicitly deny such notions. What we do suggest is that individual differences may have an impact on the prospects for effective socialization (or adequate control). Effective socialization is, however, always possible whatever the configuration of individual traits.

Other traits affecting crime appear later and seem to be largely products of ineffective or incomplete socialization. For example, differences in impulsivity and insensitivity become noticeable later in childhood when they are no longer common to all children. The ability and willingness to delay immediate gratification for some larger purpose may therefore be assumed to be a consequence of training. Much parental action is in fact geared toward suppression of impulsive behavior, toward making the child consider the long-range consequences of acts. Consistent sensitivity to the needs and feelings of others may also be assumed to be a consequence of training. Indeed, much parental behavior is directed toward teaching the child about the rights and feelings of others, and of how these rights and feelings ought to constrain the child's behavior. All of these points focus our attention on child-rearing.

Child-Rearing and Self-Control: The Family

The major "cause" of low self-control thus appears to be ineffective child-rearing. Put in positive terms, several conditions appear necessary to produce a socialized child. Perhaps the place to begin looking for these conditions is the research literature on the relation between family conditions and delinquency. This research has examined the connection between many family factors and delinquency. It reports that discipline, supervision, and affection tend to be missing in the homes of delinquents, that the behavior of the parents is often "poor" (e.g., excessive drinking and poor supervision); and that the parents of delinquents are unusually likely to have criminal records themselves. Indeed, according to Michael Rutter and Henri Giller, "of the parental characteristics associated with delinquency, criminality is the most striking and most consistent."

Such information undermines the many explanations of crime that ignore the family, but in this form it does not represent much of an advance over the belief of the general public (and those who deal with offenders in the criminal justice system) that "defective upbringing" or "neglect" in the home is the primary cause of crime.

To put these standard research findings in perspective, we think it necessary to define the conditions necessary for adequate child-rearing to occur. The minimum conditions seem to be these: in order to teach the child self-control, someone must (1) monitor the child's behavior; (2) recognize deviant behavior when it occurs; and (3) punish such behavior. This seems simple and obvious enough. All that is required to activate the system is affection for or investment in the child. The person who cares for the child will watch his behavior, see him doing things he should not do, and correct him. The result may be a child more capable of delaying gratification, more sensitive to the interests and desires of others, more independent, more willing to accept restraints on his activity, and more unlikely to use force or violence to attain his ends. . . .

In criminology it is often argued that special theories are required to explain female and male crime, crime in one culture rather than another, crime committed in the course of an occupation as distinct from street crime, or crime committed by children as distinct from crime committed by adults. We intend our theory to apply to all of these cases, and more. It is meant to explain all crime, at all times, and, for that matter, many forms of behavior that are not sanctioned by the state. . . .

Empirical Tests of the Crime and Criminality Perspective

Our stability postulate asserts that people with high self-control are less likely under all circumstances throughout life to commit crime. Our stability notion denies the ability of institutions to undo previously successful efforts at socialization, an ability other theories take as central to their position.

Similarly, our versatility construct suggests that one avenue available for the identification of persons with low self-control is via its noncriminal outlets. Other theories predict no correlation or even negative correlation between the various forms of deviance. Our conception of versatility also predicts that one can study crime by studying other noncriminal manifestations of low self-control without being misled by the results.

Our idea of crime asserts that complex, difficult crimes are so rare that they are an inadequate basis for theory and policy. Other perspectives suggest that exotic crimes are as theoretically useful as mundane crimes and just as likely to occur. Our idea of crime predicts that the vast majority of crimes will be characterized by simplicity, proximity of offender and target, and failure to gain the desired objective. Other theories make no room for failure, assuming that crime satisfies strong forces and desires and thus reinforces itself. Our perspective asserts that crime can be predicted from evidence of low self-control at any earlier stage of life. No sociological or economic theory allows such predictions. Our perspective also asserts that low self-control can be predicted from crime at any earlier stage of life; most sociological theories do not allow such a prediction.

Our perspective asserts that many of the traditional causes of crime are in fact consequences of low self-control—that is, people with low self-control sort themselves and are sorted into a variety of circumstances that are *as a result* correlated with crime. Our theory predicts that prevention of one form of deviant behavior will not lead to compensating forms of behavior, but will reduce the total amount of deviant behavior engaged in by the population in question. Other theories predict displacement and suggest constant levels of deviance in a constantly "predisposed" population.

CHAPTER

4

How Should Society React to Crime?

Chapter Preface

Criminologists have traditionally asked three questions when judging whether crime control policies are effective: (1) Do they deter crime and criminal behavior? (2) Do they incapacitate the career criminal or repeat offender? and (3) Do they rehabilitate criminal or delinquent offenders?

Theoretically, from the point of view of classical criminology and criminal law, criminal law and criminal justice serve the purpose of deterring crime. The basic view of classical criminology was that the criminal offender is rational and that punishment, or the threat of punishment, will deter criminality. This idea is consistent with the foundations of criminal law and criminal justice: The law, law enforcement, and the threat of punishment should prevent and control crime because most people will decide that crime is not worth the risk.

If the above assumptions are true, criminologists should be able to measure the value of crime control policies by evaluating their ability to deter crime. In practice, however, this turns out to be a very difficult thing to do. It is difficult to estimate how many people would be committing crime without the presence of our current criminal law and criminal justice system.

Because of the difficulties in evaluating the positive impact of deterrence policies, it has become popular to develop crime control policies that focus on incapacitating career criminals or dangerous repeat offenders. This approach also implies that career criminals have demonstrated that they cannot be rehabilitated and, therefore, attempts to reform their behavior will fail. They must be identified, removed from the rest of society, and locked up as efficiently as possible for as long as possible.

The current popularity of this policy, often called selective incapacitation, is evidenced by politicians' efforts to support the "three strikes you're out" laws. These laws would apply special sanctions and mandatory sentences to dangerous repeat offenders or career criminals.

These latest efforts abandon "corrections" in criminal justice, the idea that both juveniles and adults can be rehabilitated. Many people are much more likely to concede that the rehabilitative ideal should play a part in policies to control juvenile offenders but argue that adult offenders do not respond to it. This is related to the public's fear of becoming victims of crime. The abandonment of rehabilitation is also related to the well-publicized failures of the prison system, probation, and parole. Although we still call prisons "correctional institutions," much of the public and most politicians have almost given up on the idea.

In this chapter, the arguments for and against crime prevention and control are presented. Each has its adherents and detractors and each of these approaches is advocated as policy today.

VIEWPOINT

1

Crime Can Be Deterred by Effective and Efficient Punishment

ERNEST VAN DEN HAAG

In the following viewpoint van den Haag argues that consistent and effective punishment of criminals is the best reaction to crime. Known as the deterrence argument for crime prevention and control, it originated with classical criminology in the eighteenth century. The U.S. criminal law and justice systems have been based on the idea of crime deterrence. This argument does not rely on empirical scientific evidence as advocated by positivistic criminology. It relies more on the common sense idea that criminals calculate the risks and rewards of their actions. If the risks are too high, they will decide against harming others or engaging in behavior that might lead to humiliation and punishment. The job of criminal justice, from this point of view, is to ensure that the decision to engage in criminal behavior carries great risks of efficient and effective punishment. Criminal justice should teach a lesson

Excerpted from *Punishing Criminals: Concerning a Very Old and Painful Question* by Ernest van den Haag. New York: Basic Books, 1975. Reprinted with permission of the author.

that "crime does not pay" by getting tough on criminals. Any effort to protect the rights of the accused, to allow plea bargaining or legal loopholes, or to advocate rehabilitation instead of punishment should be viewed with suspicion. Deterrence advocates also view with suspicion efforts to exercise discretion within the criminal justice system. They want mandatory sentences for serious and dangerous criminals. Ernest van den Haag is a criminologist and faculty member at the New School for Social Research in New York. He has written extensively on the subjects of deterrence and punishment.

QUESTIONS

1. How do the costs and benefits for engaging in criminal activity influence the amount of crime we experience in our society, according to van den Haag?
2. Why does the author regard deterrence as the main utilitarian purpose of punishing offenders? What is deterrence supposed to accomplish from his perspective?
3. How does van den Haag define deterrence? What examples of deterrence does he cite?

■ ■ ■

The threat of punishment is useful inasmuch as it controls crime. When the threat has not been effective—when an offense has been committed despite it—the punishment imposed meets the obligation society undertook when threatening it and is morally justified if undertaking the obligation was. However, retribution is useful beyond being a moral obligation—above all, by making the threat of the law credible; and in three additional ways: (1) by incapacitating offenders, (2) by reforming them through intimidation or rehabilitation, and (3) by deterring others from committing offenses.

Incapacitation

For as long as it lasts, the incapacitation of detained offenders protects society from them.

The only total, permanent, and irrevocable incapacitation is execution. Other punishments, such as imprisonment, produce partial, revocable, and usually temporary incapacitation. Although some convicts commit crimes in prison, or direct extramural criminal activity from there, most do not. Imprisonment reduces the number of offenses they commit over their lifespan—if they would have continued illegal activities had they been free, and if, once out of prison, they do not make up for lost time. Two general points should be noted about this reduction of offenses. To consider these points, the incapacitating functions of imprisonment must be analytically separated from the retributive, rehabilitative, and deterrent ones. Thus isolated, the effects of incapacitation are the same whether caused by incarceration or by hospitalization.

Incapacitation does not decrease the offenses of convicts who would not have committed additional offenses anyway—e.g., of generally law-abiding citizens who committed a "crime of passion" in a specific, nonrecurrent situation. As for others, incarceration reduces their criminal activity only for the duration, unless it also affects their conduct upon release—unless prisoners are reformed. Some are. Others are criminalized, i.e., led more thoroughly into a criminal career. Most seem unaffected either way upon release; but the effects of imprisonment on criminal careers are difficult to gauge.

Whatever the effects of incapacitation on the number of crimes a prisoner commits over his lifetime, they must not be confused with effects on the crime rate: the crimes committed annually per 100,000 persons. The temporary or even the permanent incapacitation of convicts reduces the crime rate only if there is no compensating increase of crime by others. Often there is.

When illegal activities are produced as legal ones are, when crimes are produced like wheat or shoes or advertising, such an offsetting increase must be expected. When some farmers or shoemakers or ad men are incapacitated by disease, the rate of wheat or shoe or ad production hardly decreases. Nor does the rate of crime when some criminals are incapacitated—if their crimes are produced as wheat or shoes or ads are. The criminal population—or that of wheat farmers—is what it is because some are normally expected to be incapacitated. The number of farmers or criminals producing the current output would be smaller if some were not ordinarily incapacitated by various misfortunes, such as illness or imprisonment. If the rate of incapacitation increases temporarily, because of an epidemic of pneumonia or of convictions, production suffers temporarily. But the total number of persons engaged in producing shoes, or crimes, soon adjusts to produce the output determined by profitability. Hence, incapacitation will have little effect. Incapacitation is effective mainly when the forces that determine the production of crime cannot be compared with the forces that determine the supply of shoes or wheat. When is that the case?

Some crimes are produced exclusively by exceptional people, as some commodities are. If some of these people are incapacitated, production is reduced. Offenses committed almost exclusively by persons with uncommon psychological characteristics, such as psychotics, can be reduced by incapacitation: there is, at any time, only a limited and reasonably fixed supply of psychotics. Child molesting, for example, is done by offenders with an uncommon psychology (though they need not be psychotics). Incapacitating all of them would eradicate the offense. Since it is impossible to identify and incapacitate these offenders before they commit the offense, child molesting cannot be eliminated. However, incapacitating convicted child molesters reduces the rate of child molesting if, left free, they would have continued to commit the offense. Such offenders are not likely to be replaced. The "Boston Strangler" also produced the kind of crime that can be reduced by incapacitating the criminal. Whenever the crime depends on a fixed and limited supply of persons exclusively capable of committing it, and when many of these can be convicted, the crime rate can be affected by incapacitating them. The incapacitation of multiple rapists—likely to have developed a sort of addiction to raping—will reduce the rate of rape produced by them. On the other hand, increases in legal costs—punishments—are more decisive in deterring nonaddicted rapists from joining the ranks or continuing. The total rape rate is affected by both incapacitation and by the deterrent effect of punishment.

Many offenses, however, are committed by a range of fairly ordinary persons. If the psychological characteristics needed to commit the offense are not rare, those incapacitated may be easily replaced. The supply cannot be depleted by

189

incapacitation and the crime rate is not affected by it (except temporarily), whether incapacitation is caused by an epidemic or by incarceration. The time lag for replacement differs according to the attractiveness of the offense, the skill required to commit it, etc. But when crimes depend mostly on the benefit expected by reasonably rational offenders, the crime rate depends on varying that benefit through varying the cost to offenders and not simply on incapacitation of those who are caught. Punishment (cost), whether imprisonment or a fine, will affect the crime rate by deterring. But by and large crime rates will be independent of incapacitation by imprisonment, natural death, execution, or sickness of any number of easily replaceable offenders.

An imprisoned Mafia "soldier," or "capo," is prevented from committing crimes. But he is readily replaced. The total of Mafia crimes is not reduced by incapacitating Mafiosi. Or, to take a different case, when a "normal" proportion of all practicing prostitutes is incapacitated by disease or imprisonment, the rate of prostitution is "normal." If the proportion incapacitated is temporarily higher than "normal," owing to a police "crackdown," there may be a temporary decline of the activity. But if the proportion incapacitated remains permanently higher than before, the rate of prostitution will be unaffected once more: more prostitutes will be needed to provide the same level of service; more will be recruited if providing the service continues to be attractive. (We are considering here only the incapacitating effect of imprisonment, not its deterrent effect, which may make supplying the service less attractive and thus more costly to customers.) The rate of prostitution depends on factors that make the occupation attractive, not on depleting the supply of practitioners by incapacitation, unless uncommon qualifications are needed. They are not. Nor are the qualifications of car thieves, heroin dealers, muggers, or ordinary robbers and burglars rare enough for incapacitation to make much difference. (There are exceptions to which we will turn.)

The foregoing may appear a little too sweeping to some readers. The following restatement is more qualified and unavoidably more technical.

The crime rate is fairly independent of the incapacitation of actual offenders as long as an unlimited number of potential offenders is willing to replace them as soon as net benefits suffice—when the supply of offenders is elastic. In that case more people would engage in crime than do presently if the net benefit were higher (compared to legitimate opportunities); fewer, if the net were lower; and as many as do now (regardless of incapacitation) as long as the comparative net benefit does not change.

To assume an elastic supply of potential offenders is to assume that all or most "normal" people will yield to the attraction of an illicit gain, if the net benefit—the positive difference between cost and gross benefit—suffices compared to the net benefit from licit activities. This assumption may seem extreme. One may question whether people who are quite "normal," who are not deviant, who do not have something wrong with them, will engage in an illegitimate activity, even when it holds out net benefits over and above legitimate activities. We need not decide this question. Whether or not those who commit offenses when there is a net benefit have something wrong with them, there are too many to expect that the crime rate can be reduced by incapacitating some. Instead, it must be reduced in the first place by reducing the comparative net benefit from offenses, by making them less profitable.

In most cases changes in comparative cost-benefit ratios that significantly affect the crime rate depend on changes in the legal costs imposed for offenses: higher costs (punishments) reduce the comparative attractiveness of crime. However, when legal costs are held constant, net benefits also can be affected by the crime rate itself. This is the case when opportunities for crime are limited. Additional crime then requires the utilization of less good (marginal) opportunities and becomes less profitable. Bank robbing may be an instance. And the value of illegitimately obtained items, or of illegitimate services, declines as more come on the market. Thus the resale value of stolen cars and hijacked or stolen goods will decline when the supply rises. The profitability of various rackets also is affected by the availability of opportunities and the presence of competing rackets. In all such cases, crime can be made less profitable by reducing opportunities for it still further. Better burglar alarms, more guards, traveler's checks instead of cash, better lighting, and unpickable car locks all help. But the most important thing is to increase the legal cost of the offense to the offender and to those whose offense consists of merchandising the illegitimate activity or its fruits, or in buying either. All three cost increases would reduce the benefit from crime (to the original offender, to the merchandiser, and to the ultimate purchaser, respectively), thereby reducing both the supply and the demand for it.

When money is taken rather than goods, and when the opportunity to do so is unlimited—as in mugging, but not in bank robbing—the legal cost to the offender must be increased to reduce the rate at which the offense is committed. It is hard to reduce the opportunity for mugging and impossible to reduce the resale value of money.

All this is not to discount incapacitation entirely. Incapacitation plays an independent role (in the short run) when the offense requires skills that take time to acquire; or, even in the long run, when the offense has an expressive as well as an instrumental function. An unknown number of offenders may become sufficiently addicted to the expressive thrill of crime so that they will habitually continue even when the net benefit from their offenses has become quite low. Others habitually continue for other reasons, e.g., alcoholism, or ignorance of legitimate gainful activities, or inability to utilize them. To illustrate: the rate of gambling can be increased or decreased by varying the net benefit to gamblers. But some people will gamble however low the benefits are. If gambling is already unattractive to those not addicted to it, incapacitating those addicted to it would reduce the rate of gambling. So with other expressive crimes, such as rape or—in an unknown proportion of cases—robbery, often a pseudo-instrumental crime. In sum: the crime rate can be reduced by incapacitation whenever the nature of the crime, or of the criminals, is such that any part of the supply of people attracted to the crime is inelastic.

The first line of social defense is the cost imposed for criminal activity. Cost-benefit ratios are decisive for the part of the supply of offenders that is elastic. Incapacitation remains of value once the cost imposed for an offense is high enough to deter most people. Incapacitation, then, will reduce the number of professionals who have become addicted to a particular crime and who continue even when the net benefit becomes very low, and generally of those who commit it for nonrational reasons. These are mostly multiple offenders. Their number is limited, but they commit a disproportionate number of crimes—half of all those committed in certain categories.

Reform

The intimidation, or rehabilitation, of the convict is expected to lead him to law-abiding conduct upon his release.

"Rehabilitation" is meant to change the offender's intent, motivation, or even character toward law-abiding conduct. "Intimidation" causes avoidance of offenses because of fear of punishment. Whereas rehabilitation affects the offender's wish, intimidation leaves the wish unchanged—only it is not carried out because of fear. To wit: one may no longer wish to cheat, or one may wish to but control that wish for moral reasons (rehabilitation); or one may still wish to cheat but control the wish for fear of punishment (intimidation). Since internal motivations and restraints are not directly observable, the distinction between rehabilitation and intimidation cannot easily be made on the basis of statistical data. Sometimes, too, it is impossible to tell what has produced law-abiding behavior in an individual: an offender released after the age of thirty-five may become law-abiding simply because he is older—perhaps his age is a lasting form of incapacitation; perhaps he has been rehabilitated or intimidated. Nonetheless, the distinction is of some importance in penology: policies aimed at intimidation differ from policies attempting rehabilitation or merely incapacitation.

Reform, and particularly rehabilitation, assumes that the convict committed offenses because of some personality disorder that can be corrected by treatment. If the treatment succeeds he will become rational enough to see that "crime does not pay," that it is irrational. He will be reformed.

However, if a given offender's offenses are rational in the situation in which he lives—if what he can gain exceeds the likely cost to him by more than the gain from legitimate activities does—there is little that can be "corrected" in the offender. Reform will fail. It often fails for this reason. What has to be changed is not the personality of the offender, but the cost-benefit ratio which makes his offense rational. That ratio can be changed by improving and multiplying his opportunities for legitimate activity and the benefits they yield, or by decreasing his opportunity for illegitimate activities, or by increasing their cost to him, including punishment.

Replacement

If successful, rehabilitation or intimidation, though keeping the released prisoner law-abiding, still may not affect the crime rate if the rehabilitated or intimidated former prisoner is replaced. People who have committed crimes can be prevented from committing more, temporarily or permanently. But rehabilitation, intimidation, or incapacitation are unlikely to affect many crime rates as long as those incapacitated or reformed are readily and fully replaced, as they will be if their offenses are attractive enough to new recruits. In this respect, crime does not differ from dentistry. If the average working life of dentists or lawyers were shortened by fifteen years by early retirement, there would be no long-run effects if dentistry or the law remained sufficiently attractive to new recruits. So with most criminal activities. Not that the supply of prospective lawyers, or offenders, is infinite. Not everybody qualifies for either activity. But the supply is great enough for replacement rates to be unaffected by depletion.

Incapacitation and reforms are meant to affect the behavior of individual convicts. They are the most direct and tangible effects, actual or desired, of incarceration in "correctional institutions," as prisons are euphemistically called. But they are not the primary goals of punishment. And at least some offenders require neither incapacitation nor reform: they will not commit further crimes anyway. The man who kills his wife during a jealous quarrel may never marry or kill again. He needs neither reform nor incapacitation. Other offenders cannot be reformed by any known means. If incapacitation or reform were primary goals, nonreformable offenders would be imprisoned permanently, even if their offenses were trivial, while many murderers might be released upon pleading guilty. Punishment would depend on an assessment of the offender's future behavior. It would be independent of his offense. However, this would defeat not only justice but also the main utilitarian purpose of punishing offenders: deterrence.

Deterrence

Unlike incapacitation and reform, deterrence is not concerned with the convict. It is a message addressed to the public at large. The punishment of the offender deters others by telling them: "This will happen to you if you violate the law." Deterrence protects the social order by restraining not the actual offender, who, *eo ipso*, has not been deterred, but other members of society, potential offenders, who still can be deterred. As an English judge succinctly remarked: "Men are not hanged for stealing horses, but that horses may not be stolen."

What is needed for intimidation may differ from what is needed for rehabilitation; and incapacitation is needed as long as neither works. Each requires different treatment and each must be tailored to the individual offender: the length of his imprisonment ideally depends on his progress, on his current or expected future conduct, rather than on his past offense. Indeed, if the law or the court ignores the individual character and prospect of an offender, there are disadvantages: rehabilitation might be missed; imprisonment not needed to reform or incapacitate him may be imposed; or unreformed convicts may be released. On the other hand, unless the future behavior of individual offenders can be objectively predicted, individualized treatment easily becomes capricious and unhelpful—as it has become in our system.

Unlike reform, retribution depends only on the past offense of the offender; and deterrence depends only on what is expected to restrain not him but others from committing the offense in the future. Since retribution and deterrence are not addressed to the individual offender, neither depends on his current or his future conduct. The punishment required by either purpose then does not depend at all on the individual offender. It is the same for all those guilty of the same offense. Disregarding the personality of the offender has advantages. Punishment is predictable and impersonal, and arbitrary differences in penalization are minimized. Indeed, if the punishment, or its size, depends on what the judge, or parole board, thinks about the chances that the offender will be law-abiding in the future, the threat may become too uncertain to deter others readily. Deterrent effects largely depend on punishment being meted out according to the crime, so that a prospective offender can know the likely cost of the offense and be deterred by it.

Deterrence has a number of subsidiary meanings more relevant to crime prevention in general than to punishment as a specific means thereto. Thus "deterrence" may refer (a) to the fear of apprehension rather than of punishment: a police patrol, or a visible burglar alarm, deters. But apprehension probably is feared more, the more punishment is feared. "Deterrence" can also refer (b) to fear of dangers other than punishment—fear of falling off the wall one scales, or of being bitten by watchdogs, or shot by the intended victim. Further "deterrence" may refer (c) to foreclosing opportunities for crime, to the effect of protective devices, such as locks, which make it harder for the offender to accomplish his purpose. In short, one may be deterred by the difficulties and dangers involved in committing an offense, as well as by the fear of punishment.

Circumstances that deter by making it more difficult to commit crimes explain why crime rates differ among neighborhoods, and why, although it seems paradoxical, many crimes victimize the poor more often than the rich: the poor usually are easier to victimize. The rich have more to be stolen, but often they also have better locks, or guards, or dogs, or higher walls, all of which deter. Neighborhood grocers are robbed more often than banks are; the punishment might be the same and the loot greater in banks, but banks are watched better and the F.B.I. pursues bank robbers, whereas grocery robbers need fear only the local police. The number of burglaries may be reduced by stronger locks or brighter lights, as well as by more deterrent punishment; and robberies may decrease either because shopkeepers arm themselves, or because more robbers are caught and punished. However, I focus here on deterrence defined as the restraining effect the punishment of criminals has on others.

Punishment Will Not Deter Criminal Behavior

HENRY N. PONTELL

In this viewpoint, criminologist Henry Pontell presents evidence that questions the efficacy of deterrence. From the time of the classical criminologists, those advocating crime deterrence through punishment have argued that penal sanctions must be certain and enacted efficiently. Pontell points out that the real world of criminal justice does not meet this requirement. For most crimes, the risk of apprehension and arrest are low. This is where the possibilities of using the criminal justice system to deter criminal behavior fails. Sentencing practices are such that swift and severe punishment, where the punishment fits the crime, and equal justice for the same crimes does not work in the everyday reality of criminal justice administration. Therefore, the major tenets of the deterrence doctrine are not upheld in practice. Pontell predicts that current efforts to get tough on criminals, such as "three strikes and you're

Excerpted from *A Capacity to Punish: The Ecology of Crime and Punishment* by Henry N. Pontell. Bloomington: Indiana University Press, 1984. Copyright © 1984 by Henry N. Pontell. Reprinted by permission.

out" legislation, will make matters worse in the future, as far as crime deterrence is concerned. His research indicates that the more offenders we put into the system, the less capable it is of producing crime control through deterrence. Henry Pontell is a criminologist and faculty member in the program in social ecology at the University of California, Irvine.

QUESTIONS

1. Why is the reality of criminal justice not conducive to reducing and deterring crime through punishment, according to Pontell?
2. What practices of law enforcement and the courts, according to Pontell's research, make crime deterrence through punishment unlikely?
3. What is the "capacity issue" discussed by Pontell? How does it influence possibilities of crime deterrence?

■ ■ ■

Implications for Theory and Research

The implications for deterrence theory and research are clear from the findings. Current criminal justice practices, especially the extremely low probability of certain and severe punishment, indicate that the deterrent efficacy of punishment is likely to be minimal. This is not to say that deterrence does not or cannot work, but only that it is highly unlikely under present practices of criminal justice. . . . The results presented here are positive enough, however, to at least question current research on deterrence, in that there appear to be many more identifiable relationships present in the etiology of crime and punishment than merely an effect of punishment on crime. Court caseloads, influenced particularly by the degree of inequality in the population, appear to be pushing down formal penalty structures, and hence the probability of sanction. The inability of courts to produce severe and certain sanctions is also linked to the overfunding of police relative to other criminal justice agencies, especially the office of the prosecutor. Putting more cops on the beat may lead to a further erosion of the deterrent efficacy of punishment, as more violators are pushed through the "revolving door" of the courts. What defendants actually see as capricious and arbitrary practices in criminal courts can only lead to a further disrespect for law among those in the lower class who comprise the vast majority of cases in felony courts. In view of rather uncertain sanctions, and contempt for the process by which they are applied, the reality of deterrence as an effect of punishment is extremely limited for those the system aspires to deter the most—the lower class. In the words of Georg Rusche and Otto Kirchheimer:

> The crime rate can really be influenced only if society is in a position to offer its members a certain measure of security and to guarantee a responsible standard of living. The shift from a repressive penal policy to a progressive program can then be raised out of the sphere of humanitarianism to constructive social activity. . . . The futility of severe punishment and cruel treatment may be proven a thousand times, but so long as society is unable to solve its social problems, repression, the easy way out, will always be accepted.

The role of the police in the generation of crime and punishment cannot be underestimated. In studying the ineffectiveness of increased police personnel to prevent crime, Levine notes:

> To the extent that potential criminals correctly perceive the limitations of police, the credibility of legal sanctions is diminished and the deterrent capacity of the criminal justice system is undermined.

In addition to this proposition, the findings of this study indicate that a similar phenomenon is likely operating at the felony court level. The extremely low probability of severe sanctioning in court may further undermine deterrent goals of punishment. Violators who are processed through the system may become cynical of the criminal law after exposure to what might readily be perceived as arbitrary court practices, undermining a major tenet of the deterrence doctrine, according to Andenaes, namely, the legitimacy of the legal system. Thus, the irregular and minimal imposition of criminal sanctions by courts is likely to add to the ineffectiveness of increased police to prevent crime. . . .

It is presently impossible for the state to administer sanctions that are both swift and severe to the vast majority of criminal defendants. This nonpractice stands in direct opposition to the major tenets of deterrence doctrine. It appears more plausible that rates of crime, influenced by inequality, other socioeconomic conditions, and overfunding of police relative to courts and prisons, have pushed down formal penalty structures. This does not disprove deterrence, but merely documents that its effects, if they exist at all, are likely to be greatly reduced in practice. Thus, the task for future research should not be to determine whether deterrence in the abstract is capable of working, but rather whether deterrence is likely to operate given the practices and structure of American criminal justice.

Policy Implications

This study indicates that the more violators we put into the criminal justice system, the less capable it becomes in effecting crime control through deterrence. At the same time, we know that the crime problem is growing. If people are to advocate putting increased resources into the criminal justice system, they cannot argue this on the grounds that it will deter crime. If there are other grounds they wish to argue, those can be studied in turn. The results presented here indicate that deterrence is not a valid basis for increasing criminal justice resources or for pouring more money into the "fight against crime."

The foregoing analysis presents quite a different picture of crime and punishment, and one that can help inform crime control policies. The policy relevance of a system capacity perspective on criminal justice may not seem readily apparent. This is the case for two basic reasons. First, it questions the increasingly common idea that government manipulation of the legal machinery alone is effective in controlling crime. Second, and just as important, if there is a "capacity issue" that must be dealt with in formulating crime control policy, how should it be considered? Should we increase resources for official agencies, or attempt other methods to curb the flow of crime? There are no easy answers to such questions.

Nevertheless, they need to be addressed in order to understand the implications of system capacity for crime control policy.

In a recent newspaper article, well-known commentator on crime and criminal justice James Q. Wilson notes the following about "rehabilitating" the country's prison system:

> There are no inexpensive solutions to the problem. Politicians and voters who complain loudly about crime and then vote against higher expenditures for correctional facilities are being irresponsible. We cannot go on packing more persons into inadequate facilities—even if our consciences will permit it, federal judges will not.

Wilson's thoughts about the "inadequacies" of present facilities as well as the response by judges seem in line with a system capacity approach. His solutions to the problem entail "more responsibility" on the part of legislators and voters, in addition to better means of both managing and screening offenders, and the construction of more and better prisons. It is doubtful, however, that such an approach will, by itself, effect any significant degree of crime control. The amount of prison construction needed to decently house existing prisoners, to say nothing of additional ones in the future, is simply not possible given huge budget deficits at federal, state, and local levels. Without attention to the social conditions that breed crime, and thereby produce the work flows for criminal justice agencies, such an approach would likely be doomed to failure, even ignoring the fact that public monies are largely nonexistent. Caseloads would deny the possibility of deterrence.

Wilson is aware that this may indeed be true, and even argues the case in his influential work, *Thinking About Crime.*

> When thousands of felony cases must be settled each year in a court, there are overpowering pressures to settle them on the basis of plea bargaining in order to avoid the time and expense of a trial. The defendant is offered a reduced charge or a lighter sentence in exchange for a plea of guilty. Though congested dockets are not the only reason for this practice, an increase in congestion increases the incentives for such bargaining and thus may increase the proportion of lighter sentences. For those who

believe in the deterrence theory of sentencing, it is a grim irony: The more crime increases, the more the pressure on court calendars, and the greater the chances that the response to the crime increase will be a sentence decrease.

This idea is pushed to the background as Wilson argues that another reason for this pattern has to do with the belief of many judges that prison sentences are futile. Even if this is the case, however, it is still a capacity issue. If prisons were not so overcrowded and ineffective in reforming criminals, judges would likely feel differently. Nine pages later, Wilson argues that the probability of punishment should be increased in order to deter and incapacitate criminals, which is at odds with his statements concerning the "grim irony" facing those trying to effect deterrence through sentencing.

Wilson's logic concerning crime control policy is largely misleading. In yet another passage of the same book, he argues that we must increase resources for criminal justice sanctioning, after he acknowledges the influence of poverty, unemployment, and inequality in producing crime. He notes:

To a degree, anticrime policies may be frustrated by the failure of unemployment policies, but it would be equally correct to say that so long as the criminal justice system does not impede crime, efforts to reduce unemployment will not work. If legitimate opportunities for work are unavailable, many young persons will turn to crime; but if criminal opportunities are profitable, many young persons will not take those legitimate jobs that exist. The benefits of work and the costs of crime must be increased simultaneously; to increase one but not the other makes sense only if one assumes that young people are irrational.

Wilson is largely incorrect in this analysis. He ignores a central point in looking at the "costs" of crime. By increasing legitimate job opportunities and *genuinely* enhancing the benefits of work, the costs of crime will be driven up naturally, without increased resources for criminal justice. If this aspect of social inequality is reduced, and it is clearly demonstrated that legitimate and profitable opportunities are desirable and geared toward upward social mobility, the criminal justice system would be under less strain and have a greater capacity to process violators. Many middle and upper class persons choose legitimate jobs for precisely these reasons, even though they too could "profit more" from illegal activity. Unemployment, discrimination, and inequality must be reduced if the criminal justice system is to help effect crime control. This is a positive approach to controlling crime, not one that relies on negative sanctions to force people into submitting to inequitable and miserable conditions.

Building more prisons and expanding criminal justice resources may seem like "reasonable," "common sense" responses to the crime problem. Yet, not unlike many "common sense" notions, one does not have to look very far to uncover inherent contradictions.

A rather clear example of this is offered by Elliot Currie, who examines the sardonic nature of the politics of crime control in his critique of the Reagan administration's Task Force on Violent Crime. After pointing out that the Task Force "acknowledged" that violent crime reflected breakdowns in various social networks and institutions, Currie notes:

> . . . the Task Force went on to say that it hadn't concerned itself with any of those possible causes, partly because its mandate was to explore what the Justice Department, not "government" as a whole, could do about crime, but also because "we are not convinced that a government, by the invention of new programs or the management of existing institutions, can by itself recreate those familial and neighborhood conditions, those social opportunities and those personal values that in all likelihood are the prerequisites of tranquil communities." The task force was "mindful of the risks of assuming that the government can solve whatever problem it addresses."
>
> The Task Force's sense of the "limits to what government can do," however didn't stop it from proposing a variety of government interventions into criminal justice policy.

First, as Currie astutely observes, why a study group concerned with controlling "violent crime" must limit its approach to only what the Department of Justice can do is indeed curious, if not dangerous and counterproductive. Such a stance clearly limits the scope of possible interventions to increasing the size of the criminal justice system and the state's control over the individual. This "get tough" stance on crime by policy makers is doomed to failure because of prohibitive costs and the fact that it has not yet been conclusively demonstrated that increasing control resources while ignoring conditions that breed crime will serve to reduce crime rates. Rather, there is every indication that as criminal justice resources grow, so does the crime problem. . . .

The foregoing analysis does not claim that prisons aren't necessary, or that certain individuals shouldn't be incarcerated. It simply questions the current vision that society should opt for protectors with the biggest guns and prisons at their disposal. When policy makers and the public come to fully realize that what they presently do about crime (as well as other social problems) is usually first an issue of politics and second a matter of reason, science, and humanity, perhaps then the largest hurdle will be cleared to producing effective social interventions that can measurably increase the quality of life.

The criminal justice system is likely to work best when it is used least. It should not be used routinely, but exceptionally. With this major tenet as a focus for criminal justice and crime control policy, perhaps we can start to attack crime at its real sources, and allow the criminal justice system to operate effectively. Our modern system of criminal justice was born from a radical social movement in Europe two centuries ago. Perhaps it is time to seriously reexamine criminological premises and provide new directions for the future.

Criminal Justice Should Focus on Incapacitating High-Rate Offenders

KENNETH R. FEINBERG

In the following viewpoint, Kenneth Feinberg argues for targeting violent repeat offenders for selective incapacitation. This approach is currently influencing sentencing practices at all levels of government in the United States. "Three strikes and you're out" laws are based on the idea of focusing criminal justice resources on prosecuting and sentencing high-risk, high-rate offenders. Special police units and prosecution programs have been set up. Mandatory sentences and sentence enhancements have been created for career criminals. Prison and parole programs have also been tailored for this group. All of these changes in criminal justice policy were inspired by landmark studies conducted by criminologist Marvin Wolfgang. These studies found that a small percentage of

Kenneth R. Feinberg, "Selective Incapacitation and the Effort to Improve the Fairness of Existing Sentencing Practices," *New York University Review of Law & Social Change*, vol. 12, no. 1, (1983-84). Reprinted with permission.

hard-core repeat offenders is responsible for a substantial percentage of all serious crimes. If we can identify them, track them, and incapacitate them we can clear much of the serious crime in our communities. This approach assumes that dangerous criminals are different from other people and pose special dangers to the community that justifies special programs to apprehend and sentence them. Longer sentences, even life imprisonment for many felony crimes is justified, according to Feinberg. Advocates such as Feinberg assume career criminals are not deterred by the possibility of being caught and punished. They also have demonstrated that they cannot be rehabilitated. Therefore, the criminal justice system must ensure that this group of "superfelons" is incapacitated. Kenneth Feinberg is managing partner of the law firm Kaye, Scholer, Fierman, Hays & Handler in Washington, D.C. He was formerly special counsel to the Senate Committee on the Judiciary. He is also an adjunct professor of criminal law at Georgetown University.

QUESTIONS

1. How is "dangerousness" determined by those who advocate a policy of selective incapacitation for high-rate offenders?
2. What is the strategy of selective incapacitation and what predictions is it based on?
3. What are the social benefits of selective incapacitation for high-rate dangerous offenders according to Feinberg?

■ ■ ■

The principal objective of this paper is to provide a justification for pursuing a policy of selective incapacitation. This issue is extremely timely because the nation's approach to criminal sentencing and corrections policy is in disarray. Correction officials are unsure of the utility of alternatives to existing sentencing procedures and are therefore uncertain about new steps that might be taken to improve existing practices. Because priorities are confused and resources misallocated, citizens perceive that federal, state and local governments are paralyzed in their efforts to combat crime and to develop a sound, just corrections strategy. There is a disquieting, even cynical attitude among our citizens that our elected public officials, criminal justice professionals and other policy-makers are bereft of constructive ideas precisely at a time when the nation seeks innovative proposals. . . .

My defense of selective incapacitation is based on two overriding considerations. First, and of primary importance is that regardless of the imperfect state-of-the-art of predicting future criminal behavior, a policy of selective incapacitation as an important (but not exclusive) justification for imprisonment would constitute a major improvement over existing sentencing practices. A candid, public consideration of offender "dangerousness" is preferable to the arbitrary and unarticulated assumptions upon which sentencing often rests today.

Second, and of somewhat less importance to this panel, but of very real concern to the policymaker, are the financial advantages of a carefully crafted policy of selective incapacitation. The criminal justice system can no longer afford the luxury of scattering financial and technical resources in the direction of all offenders. There are not enough police to apprehend suspects, not enough prosecutors to prosecute, not enough judges to try the cases and not enough prisons to house all of those convicted.

The issue of prison capacity is of particular importance. Selective incapacitation, if properly implemented, offers the public official the way out of a thorny political thicket—either build more prisons (and confront the inevitable twin dilemmas of who will pay for the cost of construction and maintenance and where will the new prison be located) or de-emphasize the sanction of imprisonment in favor of non-incarcerative alternatives (a policy that calls for more than a modest degree of political courage). Selective incapacitation provides the way out of this political Hobson's choice by focusing on the composition of the prison population and asking who should be incarcerated and for how long. We can remedy the current prison population crisis indirectly through a more selective determination of who should occupy available prison space.

Finally, there are two errors proponents of selective incapacitation often make. First, they overstate their case by arguing that such a policy offers society a revolutionary break with past sentencing practices. Second, proponents argue that incapacitation of the high-risk offender should be the *sole* purpose of imprisonment. Both arguments are flawed and promise too much. Selective incapacitation is not new; the law enforcement community has always, to some extent, attempted to establish as a priority the apprehension and conviction of the violent criminal. What is new and promising is recent research used to justify a broad based incapacitation policy that seeks to imprison a relatively small, highly active segment of the criminal population in order to prevent high rate offenders from committing crimes in the future.

Nor should the policymaker readily discard other equally important rationales for imposing criminal sanctions. Selective incapacitation should not be viewed as the sole justification for comprehensive sentencing reform. We will always need to depend on concepts of retribution, deterrence and "just deserts" to justify the incarceration of some offenders and to help determine their length of imprisonment. In cases, for example, where there is obviously no likelihood of repetition of the offense, it may still be necessary to imprison the offender, either to acknowledge the seriousness of the offense or to deter others similarly disposed. Indeed, to the extent that a policy of selective incapacitation relies exclusively on evidence of the prior criminal history of the offender in predicting future dangerousness, it can be justified independently in terms of "just deserts," i.e., since the truly high-risk offender has a more extensive criminal track record, he "deserves" more punishment.

Defining "Selective Incapacitation" —Choices for the Policymaker

In discussing the strengths and weaknesses of selective incapacitation, we must first reach a definition of the term. For purposes of this colloquium, "selective incapacitation" is an attempt to deal with the difficult problem of offender "dangerousness." The criminal justice system can be most efficient and effective in combating violent crime by focusing its attention and limited resources "selectively" on carefully defined types of "dangerous," violent offenders.

But the policymaker who seeks to promote such selective sentencing immediately confronts formidable obstacles: What crimes should trigger the policy, how should such crimes be measured and which personal offender variables, if any, should be utilized in attempting to define accurately the so-called "high-risk" offender?

The Meaning of "Prior Criminal Activity"

In attempting to fashion a sentencing policy which targets certain offenders for imprisonment, one must determine which crimes should provoke consideration of longer sentences. This point is quite different from the issue of imperfect prediction discussed below. Imagine that one could surmount this latter obstacle, and predict with sufficient accuracy that a particular offender would, in fact, commit the *same* crime if released. We still would have to decide which criminals we should selectively incapacitate. As Professor Morris puts it, "[t]he concept of dangerousness is so plastic and vague—its implementation so imprecise—that it would do little to reduce either the present excessive use of imprisonment or social injury from violent crime."

One can appreciate this concern without concluding that selective incapacitation is forever doomed by its own "plasticity." Precise public policy choices can be made by defining which crimes satisfy the prerequisite of "dangerousness." For example, "dangerousness" could be measured in terms of crimes of violence, such as murder, rape, aggravated assault, etc.; offenses involving a risk of violence, such as weapons offenses and burglary; or the commission of any "index offense," such as violent or potentially violent crimes plus the addition of certain property crimes such as theft. Of course, as one expands this group of index offenses, "prior criminal activity" becomes a more "plastic" concept and poses a risk that too many offenders will be included in the group targeted for incapacitation.

Fortunately, this has not happened. The numerous federal legislative proposals aimed at assuring the incarceration of "high-risk" offenders also look to prior violent criminal activity as a prerequisite. It is not that our elected officials share Professor Morris' concern about "plasticity," but that focus is on the kind of violent crime that most troubles the American people. Thus, in this case at least, political considerations may very well work to the advantage of a narrower definition of prior criminal activity.

Critics who fear that selective incapacitation will be used to justify incarcerating more offenders through a codified expansion of what constitutes a "dangerous" crime may, therefore, be correct; but the validity of that concern depends on a public policy determination—whether such incapacitation is, indeed, reserved for the violent offender.

Measuring Prior Criminal Activity

Even if one relies upon prior violent criminal activity as a necessary prerequisite to the application of selective incapacitation, the problem remains as to how to measure such activity. How does one determine the incidence of such crimes? Does one consider previous arrests? If so, should the inquiry be limited to adult arrests or should juvenile arrests be considered as well? Is it more justifiable to rely only on convictions? The policymaker must decide these critical issues.

Once again, the federal proposals are very narrowly drawn. Indeed, they are too restrictive. Federal proposals limit the application of selective incapacitation to offenders with prior violent criminal activity as demonstrated by one or more convictions (no distinction is made between adult and juvenile convictions). Reliance solely on convictions poses difficulties, since convictions notoriously underrepresent the volume of reported crime. As a result, the practical value of a selective incapacitation policy is severely undercut if it is based solely on convictions. Reliance on past arrests, particularly juvenile arrests for violent crime, would seem to provide a more accurate indicator of criminal potential.

I recognize that there is a certain injustice in relying upon certain types of arrests absent any evidence of conviction. But arrests have proven superior to convictions as a basis for estimating levels of criminal activity. More to the point, arrests are currently used at every stage of the criminal justice system to justify law enforcement decisions. Consequently, one can hardly accuse the policymaker who favors the use of certain arrest data in fashioning a policy of selective incapacitation of permitting a new, inappropriate factor to enter into the decision making process.

The Use of Personal Offender Variables

A third consideration for the policymaker is what personal offender variables, if any, should be included in constructing a selective incapacitation policy. For example, do we include variables over which the individual has no control, such as I.Q. and demographic characteristics? What about variables that constitute "suspect classifications," such as race and religion? Finally, how should we treat those variables that are at least partially under the offender's control and which correlate significantly with criminal conduct, such as drug use? A purely utilitarian argument can be made that improving our ability to predict offender dangerousness justifies consideration of any variable that helps distinguish the high-risk from the low-risk offender. Yet one must exclude, even at the expense of accurate prediction, both those variables over which the individual has no control and those deemed constitutionally "suspect." . . .

The most accurate predictors appear to relate to the prior criminal activity of the offender. These include age at first arrest, the number and type of prior arrests and the time recently served in jail. Other accurate predictors reflect variables over which the individual has some degree of control, such as drug use and unemployment. Thus, it is unlikely that the reluctance to use such individual variables will compromise the effectiveness of a selective incapacitation program. Instead, the new policy considers only those variables associated with the offender's prior criminal activity and factors primarily under the offender's control. . . .

Selective Incapacitation: The Problem of Imperfect Prediction

Even if proposed selective incapacitation policies are based primarily on carefully measured prior criminal activity with only limited use of voluntary control variables, a major obstacle still remains: how does one determine which individual offenders should, in fact, be subjected to such a policy? It is one thing to maintain that an effective law enforcement strategy should be based on the idea of incarcerating the so-called high-risk offender. But how does the policymaker guard against the problem of the imperfect prediction, which can lead to the unjust, lengthy incarceration of a "low-risk" offender? The legitimacy of selective incapacitation is placed in question by this issue. In attempting to predict future criminal behavior, how justifiable is it for the policymaker to rely on past data in deciding whether to imprison today? The effort to predict future criminal behavior by making questionable distinctions among offenders may produce errors resulting in low-risk offenders being swept into the high-risk group.

There are various answers to this dilemma. One could, of course, maintain that the problem of the false prediction is not a problem at all, that the policymaker need not be particularly concerned with sending too many present offenders to jail for too long a period of time. The offender has, after all, already been convicted of a crime; any cries of unfairness directed at the length of her imprisonment have a particularly hollow ring.

But surely this is not a satisfactory answer. Even if one refuses to recognize the injustice of sentencing an offender to a lengthy term of imprisonment based upon a false prediction of "high-risk" future criminality, there are important pragmatic reasons for rejecting this approach. Where would society house this expanding group of offenders? Who would pay for the expensive construction and maintenance of new prison facilities? To what extent does such a nonselective policy repeat past errors by spreading the resources of the criminal justice system too thin? These and other practical questions cannot be ignored. . . .

Selective Incapacitation and the Promotion of Equity

In defending a policy of selective incapacitation, one must first compare it to present sentencing practices. Today, sentencing decisions are often made in the dark. As a result, the criminal justice system is seriously flawed in two important respects.

First, and of most visible concern to the public, is the justifiable perception that too many high-risk offenders who should be incarcerated are slipping through the system. This perception provokes the almost universal call to "get tough" with the violent criminal through increased use of incarceration. If a formal theory of incapacitation cannot justify such a policy on the ground that predicting future violent behavior is a difficult business fraught with inequity, the policymaker will simply find other justifications for imprisonment.

Second, the opposite problem, often ignored by the policymaker on grounds of political inconvenience, is that indifference towards the fate of false positives leads to imprisonment of the low-risk offender. Unarticulated sentencing assumptions and criteria are used to justify the sanction of imprisonment. Imprisoning false positives fails to assure that the limited prison space will be reserved for the high-risk offender. The result is that today unnecessarily harsh sanctions are inflicted on those demonstrably less dangerous. At the same time, others, more dangerous, either avoid imprisonment altogether or are released on parole after serving only a portion of their sentence. The result is clear. Our current prison crisis is, in large part, a "composition crisis," with too many of the wrong people occupying limited available prison space.

When compared to these existing sentencing practices based on implicit, unarticulated variables, candid reliance on selective incapacitation data, whatever its limitations, should be viewed as an important improvement in current law. Such "sunlight" can promote due process, place all the players in the criminal justice system on notice concerning the factors to be considered in deciding an appropriate sentence, and increase the possibility that like cases will be treated alike. Before critics raise the red flag when it comes to a policy of selective incapacitation, they should compare proposals for reform with the sad state of existing law. Such comparison lends credence to the pursuit of a new candid incapacitation policy.

Selective Incapacitation: Beneficial Side Effects

What are some of the beneficial side effects of a policy of selective incapacitation that may be ignored in the course of the debate? It is a mistake from a public policy perspective to view selective incapacitation as an inevitable harsh instrument of injustice; it can be an effective instrument for reconstituting the current prison population. Perhaps most importantly, implementing such a policy *would* force public officials to acknowledge the need to develop non-incarcerative alternatives for the low-risk offender. Programs based on community service, restitution, probation, and work release, would assume a new importance if premium prison space were reserved for the high-risk offender.

Selective incapacitation also encourages the other components of the criminal justice system, especially the police, to pay less attention to less serious crimes and criminals. This welcome side effect is especially important today as depleted budgets have compelled all components of the criminal justice system to prioritize their needs and goals. A policy of selective incapacitation can offer the law enforcement community a justification for spending limited criminal justice resources primarily on combating violent crimes committed by the high-risk offender.

Such prioritizing may, of course, promote short-term political flack, particularly among citizens who look to the police for the resolution of all disputes, however minor. General maintenance of community order, however, must be balanced against the need to investigate, apprehend, prosecute and imprison the high-risk offender. In the long run, selective incapacitation can be a catalyst for a beneficial reallocation of resources.

Finally, a carefully crafted policy of selective incapacitation can do indirectly what policymakers are reluctant to do directly—acknowledge that many crimes currently on the statute books are simply not worth enforcing. Selective incapacitation provides the policymaker with a convenient "out," an indirect way of acknowledging that society is not willing, or financially able, to prosecute all crimes, however minor or inconsequential. A policy would indicate that certain conduct should not be deemed criminal or, at the very least, that the limited law enforcement resources and the severe sanction of imprisonment should be reserved for commission of the most serious offenses.

Conclusion

Selective incapacitation cannot be labeled per se "liberal" or "conservative," "pro law enforcement" or "pro defendant." In the hands of the policymaker, it can be either a harsh instrument for expanding an already overflowing prison population or a means for carefully restricting the use of incarceration. There is nothing inherently illiberal in championing a policy of selective incapacitation as the primary rationale for comprehensive sentencing reform. How selective incapacitation is defined and implemented determines whether it will be used as a method of controlling the size and nature of our prison population, or merely as one more political symbol of crime control, offered by those who promise success against crime only if we "get tough" with criminals.

Regardless of one's views about selective incapacitation, one should not be misled into believing that it constitutes a watershed in dealing with the high-risk offender. Selective incapacitation is not new. Our criminal justice system continues to focus the bulk of its resources on the dangerous offender. The flawed capacity to predict such dangerousness is a common, integral aspect of the existing system. Decisions to imprison are made every day by criminal justice officials relying on flawed predictions.

Opposition to any policy of selective incapacitation is based upon the need for increased use of imprisonment, which will result in a vast expansion of our prison population and the spawning of a harsher criminal justice system. Though legitimate, these concerns are based on a political judgment. Opponents assume that the potential benefits associated with selective incapacitation such as greater fairness in the handling of offenders, targeting the limited law enforcement resources at the most dangerous offender, more effective crime control at less cost, and new respect for the criminal law, are outweighed by anticipated harms or will simply not be realized. If compelled to evaluate the strengths and weaknesses of selective incapacitation in a public policy vacuum, without the benefit of comparison with existing criminal justice procedures, I might very well conclude that the downside risks outweighed the potential benefits. Innate political cynicism concerning how the public policy balance would ultimately be struck might lead me to side with the critics.

The current situation is, however, not that simple. We are not starting from square one; we have not been asked to fill a public policy vacuum. The criminal justice system practices a policy of selective incapacitation in the dark, and functions all too often through the use of "hunch, guess and gut reaction" when it comes to the critical issue of predicting dangerousness. I would opt instead for a policy of selective incapacitation designed to bring increased candor and accountability to the process. I acknowledge the limitations of my argument. Not only is candor no guarantee that unbridled law enforcement discretion will become more principled, but there is also the very real possibility that the policymakers will exercise their option to favor increased use of imprisonment. In addition, constitutional principles and considerations of justice and fair play preclude the use of certain variables, now used informally, that aid in the prediction process. Candor is not the answer to all of the problems surrounding selective incapacitation.

I conclude that a properly implemented policy of selective incapacitation can be an important part of a comprehensive criminal justice reform strategy. Though unlikely to have much of an impact on the violent crime rate, a policy of selective incapacitation can significantly reduce the current injustice in the criminal justice system. To those supporters and critics who view selective incapacitation simply in terms of crime control, this could prove to be the biggest irony of all.

Selective Incapacitation of High-Rate Offenders Will Not Work

SAMUEL WALKER

In this viewpoint criminologist Samuel Walker examines the evidence for selective incapacitation for high-risk, high-rate offenders. He concludes that the evidence shows that efforts to predict dangerousness are not workable in practice. He also claims that advocates of policies such as the "three strikes and you're out" approach are not being realistic about the costs of imprisonment that would result from its implementation. According to Walker, this approach creates grave due process problems. Walker indicates that these policies can have unintended and undesirable side effects. Walker also examines the impact of special career criminal prosecution programs. These are intended to remove discretion from decisions made by criminal justice personnel. However, they do not really accomplish this goal, according to Walker. He concludes that they may also have undesirable and unintended consequences. Samuel Walker is a faculty member at the University of Nebraska at Omaha. He is the author of many books and articles on criminal justice history and policy including *Sense and Nonsense About Crime and Drugs: A Policy Guide* from which this viewpoint is excerpted.

QUESTIONS

1. What does Walker mean by the "prediction problem" and how does it affect selective incapacitation policies?
2. How has mandatory sentencing policy affected the war on drugs and crime, according to Walker?
3. Why don't career criminal prosecution programs accomplish what their advocates intend, according to Walker?

■ ■ ■

Incapacitation seeks to reduce crime by imprisoning repeat offenders. If they are in prison, they will not be able to victimize law-abiding citizens. Actually, there are two kinds of incapacitation policy. Gross incapacitation involves locking up large numbers of people. Selective incapacitation calls for locking up only the few "high rate" "career criminals." Like preventive detention, selective incapacitation builds on Marvin Wolfgang's career criminal research and seeks to lock up that small group of career criminals. . . .

Selective incapacitation became one of the hottest ideas in criminal justice in the late 1970s and early 1980s. James Q. Wilson gave it a strong endorsement in his 1975 book, *Thinking about Crime,* claiming that serious crime could be reduced by *one-third* if each person convicted of a serious crime received a mandatory three-year prison sentence. He drew upon a study by Shlomo and Reuel Shinnar, who claimed that selective incapacitation could reduce crime by 80 percent.

These extravagant claims generated much excitement. A number of researchers attempted to test them by developing sophisticated models of incapacitation policies. The most important effort was a 1982 Rand Corporation study, *Selective Incapacitation,* by Peter Greenwood. It estimated that a fine-tuned sentencing policy could reduce robbery by 15 percent while also reducing prison populations by 5 percent. This increased imprisonment of career criminals would be offset by not incarcerating low-risk offenders currently being imprisoned. Like so many crime control proposals, the Rand report seemed to offer the best of all possible worlds: more effective crime control at less cost.

If this seems too good to be true, that's because it was. Selective incapacitation fails on several points. My argument is: *Selective incapacitation is not a realistic policy for reducing serious crime.*

At first glance, it would seem that selective incapacitation would be relatively easy to implement. The time that elapses between conviction and sentencing would allow for the careful consideration of the offender's prior record and other factors that might be relevant to the sentence. This is what probation officers normally do in developing the presentence investigation (PSI) report for the judge. Selective incapacitation seeks to refine this process by developing a more precise formula for identifying the career criminals.

Unfortunately, it isn't that easy in the real world of the criminal justice system. Let's take a close look at the Rand report and see what obstacles arise.

Selective Incapacitation: The Rand Report

The Rand report, *Selective Incapacitation*, was based on interviews with 2,190 prison and jail inmates in California, Texas, and Michigan. The Rand Inmate Survey (RIS) has been very influential in criminal justice research. The technique of using self-reported criminal activity to estimate average annual offense rates is the cornerstone of selective incapacitation. California prisoners convicted of robbery did an estimated average of 53 robberies every year, 90 burglaries, 163 thefts, and 646 drug crimes. Imprisoned robbers in Texas, meanwhile, committed an estimated average of 9 robberies, 24 burglaries, 98 thefts, and 356 drug offenses. These figures are incredibly high and would appear to clinch the case for selective incapacitation. Look at how much crime would be prevented by locking up one California robber for one year! Or five years!

These figures present a number of problems, however. First, they are estimates, based on the self-reported recollections of prison inmates. Second, and more serious, these figures are *averages* that are inflated by the extremely high rates for a very select group of offenders. The Rand report observes that "most offenders reported fairly low rates of crime." For all 2,190 prisoners interviewed, the median robbery rate was only five per year. The worst 10 percent of these criminals (or the 90th percentile) committed eighty-seven per year! This latter group includes the truly high-rate offenders. As these data indicate, there is no such thing as an "average" offender. Even those we label "repeat" offenders or "career criminals" have rather low annual averages (five robberies a year, according to Rand).

This brings us to one of the basic issues in career-criminal research: estimating the number of crimes committed by high-rate offenders.

How Big Is *Lambda*? Or, How Much Crime Do They Commit?

The crime reductions promised by Rand, Wilson, and the Shinnars are based on estimates of the number of crimes a career criminal commits each year. These estimates have become one of the central issues in career criminal research over the past fifteen years. While it is an extremely technical question, one that has been the subject of intense debate among criminologists, this issue has enormous policy implications. If the average career criminal commits more than 100 crimes a year, then incarceration would achieve considerable crime reduction. But if the average is less than 10 a year, the crime reduction will be relatively small.

In career-criminal research, the average annual offending rate is referred to as *lambda*. Unfortunately, there is no consensus on the size of *lambda*. The Shinnars assumed that each career criminal committed 10 reported crimes a year. A highly controversial Justice Department report by Edwin Zedlewski assumed an average of 187 crimes per year. Other criminologists estimate offense rates as low as between 0.5 or 3.3 crimes per year. There is a rough consensus that the average for all high-rate offenders is about 18 per year.

As we have already indicated, the idea of an "average" is meaningless. Consider the Rand inmate self-report data. Those 2,190 inmates are a pretty select group to begin with. They are among the very few who got arrested, convicted, and imprisoned. . . .The problem is that the really high-rate offenders we are looking for are already in prison. It is not clear that we can identify and imprison other high-rate offenders.

The advocates of selective incapacitation claim to be able to improve on normal operations by being more precise about whom they select for incapacitation. And there lies another major problem. As the Rand report itself put it, "The difficulty lies in identifying those with high rates." It might have added, "and identifying *only* those with high rates." This brings us again to the prediction problem.

The Prediction Problem

There are three different methods of prediction. *Statistical* predictions compare patterns of the individual with the behavior of similar kinds of people (everyone else in your fraternity flunked this course, therefore you will too). *Anamnestic* predictions are based on repeat behavior by an individual (you flunked the first three tests in this course, therefore you will probably flunk the next test). *Clinical* predictions are based on evaluations of an individual by trained experts (after talking with you and assessing your personality, the teacher concludes that you will flunk this course).

To identify the candidates for selective incapacitation, Rand used an actuarial method of prediction. Using the self-reported social and criminal histories of the 2,190 inmates, it identified thirteen characteristics that would predict high rates of criminal activity. Only those characteristics that were legally relevant and appropriate were used. An offender's race is not a legally appropriate factor, for example. Rand then used this data to develop a seven-point prediction scale (Table 1). Offenders with four or more points were then predicted to be high-rate offenders; those with two to three points were predicted to be medium rate, and those with only one or no points were low-rate offenders.

221

TABLE 1 Seven-point scale of factors affecting prediction of offense rates

1. Prior conviction for the instant offense type
2. Incarcerated more than 50 percent of preceding two years
3. Conviction before age 16
4. Served time in a state juvenile facility
5. Drug use in preceding two years
6. Drug use as a juvenile
7. Employed less than 50 percent of the preceding two years

SOURCE: Peter W. Greenwood, *Selective Incapacitation* (Santa Monica, Calif.: Rand Corporation, 1982), p. 50.

To determine how well the prediction device would work, Rand then correlated the prediction scores with their actual reported criminal activity. The results appear in Table 2. It turned out that the prediction device was correct only 51 percent of the time. You and I could do as well by flipping a coin. We reach the 51 percent figure by adding the predicted low-risk offenders who proved to be low risks (14 percent), the predicted medium risks who proved to be medium risks (22 percent), and the predicted high risks who actually proved to be high risks (15 percent). The prediction device was *grossly* wrong in 7 percent of the cases: the 4 percent who were predicted to be high risks but who turned out to be low risks (false positives) and the 3 percent who were predicted to be low risks but proved to be high risks (false negatives). The prediction device was only *moderately* wrong in the remaining 42 percent of the cases.

TABLE 2 Predicted versus self-reported offense ratio for robbery and burglary

Score on prediction scale	Self-reported offense rates			
	Low	*Medium*	*High*	*Total*
Low (0-1)	14%	10%	3%	27%
Medium (2-3)	12	22	10	44
High (4-7)	4	10	15	29
Total	30%	42%	28%	100%

Source: Peter W. Greenwood, *Selective Incapacitation* (Santa Monica, Calif.: Rand Corporation, 1982), p. 59.

We can hardly expect any system to be perfect. The relevant question is whether the Rand prediction device is more precise than existing sentencing practices. If it led to an improvement that was substantial, even though less than perfect, the device would be useful. Greenwood took his sample of offenders and recategorized them as low, medium, or high risks according to their prison sentences. The judges' sentences were "correct" 42 percent of the time—that is, the sentencing judges correctly identified the high-rate offenders and sentenced them to long prison terms 42 percent of the time. Meanwhile, the judges were grossly wrong 12 percent of the time. In other words, the extremely sophisticated Rand prediction device was only slightly better than what judges had in fact already done with these offenders (51 percent versus 42 percent).

These results are not reassuring. Perhaps a clinical method of prediction would be more accurate. On behalf of the National Council on Crime and Delinquency, Ernst A. Wenk, James O. Robison, and Gerald W. Smith applied this method to a sample of 4,146 youths committed to the California Youth Authority. Of this group, 104 subsequently became "violent recidivists." Wenk and his colleagues sought to develop a prediction device that would have identified these 104 violent recidivists in advance.

The most obvious prediction of violence would be a prior record of violent behavior. But only half of the 104 subsequently violent youths had any previous history of violence. Using only prior violence as a predictor, then, would allow the other 52 to slip through the net. They would be false negatives. Wenk, Robison, and Smith then asked professional clinicians to develop indices of "violence-proneness" to help identify the potentially violent. These indices included, in addition to previous violent behavior, evident emotional problems, and drug or alcohol abuse. Using these indices, they concluded that, at best, they could have accurately identified half of the juveniles who actually became violent. Unfortunately, these factors included a 10 percent error rate. This may not sound too bad until we look at the results in Table 3. A 10 percent error rate yields 404 false positives—people the index would incorrectly predict to be violent. In short, we would imprison 8 people unnecessarily for every violent person we correctly identified

223

and locked up. Meanwhile, there are the 52 false negatives who slipped through the net. The clinical prediction method used by Wenk and his colleagues was no more accurate than the actuarial method used by Rand.

TABLE 3 Numbers of youths predicted to be violent and nonviolent who proved to be violent and nonviolent, California, 1972

	Predicted violent	Predicted nonviolent
Actual violent	True positives: Violent persons correctly identified as violent and incarcerated 52	False negatives: Violent persons incorrectly identified as nonviolent and not incarcerated 52
Actual nonviolent	False positives: Nonviolent persons incorrectly identified as violent and needlessly incarcerated 404	True negatives: Nonviolent persons correctly identified as nonviolent 3 ,638

Source: Ernst A. Wenk, James O. Robison, and Gerald W. Smith, "Can Violence Be Predicted?" *Crime and Delinquency*, 18 (October 1972): 393-402.

The Cost of Imprisonment

One of the more interesting features of the Rand *Selective Incapacitation* proposal is its attempt to deal with the cost of imprisonment. The huge cost of keeping someone in prison—$25,000 a year, not including construction costs—is one of the main problems facing the criminal justice system and American society as a whole. Soaring prison populations and the attendant costs have spurred the development of cheaper alternatives: intensive probation, boot camps, home confinement, and electronic monitoring.

Selective Incapacitation addressed the cost problem by balancing the longer prison terms for high-risk offenders with shorter terms—or no prison sentences at all—for low-risk offenders. Rand actually projected a 5 percent reduction in the prison population through the "savings" that would result from not sentencing many low-risk and medium-risk offenders to prison or from cutting the length of their prison terms.

This looks great on paper, but it does not work out in practice. Not imprisoning low-risk and medium-risk offenders is exactly what liberal reformers have been advocating for years. The National Council on Crime and Delinquency, the National Moratorium on Prison Construction, the National Prison Project of the American Civil Liberties Union, the Sentencing Project, and other organizations of experts have long maintained that we unnecessarily lock up too many people and that we should limit incarceration to the really dangerous offenders.

These authoritative voices were completely ignored as the prison population tripled. The reason is clearly the tremendous public demand for getting tough with criminals. Legislatures have responded by enacting laws with lengthy mandatory minimum terms. Judges have sentenced more offenders to prison and increased the length of prison terms, generally at the request of prosecutors. Parole authorities have been reluctant to grant early release, except when compelled to by overcrowding. In the face of this public pressure, the "savings" promised by Rand will simply not materialize. . . .

Due Process Problems

Perhaps the most shocking aspect of the Rand *Selective Incapacitation* report is the use of employment history as a criterion for sentencing. An offender would acquire one point for having been unemployed for more than half of the two preceding years. On the seven-point scale, unemployment is as serious as a prior conviction for the present offense or as incarceration for more than half of the two preceding years. Under the proposed Rand formula, each point carries major consequences. A second point, for example, transforms the person from a low-risk to a medium-risk offender and thus would mean the difference between jail and prison.

It is outrageous that anyone should seriously recommend basing imprisonment on unemployment. But that is precisely what the Rand formula does. The policy would take us back two hundred years, to the days of imprisonment for debt. Fortunately, we are not likely to be called upon to endure this policy. In every legislature voices would be raised to point out the reactionary nature of this idea and vigorously oppose it. Even many law-and-order conservatives would hesitate to criminalize unemployment. And even if such a policy were to become practice somewhere, it would immediately be challenged in court. It is safe to say that most lower federal courts would throw such a case out on due process grounds. Current case law already forbids the criminalization of conditions such as vagrancy, drug addiction, and chronic alcoholism, and the current Supreme Court is likely to agree.

Before we leave this issue, let me emphasize that the assignment of a point for unemployment was not an arbitrary decision by the Rand experts. Their sophisticated analyses determined that unemployment was one of only seven factors that were highly correlated with future criminal behavior. Take any one of those seven away and the entire formula begins to crumble; that is, their "success" rate would fall below the 51 percent they currently propose. They would then be doing no better than judges currently do, using a combination of pre- sentence investigations and pure hunch.

Probably unemployment *is* highly correlated with criminal activity. The rational and humane way to deal with that problem is not to punish people for being unemployed but to provide employment opportunity.

Unintended Consequences

A final problem with most incapacitation proposals—Rand's and others—is that they would have a significant impact on the criminal justice system. To a great extent this has already happened. The massive increase in the prison population has, in spite of a massive effort in prison construction, led to serious overcrowding. Several things happen as a result. Many states have passed emergency or "safety valve" laws to deal with prison overcrowding. These laws place a cap on prison populations and mandate early release of current prisoners before new ones can be admitted. Inmates' parole dates are moved forward so that they can be released early.

This process has been repeated many times. The quadrupling of prison sentences in Florida, from about 10,000 in 1980 to almost 44,000 in 1989, led to an overcrowding crisis that in turn led to a lawsuit on prison conditions. To comply with the resulting consent decree, state authorities began an aggressive early release program that cut the average prison term in half. In Tennessee, a tough new sentencing law led to overcrowding, a suit, and a forced reduction in prison terms. Massive arrests in New York City in the early 1980s produced the same sequence of events. Eventually, the police backed off from their aggressive arrest policy and the jail overcrowding problem became less serious.

In short, the incapacitation strategy was self-defeating: locking more people up resulted in people being locked up for shorter periods of time. The crime reduction gains promised by incapacitation were canceled out by early releases. . . .

Conservatives believe that a lot of truly dangerous criminals beat the system without being adequately punished. The complaint is that many of those who are arrested slip through "loopholes" in the system: their cases are dismissed, they are allowed to plead guilty to lesser offenses, or if convicted they are not sent to prison. As a result, they return to the streets and commit more crimes.

Prosecute the Career Criminal

One alleged loophole is the product of sheer neglect: dangerous offenders are not sufficiently punished because prosecutors don't concentrate on them. To overcome this problem a number of jurisdictions have created special "major-offender" or "career-criminal" programs targeting career criminals. The basic idea is to concentrate on the few career criminals and make sure they are prosecuted, convicted, and incarcerated. Like the police career-criminal programs . . . these programs are based on Wolfgang's findings about the high percentage of crimes committed by the few career criminals.

The San Diego Major Violator Unit targets robbery and robbery-related homicide cases in which the defendant is charged with three or more separate robbery-related offenses or has been convicted of one or more serious offenses in the preceding ten years. The individual prosecutor who is assigned a major-violator case follows it through to completion. This *continuity of prosecution* is the key to the program, designed to correct what many people believe to be a major weakness of normal procedures. Criminal cases typically pass through the hands of several prosecutors, with different attorneys handling the initial charge, the preliminary hearing, and so on. Continuity is designed to heighten personal involvement in each case and prevent mistakes resulting from lack of familiarity with the case. San Diego prosecutors, for example, maintain close personal contact with witnesses. (The failure of witnesses to cooperate fully is often one of the main reasons that cases are dismissed.) Prosecutors are also involved in the preparation of the presentence investigation (PSI) report, and they submit an independent sentence recommendation to the judge, often asking for a stiff sentence.

Career-criminal programs typically involve limitations on plea bargaining. San Diego prosecutors will accept a plea only to the top felony count. This prevents the defendant from avoiding prison by pleading to a misdemeanor or a lesser felony and getting a sentence of probation.

Alas, the idea of prosecuting serious offenders "to the fullest extent of the law" is another idea that fails to deliver on what it promises. My position is: *Career-criminal prosecution programs do not produce higher rates of prosecution or punishment.*

Career criminal prosecution programs fail for a very simple reason: we are already tough on so-called career criminals. Contrary to popular belief, these defendants do not slip through the system and get off easy.

Data from San Diego confirms the fact that prosecutors there were already tough on career criminals. The Major Violator Unit won conviction in 91.5 percent of its cases. This sounds very impressive until we discover that they normally convicted 89.5 percent of all career criminals. The Major Violator Unit did produce a slight increase in the percentage incarcerated, from 95.3 percent to 100 percent. But they were already pretty tough on serious offenders in San Diego without a special program.

Rehabilitation Should Be the Goal of Crime Control

CLEMENS BARTOLLAS

Criminologist Clemens Bartollas reviews the philosophy of rehabilitation, the goals of rehabilitation, and the arguments for rehabilitation in this viewpoint. The philosophy of rehabilitation is consistent with positivistic criminology as it is grounded in the idea that factors outside the control of the offender cause criminal behavior. Bartollas discusses three models of rehabilitation: the medical model, the adjustment model, and the reintegration model. He explains how rehabilitation approaches underlie what takes place in both juvenile and adult corrections. Bartollas also discusses various defenders of the rehabilitative ideal and their reasons for arguing that rehabilitation should be the goal of criminal justice and crime control. In recent years, this ideal has almost disappeared as a serious goal for adult offenders. It still retains influence on programs for juvenile offenders. However, Bartollas presents the argument that we should not

From Clemens Bartollas, *Correctional Treatment: Theory and Practice*, © 1985 by Prentice-Hall, Inc., pp. 25-34. Reprinted by permission of Prentice Hall.

give up on the rehabilitative ideal. This has been the traditional justification for corrections and prison reform. Clemens Bartollas is a faculty member at the University of Northern Iowa. He is the author of numerous books on criminology and criminal justice including *Correctional Treatment: Theory and Practice*, from which this viewpoint is exerpted.

QUESTIONS

1. How do the assumptions of the medical model, the adjustment model, and the reintegration model of rehabilitation differ, according to Bartollas?
2. What are the main defenses for rehabilitative philosophy discussed by the author? Which defense do you think is the strongest?
3. Based on this information, what role do you think rehabilitation should play in crime control in the future?

■ ■ ■

The rehabilitative ideal traditionally has been identified with the medical model, but because the adjustment and reintegration models are also committed to changing the offender, they too should be included under the more inclusive term of "rehabilitative philosophy." The three models have some important similarities and differences.

Philosophical Underpinnings of the Medical Model

Donal E. J. MacNamara, in his noteworthy essay on the medical model, provides a definition of the model:

> In its simplest (perhaps oversimplified) terms, the medical model as applied to corrections assumed the offender to be "sick" (physically, mentally, and/or socially); his offense to be a manifestation or symptom of his illness, a cry for help. . . . Basic to the medical model, although rather surprisingly denied by many of its proponents, is that the criminogenic factors are indigenous to the individual offender and that it is by doing "something" for, to, or with him that rehabilitation can be affected.

Francis Allen, in an essay which has become a classic on the rehabilitative ideal, clarifies the basic assumptions of the medical model: (1) that "human behavior is the product of antecedent causes"; (2) that it is the obligation of the scientist to discover these causes; (3) that knowledge of these antecedent causes makes it possible to control human behavior; and (4) that measures employed to treat the offender "should be designed to effect changes in the behavior of the convicted person in the interest of his own happiness, health, and satisfaction."

The American Friends Service Committee's *Struggle for Justice* defines the underlying rationale of the medical model:

> [T]he dispassionate behavioral expert displaces judge and theologian. The particular criminal act becomes irrelevant except insofar as it has diagnostic significance in classifying and treating the actor's particular criminal typology. Carried to an extreme, the sentence for all crimes would be the same: an indeterminate commitment to imprisonment probation, or parole, whichever was dictated at any particular time by the treatment program. Any sentence would be the time required to bring about rehabilitation, a period which might be a few weeks or a lifetime.

In short, proponents of the medical model believe that crime is caused by factors that can be identified, isolated, treated, and cured. Punishment should be avoided because it does nothing to solve offenders' problems and it only reinforces the already negative concept that offenders have of themselves. The medical model also assumes that the criminal lacks the ability to exercise freedom of choice or to use reason.

Advocates of the medical model further contend that the legal definition of delinquency and criminal behavior should be broad and that victimless crimes and status offenses for juveniles, as well as crimes against victims, should remain on the books. Those competent in diagnosis and knowledge of human behavior, according to the medical model, should have wide decision-making authority in the juvenile and adult justice system. This model also encourages a much wider use of mental health facilities.

Philosophical Underpinnings of the Adjustment Model

In the late 1960s and 1970s, some proponents of rehabilitation became dissatisfied with the medical model. Although they agreed with the medical model that offenders are different from nonoffenders, need treatment, and can be "cured" by the scientific expert (a person trained in a particular counseling technique), they claimed that offenders are still able to be responsible and to make law-abiding decisions.

The adjustment model is based upon four assumptions. First, offenders need help, or treatment, to conform to societal expectations. They need to be shown that their maladjustive behavior, negative attitudes, or inappropriate interpersonal relationships led them to an involvement with crime. Second, offenders have the capacity to live a crime-free life and, therefore, the emphasis of correctional treatment should be on the belief that offenders are responsible for their present actions. That is, while offenders cannot change the facts of their emotional and social deprivations of the past, they can demonstrate responsible behavior in the present and can avoid using their past problems as an excuse for delinquent or criminal behavior. Third, the larger social environment and the individual's interaction with this environment are important factors in understanding antisocial behavior. Individuals can be taught alternatives that will allow them to live crime-free lives. Finally, punishment is seen only to increase offenders' alienation and behavior problems. . . .

Philosophical Underpinnings of the Reintegration Model

A basic assumption of the reintegration model is that offenders' problems must be solved in the community where they began. Another basic assumption is that society has a responsibility for its own problems and that it can partly fulfill this responsibility by helping law violators reintegrate themselves back into the social order. Thus, the community must offer the offender the opportunities to develop law-abiding behavior, and the offender must learn how to utilize these opportunities. A third assumption is that meaningful community contacts are required to achieve the objectives of reintegration. Offenders must be provided opportunities to assume the normal roles of citizens, family members, and employees. Offenders also need opportunities for personal growth in nonsecure environments. Finally, proponents of reintegration philosophy recommend community-based corrections for all but the hardcore criminals, and they would offer those offenders who must be institutionalized a wide variety of reentry programs, permit confined offenders to be brought into the decision-making process so that they may choose their prison programs, and provide the necessary services so that offenders can restore family ties and obtain employment and education.

The process by which change takes place in the reintegration model is known as internalization. To achieve internalization, offenders must be presented with such options as education, employment, recreation, and any other activity needed to provide direct or indirect alternatives to criminal behavior. Proponents of this model reason that through a process of experimentation, offenders can learn how to meet their needs in law-abiding ways. Because such offenders choose their own means to achieve successful habilitation in the community, their change in attitudes and values reflect their new view of self. In other words, the change is internalized, and socially unacceptable values and behaviors are altered. . . .

In summary, the philosophy of reintegrating the offender back into the community clearly contains the mandate that the offender must be changed by community-based corrections so that he or she will become a law-abiding citizen. Proponents strongly support the notion that this change process is more likely to occur in community-based programs than in fortress-like institutions. Thus, the community is further charged with becoming involved in the change process. . . .

Defense of Rehabilitative Philosophy

The much-maligned advocates of the rehabilitative ideal have used various arguments in defense of correctional treatment: The widespread criticism of rehabilitation is unfair because the "nothing works" thesis is incorrect. Rehabilitation has not really been tried because it has never been given more than lip service in American corrections. Rehabilitation is a necessary part of a humane correctional process, and it is too compelling an ideal to give up. . . .

Correctional Treatment Has Yet to Be Tried

Advocates of correctional treatment charge that rehabilitation has not been given an adequate chance. Seymour L. Halleck and Ann D. Witte put it this way:

> Correctional rehabilitation programs have generally been per-functory, underfunded, understaffed and carried out in settings certainly not ideal. . . . With programs so limited in duration and quality, limited rather than dramatic chances in lifestyles would seem likely.

Supporters of rehabilitation correctly surmise that programs are so few that they can serve only a small minority of inmates in adult prisons. Joan Petersilia, in reporting the findings of a national survey conducted by Rand, revealed that no more than 40 percent of the inmates in state prisons participate in a treatment program while incarcerated, and that only "one in four or five inmates with identified needs participate in prison treatment programs related to his needs."

In addition, programs have been sabotaged by custodial staff in several ways. Staff members sometimes "forget" the days that certain inmates are to attend programs. Security staff members may recommend to prisoners that they not become involved in programs, and, at times, do not even permit treatment staff to see inmates on the cellblock or in other areas of the prison.

In addition, lack of follow-up in the community clearly negates the effects of treatment upon offenders. An offender may have profited from treatment and left the community-based facility or the prison intending to go straight, but any number of debilitating factors, including a failure to receive adequate support services in the community, may unravel the good accomplished by correctional treatment.

Rehabilitation Is a Necessary Part of the Correctional Process

Halleck and Witte explain the rationale behind the defense of rehabilitation as a necessary part of corrections:

Prisoners need the hope that rehabilitation brings. . . . There is good reason to fear . . . that a correctional program that doesn't include rehabilitation will be extremely difficult to implement, will be absurdly expensive, and will encourage us to ignore critical ethical issues.

Francis T. Cullen and Karen E. Gilbert question what the criminal justice system would look like without rehabilitation. They contend that the state's handling of offenders would have been more repressive without the evolution of the rehabilitative ideal. Today, because of the increased acceptance of repressive methods to handle offenders, they argue, the retention of rehabilitation is necessary to maintain humanitarianism in the criminal justice system. Indeed, they state that "rehabilitation is the only justification of criminal sanctioning that obligates the state to care for an offender's needs and welfare."

Many offenders need the expert help provided by treatment because their past failures clearly indicate that they cannot make it on their own. This inability is especially true of repeat or multiple offenders and offenders involved in compulsive crimes. Unless repeat and multiple offenders make conscious decisions to walk away from crime and find support systems to help them succeed in this goal, they may end up spending a large portion of their lives in prison. Unless compulsive sex offenders, for example, receive intensive psychotherapy, they are likely to commit other sex crimes as soon as they are released from confinement.

Proponents of rehabilitation warn that without treatment, the victimization of society will increase. That is, society cannot afford to have untreated offenders released from correctional care because society needs the benefits of treatment for its own self-protection. Rehabilitation, in other words, serves the useful purpose of deterring property and personal crimes in American society.

Rehabilitation Is Too Compelling an Ideal to Give Up

The Panel on Research on Rehabilitative Techniques underlined the compelling nature of rehabilitative philosophy:

The promise of the rehabilitative ideal is so compelling a goal that the strongest possible efforts should be made to determine whether it can be realized and to seek ways to realize it before it is abandoned. Our society cannot avoid the perplexing and recurring problems of how to deal with criminal offenders and the consequences of its penal policy. It is crucial, therefore, that we avoid simplistic solutions and continue efforts to systematically develop, implement, test, and evaluate a variety of intervention programs in the search for a more humane and effective correctional policy.

Proponents argue that it is not necessary to give up on the compelling ideal of rehabilitation because correctional interventions made significant progress during the 1970s. In this decade, the reintegration and adjustment models largely replaced the controversial medical model, and compulsory programs received lessening support from advocates of rehabilitation. Equally as important, programs became more varied, especially in community-based corrections, and the technology of interventions became more sophisticated. Furthermore, the overall quality or integrity of programs improved, and far more adequate research methods were used to evaluate correctional interventions. Proponents are now predicting that it will soon be possible to predict more accurately what interventions will work for which offenders in what contexts.

Rehabilitation Is a Costly Myth

FALCON BAKER

In this viewpoint, Falcon Baker assesses the worth of rehabilitation programs for juvenile offenders. He finds them not only ineffective but a costly waste of resources. He argues that they lead to juveniles becoming more antisocial in the long run. He attributes this state of affairs to the fact that Americans have blind faith in the ability of science to change behavior. Baker reviews a variety of highly acclaimed institutional and community programs for delinquent youth. He finds that those who have advocated these programs ignore valid evaluation of their worth. They deceive themselves, the public, and policy makers about the real worth of juvenile corrections and rehabilitation. He concludes that the problems of youthful offenders are so entrenched by the time they are committed to rehabilitation programs that no amount of coerced therapy can overcome them. Their criminality is

Excerpted from *Saving Our Kids from Delinquency, Drugs, and Despair* by Falcon Baker. New York: HarperCollins, 1991. Copyright © 1991 by Falcon Baker. Reprinted by permission of Curtis Brown Ltd., for the author.

deeply rooted in adverse social conditions that must be addressed and overcome if real help is to be offered to juvenile offenders. Falcon Baker was director of Juvenile Studies for the Kentucky Crime Commission and director of Delinquency Prevention Programs in the Louisville public schools. He is the author of many articles on youth problems and programs.

QUESTIONS

1. What evidence does the author present that juvenile rehabilitation is a myth?
2. According to the author, what do the recidivism statistics show about the worth of the programs that he reviews?
3. What solutions might be offered for the problems of juvenile crime that have a chance of reducing future criminality?

■ ■ ■

> **MYTH:** *Juvenile judges save delinquents from lives of crime by committing them to programs for rehabilitation.*
>
> **REALITY:** *The belief that delinquents can be forcibly rehabilitated has been a costly bit of wishful thinking. The vast majority become far more delinquent because of their rehabilitative experience.*

Regardless of the euphemistic names given to delinquency institutions—reformatory, state training school, boys' industrial school, boys' camp, forestry camp—they brutalize children. It is claimed that these schools teach juveniles a trade. They do. The trade is crime. It is claimed that these schools change a delinquent's mental attitude. They do. He learns to hate. It is claimed that these schools can redirect a youth's motivation. They do. He becomes dedicated to getting even with a society that has excluded him.

How can it be that honorable men deliberately and knowingly submit juveniles to injustice and cruelty?. . . The answer is simple. They do it with a clear conscience because America embraces a myth—the myth of rehabilitation. Americans have blind faith in the ability of science to accomplish miracles. It is easy to transfer this faith into a naive belief that some vague psychological activity, optimistically described as "therapy" or counseling, can change a delinquent youth into a law-abiding, responsible citizen.

The myth has been an expensive one—expensive in terms of the billions of dollars that have been wasted in the vain pursuit of therapeutic goals, even more expensive in terms of the thousands of young people whose lives have been mangled and futures destroyed. It is truly one of the great mysteries of the twentieth century how society has maintained the myth of rehabilitation despite the overwhelming evidence that coercive therapy simply does not work. But compassionate people are so fervent in their wish for it to work that they are blinded to disturbing facts.

For decades administrators and program directors managed to conceal the truth from the general public. But in the 1960s many people began to raise questions, among them the California legislators. They had become weary of being called upon, year after year, to build another and yet another juvenile institution. They demanded to know just what was going on. In response the California Youth Authority, which operates the world's largest juvenile correctional system, undertook a massive study of four thousand formerly institutionalized delinquents.

Their report, published in 1966, told the story of what had happened to those youths in just five years following discharge. Despite their rehabilitation, 44 percent of the males had already ended up in prison. Most of the remainder had been convicted of crimes for which they received jail sentences or fines. This study was particularly disheartening in that California is generally considered to have some of the most progressive juvenile programs in the nation.

Since then many studies have demonstrated the almost total failure of institutional programs in the rehabilitation of juveniles. Most surveys are even more discouraging, showing recidivism rates as high as 75 or 80 percent. Three out of four chronic juvenile offenders graduate into adult crime.

Massachusetts, under the leadership of Jerome Miller, then commissioner of the Department of Youth Services, was the first state officially to recognize and admit this failure of rehabilitation within an institution. In 1972, after discovering that the entrenched staffs of the scandal-ridden institutions were resistant to reform, Miller closed all of the state's large training schools. To the amazement of his critics, juvenile crime did not soar. *Instead, when the courts stopped sending delinquents to institutions, serious juvenile crimes declined. . . .*

Maturational Reform

As has been previously noted, most delinquent youths grow out of their antisocial behavior—provided nothing disturbs that natural process. "Maturation reform" is the term devised by David Matza for this phenomenon whereby juveniles tend to become progressively less delinquent as they move toward adulthood. The maturing youth faced with paying the rent, buying diapers, and putting groceries on the table becomes weary of sowing wild oats and other juvenile peccadilloes.

Maturation reform seems to occur regardless of whether an individual juvenile is treated, punished, or ignored. But it seems to occur more readily among those youths who are not caught or given "treatment."

For this reason it is understandable that Allan Breed, for many years director of the California Youth Authority, declared that *"nothing in 25 years' experience has changed my early reaction that institutions do more harm than good."* And the similar conclusion of Milton Lueger, longtime director of the other large state juvenile correctional system, the New York State Division of Youth, bears repeating here: "With the exception of a relatively few youths, it is probably better for all concerned if young delinquents were not detected, apprehended, or institutionalized. Too many of them get worse in our care."

GGI and the Highfields Fad

As the failure of large institutions became apparent small ones housing only twenty to forty youths came into favor. Attention focused on the Highfields (New Jersey) Treatment Program, a small residential institution which in the early fifties was set up in the former mansion of Charles Lindbergh, the site of the famous kidnapping. Staff reports claimed sharply more success than had been achieved in traditional large institutions.

And despite the absence of independent evaluation, the program suddenly became the glamorous star of the correctional world. Program planners from across the nation beat a path to Highfields.

Here the treatment relied heavily on Guided Group Interaction (GGI), also known as Positive Peer Group Pressure and Positive Peer Culture. It was a technique so simple and so inexpensive that in the 1970s it became a widespread fad. Those who copied the program discovered that just any worker, trained or not, could run the groups. The fad grew into a national phenomenon, becoming the backbone of most juvenile correctional programs.

In 1969 the Select Committee On Crime of the U.S. House of Representatives conducting a two-year study of juvenile corrections visited institutions across the nation. Among them was the Red Wing (Minnesota) School for Boys, where the staff stated that recidivism had dropped from 40 percent to 19 percent since they instituted the Positive Peer Culture method. The congressional committee was so impressed that in 1971 it published a report to the nation declaring that the program could rehabilitate virtually any type of delinquent. Furthermore, most any juvenile institution could be converted quickly and inexpensively to the new system.

Hosanna! Success at last!

As the name implies, the GGI system attempts to utilize the strong influence that adolescent peers have upon each other. Within the residential facility groups of eight to twelve youths live, work, play, study, and eat together. A two-hour formal group session is usually held daily; in the presence of the adult leader the teenagers probe the causes of their undesirable behavior.

When an individual is on the hot seat he or she is pressured to confess all past sins and to describe each transgression in gory detail. At times the pressure is painful physical force—being sat upon, slapped, screamed at directly into the ear, and subjected to other more severe "unapproved" actions. (A number of fatalities have occurred, as at a Kentucky youth camp where an asthmatic youth's arms were held tightly crisscrossed beneath his chin until, after twenty minutes, he stopped breathing.) From a list of character defects the group members decide which caused the delinquent to go wrong, tell him how he must change, and finally badger and harass him until he agrees to alter his attitude and behavior.

Outside the meetings the youths watch each other for violations of institutional rules or of group-imposed sanctions. Tattling is encouraged. This is "showing concern for others." In one group session I sat in on, a boy garnered points with the staff by squealing on four buddies. One was thinking about running away, a second had goofed off at the work detail, another had stolen a cigarette, and a fourth had been masturbating in the rest room. If one member breaks a major institutional rule—goes AWOL, hits a staff member, destroys public property—*all* members are punished by the staff along with the culprit: the others failed to show concern. Such a policy turns everyone into a vigilante.

Obviously, institutional staffs are loud in their praise. Their lives become much easier, since discipline is maintained by the inmates themselves. To obtain release from the institution, the youth must first obtain his group's agreement that he has satisfactorily "worked through his problems." This must then be confirmed by the staff. Getting out becomes a con game—conning both the peer group and the staff.

On my first visit to a juvenile camp where GGI was utilized, I came away filled with enthusiasm. It was true. That elusive cure for delinquency had been found. I had talked at length with four boys who the staff informed me were nearly ready for release. The boys freely discussed with me their past mistakes and were profuse in their professions of determination to go straight. One boy wasn't even going to see his girl except on weekends—he'd need other evenings to study.

My enthusiasm collapsed three months later when I looked up those four boys. Two were already back in the detention center awaiting court hearings on new charges, one for breaking and entering, the other for purse snatching. The would-be student had been kicked out of school: he had been unable to adjust in a school that didn't want to bother with a former institutionalized delinquent. Only one had apparently managed to remain trouble-free for a whole three months.

These youths had not only conned the staff and their group, they had conned themselves. At the time, most genuinely believed that they could make it when they returned home—returned to the same home and the same community environment that had spawned their delinquency in the first place. The only real change had been that now they possessed an opportunity-limiting label—"reform school graduate." As such they were no longer welcomed in law-abiding company, in school, or by prospective employers. All they had really learned was how to be a con artist.

A Second Look at GGI

Long after programs modeled after Highfields had been established across the country, criminologists began to take a second look at the validity of the claims. Many flaws in the research method were discovered. Subjects had not been randomly assigned either to Highfields or to Annandale, the traditional large institute with which it was compared. Instead, Highfields's subjects had been hand-picked by the judge as promising candidates. Furthermore, the staff had been permitted to expel uncooperative, disruptive youngsters (and not include them in the statistics), a luxury the staffs of traditional institutions did not enjoy. When all significant variables were considered, the outcome at Highfields was little different from the conventional reform school's.

A year after the enthusiastic congressional report on Positive Peer Culture at Red Wing, the Minnesota Department of Corrections published its research findings. The failure rate of boys approximately two years after release had already reached 55 percent, a far cry from the 19 percent reported to the congressional committee and considerably worse than Red Wing's record before adopting the new approach. In a slight understatement, the juvenile delinquency program planner for the Minnesota Crime Commission wrote me that "people are not as enthusiastic as they originally were about using the technique as a cure-all for all troubled kids."

Since that time dozens of research studies have consistently demonstrated that programs utilizing Guided Group Interaction have little positive effect. But amazingly, these carefully documented studies have failed to dampen the enthusiasm with which the "treatment" is embraced by administrators, even today. It is embraced because, as I have pointed out, it is an effective way to maintain discipline, it is inexpensive, and it brings joy to the soul of a counselor to hear a delinquent confess the error of his or her ways and promise to reform. The counselor is not around a few months later to witness the decay of those artificially induced promises.

Considerable space has been devoted here to Guided Group Interaction as a therapeutic tool, not because it is so much more unsuccessful than other strategies but because it points to the paucity of successful techniques and the inability to forcibly rehabilitate juveniles. Probably the principal reason for GGI's continued use is simply that the juvenile corrections industry has nothing more hopeful (or cheaper) to offer.

"Deinstitutionalization"

It became increasingly apparent that regardless of the therapy technique utilized, confinement in institutions was most often detrimental. (In addition to other failures, in 1986 seventy-four juveniles died while being rehabilitated, including twenty-one suicides and twenty-eight homicides.) So the battle cry of reformers changed to a fancy mouthful of a word, "deinstitutionalization." Professional journals were crammed with articles urging judges to commit delinquents to treatment programs in an open setting rather than to institutions. "Deinstitutionalization" became a code word that every program planner had to include in his application for grant money in order to show that he was hip to the latest fad. And fad it was.

The key to keeping youths out of institutions was to be community treatment. Basically this meant probation combined with some form of therapy. This could be as comprehensive as commitment to a nonsecure group home or as minimal as a once-a-week counseling session.

Hope springs eternal that the magic pill will be found. And again it seemed that the discovery had been made. Just as Highfields had become the guiding light in the movement for smaller institutions, now Achievement Place, a group home utilizing *behavior modification* techniques, became the star of the deinstitutionalization movement. Again administrators rushed to examine the new technique that was producing such exciting results: improvement in school performance, emotional behavior, conversational and social skills, attitudes, self-concepts, self-maintenance behaviors . . . and greatly reduced delinquent behavior.

Behavior Modification—the New Cure

Behavior modification is as old as the human family. Parents mold the behavior of children through rewards for good behavior, punishment for bad. Psychologists at the University of Kansas in 1967 adapted this concept to a group home for delinquents in Lawrence, Kansas. The idea was to give improperly socialized youths the home environment and character training they had missed. The most significant component of the program was the professional training given the foster parents before they were placed in charge of a home.

In the Achievement Place model, six to eight delinquents live in an open home with a married couple as teaching parents. Motivation for change is based on awarding points for good behavior and taking them away for improper behavior. A posted list specifies the points for over two hundred actions covering virtually everything conceivable. Among them: +50 for peeling a carrot, +100 for carrying in a grocery sack, +1,500 for doing a large homework assignment, -10,000 for fighting, -2,000 for forgetting school lunch money, -10,000 for lying. Points are given out on the spot and tabulated at the end of the day. Accumulated points may be exchanged for privileges such as snacks, watching TV, getting out of regular work, going to town.

The teaching parents are also instructed to provide social reinforcement with praise, affection, and support. As in the Guided Group Interaction technique, the youths are rewarded for reporting peer misbehavior, punished for not reporting. Residents quickly learn that if life is to be bearable they must do what the teaching parents "suggest." Again it is a technique successful in maintaining discipline and getting work done.

By 1981 when the government's Institute for Juvenile Justice and Delinquency Prevention released a book touting Achievement Place, it was already possible to list some eighty other books, journal articles, and Ph.D. dissertations that dealt with this newfound cure for delinquency. Across the nation new homes were being cloned almost daily. The National Teaching-Family Association was formed to coordinate these efforts. Six regional sites were established to train couples in behavior modification technique.

Only after the teaching-family model had begun its wild-fire spread did the National Institute of Mental Health fund Mark R. Weinrott, Richard R. Jones, and James R. Howard to do a comprehensive evaluation of the approach. A longitudinal study was made of twenty-six teaching-family homes (including the original Achievement Place) that were alternative placements for delinquent youths. Follow-up data of these youths, three years after their release, were reported in 1982.

The evaluation report sounded like a rerun of the evaluation of the Guided Group Interaction fad of a decade earlier. Just as the early promise of Highfields did not stand up under careful scrutiny, now Achievement Place failed to live up to its promise. Delinquent activity was reduced only while the youths were living in the teaching family homes. A year following treatment there was no significant difference between them and youths from comparison programs.

Again, in what sounds like a rerun, the negative findings of this definitive study failed to have a chilling effect on the enthusiasm. In the year the report was made there were 170 homes officially utilizing the program; two years later, in 1984, despite the report the number had increased to over 250.

Reasons for the failure are virtually the same as those that accounted for the failure of Guided Group Interaction. While he or she is in a behavior modification program a youth's actions are controlled by the promise of rewards and punishment. But not so afterward. In the real world the youth is no longer rewarded for being good; but crime provides rewards for being bad. And as with other rehabilitative programs, *in the end the delinquent is dumped back into the same family, the same community, the same problems that existed before the "rehabilitation.".* . .

Master of One's Fate

It has been naive to hope that deep psychological scars from years of emotional stress or social and physical deprivation could be erased by forcing a kid into a few hours of something posing as therapy. Perhaps the failure is wrapped up in the human need to feel that one is master of his own fate. A youth sees society trying to force him to behave in a certain way. And while bowing his neck, the juvenile vows that nobody, but nobody, is going to tell him what to do.

This is "reactance," a psychological phenomenon that in varying degrees is common to us all, a phenomenon that makes it virtually impossible to control anyone's behavior by force except during the time the individual is under close surveillance and faced with punishment.

Reactance is not solely a juvenile phenomenon. It destroys the effectiveness of adult therapeutic programs that demand participation. Court-ordered rehabilitation programs for drug and alcohol abuse, for example have been miserable, costly failures. Human behavior can be changed, but only if the individual *wants to change*. There were dire predictions about the hordes of junkies who would return from the Vietnam War: heroin use had been widespread. But the vast majority of addicted soldiers made the transition to a drug-free life with relative ease. Removal from the environment that nurtured the drug use, combined with a personal motivation to lead a normal civilian life, was all that was necessary.

The success of Alcoholics Anonymous and similar self-imposed programs can be attributed largely to their voluntary aspect. The alcoholic comes to AA wanting help, wanting to change, and frequently he does. When attendance is merely a court-ordered alternative to jail, the prognosis is far less hopeful. Similarly, many juvenile programs that would be helpful on a voluntary basis are destroyed by the demand to participate.

Delinquents will alter their antisocial behavior of their own volition if they can be shown that reform will bring a better life. Unfortunately, for many uneducated youths of the underclass legitimate opportunities are not readily available. For them crime holds the most hope for sharing in the material bounty of America.

No amount of "therapy" is going to overcome fourteen or fifteen years of the corrupting influence of family, friends, and environment. This influence began early in life, for some even dating back to inadequate prenatal nourishment or maternal drug or alcohol addiction. Showing concern for these troubled juveniles in their teenage years is at least a decade too late. Their criminality is rooted in deeper social problems which society must address if crime is to be reduced.

CHAPTER

5

What Is the Future of Criminology?

Chapter Preface

The study of crime, criminality, and crime control draws diverse researchers and theorists from a variety of academic backgrounds. It should not be surprising that points of view about what criminologists should study and how they should study it diverge, and will continue to do so in the future.

Criminology will also change as crime and criminals respond to social changes that affect all of us. Criminologists will have to study new crimes, new kinds of criminal behavior, and new technologies' effects on crime and crime control.

For example, some feel criminology should focus on problems emerging as society undergoes rapid technological change in the area of computerized information networks. Criminals, like the rest of society, will adapt to changes in communications technology and information processing and learn to exploit them. Information has become a valuable though sometimes intangible commodity and the theft of this valuable commodity is on the rise. Computer-related crime is already recognized as a major problem worldwide. Controlling this problem will be a continuing focus of criminology and the work of criminologists.

Already, computer bulletin boards are being used to exchange illegal information of various kinds. Arms dealers, for example, exchange information on sources of illegal weapons. But, turning the technology to their own advantage, police departments are making crime data available to citizens via their own computer bulletin boards to enlist citizens in crime prevention efforts.

Changing technologies will affect society in other ways, including decentralizing government services, making government agencies reflect a consumer society's concerns about costs and conservation of resources, and empowering citizens to be more involved in localized problem solving. Some criminologists emphasize study in the area of "natural crime prevention." This concept is based on the idea that the best protection against crime comes from the vigilance and security provided by citizens protecting their own "turf." From this point of view, crime prevention can be incorporated and ingrained in the everyday activities of citizens going about their daily business. To that end, these everyday activities and the procedures designed to enhance safety and law-abiding behaviors need to be studied by criminologists.

Simultaneously, our traditional crime control agencies will need to reorient themselves to cooperate preemptively with the public rather than only reacting to crime after situations veer out of control. Crime fighting in our society will become a joint effort of public agencies, private agencies, and citizens anticipating the onset of crime problems. Community policing and problem-solving policing enlists citizens and the business community to help identify problems, set priorities for crime prevention and control, and work together with the police in projects such as community cleanups, graffiti removal, and identification of criminal violators and fugitives.

A priority for other criminologists in the future will be the issue of violent crime prevention. The United States is the most violent of all Western industrial societies. Violence permeates families, schools, neighborhoods, and workplaces. Criminologists will study all aspects of the causes of violence and its prevention. Perhaps the answer to violence prevention in our society, some suggest, lies in the relationship between family violence, advertising, entertainment, and the negative example provided by social policy which relies on a combative approach to problem solving. As you will see in the following viewpoints, criminologists have different ideas about which direction criminology must take in the future.

Future Technology Will Solve Old Crime Problems

GENE STEPHENS

This viewpoint gives us some predictions about advances in our ability to respond successfully to crime problems and the problems of illegal drugs in the future. New technologies and therapies will change the offender and prevent these problems from overwhelming our society. Technological advances not only create new crime problems but open up the possibility of developing more successful crime prevention techniques. According to Gene Stephens, new communication technologies will allow the police to respond more efficiently and create better tracking systems. Community-based solutions to the crime problem will also become more important in the future, according to Stephens. A more participatory, mediation- based system of crime control will emerge. Stephens warns that technology contains the potential for improved crime prevention and control but it also provides the opportunity for abuse and attacks on our basic rights as citizens. Gene Stephens is a

Gene Stephens, "Drugs and Crime in the Twenty-First Century: New Approaches to Old Problems," *The Futurist*, May/June 1992. Reproduced with permission from *The Futurist*, published by the World Future Society, 7910 Woodmont Ave., Suite 450, Bethesda, MD 20814.

professor in the College of Criminal Justice at the University of South Carolina. He is also criminal justice editor for the journal *The Futurist*, from which this viewpoint is excerpted.

QUESTIONS

1. How will we learn to fight the illegal drug problem with new drugs, according to Stephens?
2. What kinds of new crime prevention technologies will reduce crime, according to Stephens?
3. What examples of criminal justice innovations does Stephens claim will allow us to be more successful in responding to crime in the future?

■ ■ ■

Crime should have been added to "death and taxes" as inevitable facts of life. But in the twenty-first century, technology and new crime-management methods will be able to significantly reduce street crime—the theft and violence that frightens citizens most.

There is no shortage of scientific and technological advances that will help police in their efforts to curtail drugs, crime, and violence in the twenty-first century. In fact, breakthroughs in information technologies, medicine, new materials, and a number of other areas will have important implications for crime prevention and criminal justice.

According to the National Crime Victimization Surveys conducted by the Department of Justice, the crime rate decreased significantly in the United States during the 1980s. The aggregate number of households touched by crime was down from one in three in 1975 to one in four by 1990. But the rate of decline leveled off in the early 1990s, and a few types of violent offenses increased somewhat. Today, U.S. prisons are filled to overflowing, and the fear of crime—particularly violent crime—continues to grow.

Law-enforcement efforts, no matter how skilled or effective, will never completely eradicate the problems of drugs and street crime. But these problems will be greatly alleviated by applying the technologies of the Information Age to the age-old problem of crime and justice. Crime itself can never be eliminated, but the number of crimes committed—and even the opportunities to commit crimes—can be dramatically reduced.

Fighting Drugs with Drugs

Much of the public's concern about crime—as well as an enlarged correctional population—can be directly attributed to the "war on drugs," as drug-related arrests have escalated rapidly during the past decade. Twenty to forty-five percent of the new prison inmates are drug abusers, and a significant proportion of violent offenders are either drug suppliers fighting over territorial rights or drug abusers desperately seeking the means to feed their addiction.

Advances in our understanding of drugs and the development of new therapeutic medications—along with the redefinition of law-enforcement problems and a redirection of social policy—will assist in the war on drugs and crime in several significant ways. For example, while the drug problem in the United States is most often associated with "hard" drugs such as cocaine or heroin, most of the problem actually comes from alcohol use. A drug now being tested promises to alleviate the massive problems caused by alcohol. RO15-5413, first tested by a Swiss pharmaceutical firm, sobered up heavily intoxicated rats in two minutes. Later tests found that, if the drug was taken before drinking, the rats did not get drunk; if it was taken over a period of time, the rats lost interest in alcohol. Early reports indicate that the same results will be found for humans, leading to a "sober-up" pill.

Police have expressed concern that a driver might kill someone while under the influence of alcohol and then take a sober-up pill in an attempt to hide the "evidence," but since the drug works by blocking the impact of the alcohol on the brain rather than actually lowering the body's blood-alcohol content, the alcohol in the bloodstream should still be detectable with blood tests. Since half of all street crime and traffic fatalities are associated with alcohol, this should be a great boon to curbing the nation's biggest drug problem.

Similar impact-blocking compounds are already being tested and show promise of having the same effect on amphetamine and barbiturate users and even crack-cocaine addicts.

Understanding and Controlling Criminal Behavior

Another aid to curtailing dangerous drug use in the future will be the increased knowledge and new therapeutic medications that should result from the current Human Genome Project. Launched to discover the genetic causes and thus treatments for brain-related diseases such as Parkinson's disease and epilepsy, the project is expected to result in a map of the chemical and electrical circuitry of the brain, as well as decoding, the body's genetic structure.

In a few years, the genetic keys to understanding and controlling behavior—from apathy to hyperactivity, from gentleness to violence—should be known. Through synthesis of the body's own chemicals and time-release implants of powerful therapeutic medications, behavior could be kept in constant check: drugs fighting drugs.

The next step might be the use of nanocomputer implants to keep track of and control the behavior of public offenders. These implants could be placed in the brain and could be equipped with microscopic transmitters to constantly monitor behavior and to send subliminal anti-crime messages to the offender (e.g., "Do what the law requires" or "Help, don't harm"). The nanocomputer could also release control chemicals on a set schedule and even diagnose changes in behavior and take necessary action to calm the individual.

Such technologies raise serious questions about the invasion of privacy of private citizens and how broad the monitoring and behavior-modification powers of the police will be allowed to grow. But as long as the American public's concern about drugs and crime remains high, increased surveillance and behavior modification are likely to be viewed as acceptable crime-fighting measures.

Advanced Crime-Prevention Technology

The best approach to solving crimes is to anticipate them and prevent them from occurring in the first place. Advances in technology soon will make it far easier to deter or discourage property crimes such as burglary or theft.

For example, the "smart house," which features a central computer that controls functions ranging from heating and cooling to turning lights on and off, will likely play a major role in crime prevention. Today, smart houses are described in terms of convenience, but the security aspect is impressive. Intruders can be videotaped and police or security called by the central computer. A combination of retina-scanning equipment for identification and pressure- and heat-sensitive floors and walls could be installed in homes, allowing for the programming of "'authorized" resident and guests in a smart house and the detection of "unauthorized" visitors. In the future, DNA "bar codes"—taken from a single drop of blood or other body chemical or cell—will make such identification even more certain.

With the cost of centralized home computers falling rapidly, millions of smart houses will be built in the next few years. To consider home security and crime prevention without taking these inventive homes into consideration would be a serious flaw in any future law-enforcement policy decisions.

Much technology that can deter crime is already on the market. Audio devices that can hear through walls are in use today and will soon be joined by heat-sensing cameras that can "see" through walls. And as satellite equipment becomes less expensive and easier to use, it will become an increasing part of the surveillance arsenal used by the police. And soon, the capacity of police to keep up with information on all citizens will be enhanced by universal dossiers keyed to genetic fingerprints taken from all individuals at birth. The dossier would include every incident of trouble in an individual's life—from fighting in school to posing a credit risk—and such data would be collected, stored, and disseminated from cradle to grave.

Other technologies will help police to solve mysteries and close cases. At the Medical University of South Carolina, a new technique called bullet cytology is being used to identify which bullet struck which body organ when the victim is shot more than once. By washing bullets in a saline solution, the forensic scientist can determine from the residue which bullet passed through the heart or which one passed through the liver, helping to pinpoint the cause of death and strengthening the case against the assailant.

The voice-stress analyzer may soon become a standard item that police carry. Such analyzers will be refined to the point where they can be placed in a shirt pocket and be voice-activated when the police officer questions suspect or witness. The analyzer can be quickly checked to determine when the suspect or witness felt stress during the questioning (indicating that he or she might be giving a dishonest answer), much the way that polygraph machines or "lie detectors" are used today.

Another major problem for police—communications—will be overcome by two innovations: the "Dick Tracy" wrist communicator and the universal translator. The wrist communicator—an ultra-small, two-way cellular phone—will allow police officers to be "on duty" at all times and to be constantly in touch with headquarters, with fellow officers, or, indeed, with anyone around the world. The universal translator—a small computer that will instantly translate speech from one language to another—will allow police officers to question suspects, witnesses, or crime victims without the language barriers that they often encounter today.

Bionics, too, could have a dramatic impact on crime fighting in the future. Already more than a score of body parts, from arms and legs to hearts, can be replaced by mechanical parts that often work as well as or better than the original. In particular, two replacement parts—both of which are being researched today—could have far-reaching effects: bionic eyes that are powerful enough to see for miles and bionic eardrums that are so sensitive that they can hear a pin drop behind a closed door.

Such bionic eyes and eardrums would greatly enhance a police officer's surveillance capabilities, while redefining citizens' expectations of privacy. But a dilemma emerges. Just who would be allowed to have these bionic parts: only those police officers who needed to have their eyes or ears replaced due to illness or injury, or any officer who chooses to replace his healthy eyes and eardrums with bionics in order to improve his performance? And would other citizens—including potential criminals—be allowed to obtain high-powered bionic parts? No doubt the ethical implications of such replacement parts will be a part of any future law-enforcement debate.

These and other technological innovations can be expected in the decade of the 1990s or early in the twenty-first century. But innovations in the way the U.S. criminal-justice system operates will emerge as well.

Criminal-Justice Innovations

"Community policing" is an innovation whose time has come. It is in harmony with the American society of the late twentieth and early twenty-first century: heterogeneous and culturally pluralistic. In this type of world, the police's role clearly must be to work with the community to tailor service to the community's needs. The "western marshal" or "gunfighter" approach simply is inappropriate for the modern world.

Closely aligned with community policing is the need to expand the scope of the criminal-justice system. If an offender is undereducated, poverty-stricken, medically or mentally ill, or mentally retarded, he or she often can be better dealt with by educators, social workers, doctors, or mental-health specialists than by western-marshal-style police officers. Police could coordinate crime prevention efforts with other social-service agencies and citizens in the community to develop truly pro-active strategic plans to provide the education, poverty assistance, medical attention, and mental-health treatment that would get to the heart of the crime problem.

Another innovation that has started to make inroads in the criminal-justice system is "participatory justice"—the use of mediation, arbitration, and other alternatives to the adversarial system of handling civil and criminal cases. Already, hundreds of small centers are settling disputes efficiently and effectively without the need for the threats and intimidation inherent in traditional criminal courts.

In Atlanta, for example, cases are referred directly from courts and social-service agencies to the Neighborhood Justice Center, where they are usually mediated within 72 hours of the referral. The mediator, a trained volunteer, brings all parties to the alleged offense to the negotiating table and seeks to achieve a consent agreement among the parties. In most cases, such a consent is achieved, and remedies range from paid restitution or apologies to counseling. In an evaluation conducted by the

Department of Justice, it was found that in 88% of cases handled both sides were satisfied with the process. This type of process provides the possibility of "win-win" justice and thus is in harmony with a heterogeneous world in which people increasingly will have social conflicts based on differences in lifestyles and expectations of their community.

Justice in the Twenty-First Century

Justice is in the eye of the beholder. Traditionally, neither the defendant nor the complainant has felt justice was done in the adversarial legal system. Defendants feel that the reasons for their actions are ignored and that the penalties are too harsh; victims receive little or nothing in repayment for their physical or financial losses and often feel that defendants don't receive long enough sentences.

In a more participatory system, using the mediation process, both sides must be satisfied or no agreement is signed, leading to a better understanding by both parties of why a sentence was imposed and a deeper sense of "closing the case."

Participatory justice can help victims—and victimizers—to achieve the understanding and empathy necessary to move beyond revenge to reconciliation. In the end, peace of mind as well as freedom from crime must be the result of any successful law-enforcement efforts.

From a crime-and-justice standpoint, the twenty-first century could be either heaven or hell. Police will have new tools that will allow them to better fight crime—or prevent crime from occurring in the first place. These same tools will have the potential for abuse—particularly in the area of invasion of privacy. One thing is certain: Both the technological and social innovations that can lead to criminal-justice heaven or hell are on the way.

VIEWPOINT

2

Criminals Will Become More Sophisticated

RICHTER H. MOORE JR.

The "information highway," which includes the linking of computer networks, television, telephone, financial services, etc., is a matter of top priority for the leaders of the United States. In this viewpoint Richter H. Moore Jr. describes the ways these technological developments will also be used for the purposes of organized crime. He predicts that criminal organizations will include the most skilled computer hackers to penetrate financial institutions. This will make the bank robberies of the past look insignificant by comparison. Privacy will be jeopardized for all as organized criminals gain access to computerized transactions. Criminals will utilize the most sophisticated new technologies, including satellites, genetic manipulation, and nuclear devices to increase their power and profits. Criminal organizations will offer new opportunities to those seeking wealth and power. In some

Richter H. Moore Jr., "Wiseguys: Smarter Criminals and Smarter Crime in the Twenty-First Century," *The Futurist*, September/October 1994. Reproduced with permission from *The Futurist*, published by the World Future Society, 7910 Woodmont Ave., Suite 450, Bethesda, MD 20814.

cases they will be able to control governments and operate with immunity from prosecution. This frightening scenario not only poses new challenges for crime control agencies. It offers new opportunities and challenges to criminologists who need to understand charges in crime and criminality for the next century. Richter H. Moore Jr. is a professor of criminal justice at Appalachian State University in North Carolina and a former president of the Academy of Criminal Justice Sciences.

QUESTIONS

1. In what new ways will criminal organizations of the next century use knowledge to enhance their power and control, according to the author?
2. How will organized crime and legitimate businesses work together in the future, according to the author?
3. How does the author predict that information theft will affect our society in the future?

■ ■ ■

Organized crime has invaded the Information Society. With today's satellites, telecommunications, video technology, and computers, the world of information is open to everyone, and the ability to use information—to turn it into knowledge—is a source of power.

Criminal organizations of the twenty-first century will continue to use violence and wealth (their most common sources of power in the twentieth century), but they will also increasingly use knowledge to enhance the power they already have. The top guns of twenty-first-century criminal organizations will be educated, highly sophisticated, computer-literate individuals who can wield state-of-the-art information technology to the best advantage—for themselves and for their organizations.

One of the top targets of twenty-first-century organized crime will be financial institutions. In the last quarter of the twentieth century, organized crime has become a major international financial force. Profits from drug trafficking have built major cartels and international conglomerates, with financial power rivaling many of the world's major corporations. Drug entrepreneurs blithely write off "business" losses greater than some countries' entire budgets. They use their illegal profits to establish giant financial empires, which usually include some major investments in legitimate businesses. Their dabblings in legitimate activities give these operators knowledge of the vulnerabilities of financial institutions. And insiders might be lured by opportunities for great wealth to hook up with criminal organizations.

Banks will be handling increased amounts of customer information valuable not only to them, but to criminal organizations as well, so criminal organizations of the future will routinely place their own operatives in financial institutions, or develop contacts with those already there. These "moles" will provide information such as computer passwords and access codes, which will allow criminal organizations to invade without casting suspicion on their insiders. To further elude detection, pairs of insiders could work in different parts of the organization—perhaps even in different countries.

Hijackings on the Information Highway

Some futurists predict that the developed world will become a cashless society within the first quarter of the next century and that this will solve the problem of drug trafficking. Unfortunately, the criminal organizations of the future will be ready for a cashless society. Their electronic, financial, and legal experts will simply establish new ways of doing business.

In drug trafficking, for example, the street dealer who today collects cash for his transactions will be able to accept "plastic," and the buyer will be provided with an adequate credit line with which to make purchases. The seller of illegal goods and services can use a legitimate business operated by the crime group as a means of recording the sale. The sale of drugs may show up as merchandise on the records of a restaurant, bar, or convenience store.

Computer extortion will be a steady moneymaker for criminal organizations of the future. The introduction of a virus into the computers of a multinational corporation could be disastrous. The loss or vandalism of computer data could result in a complete work stoppage or, if related to an assembly line, to defective products. Tomorrow's viruses will be even subtler and more vicious than today's. They will be able to attack mainframes and even destroy hardware without being detected.

Theft in the new century will far exceed anything in the old in terms of sophistication and specialization. Already we see harbingers of what is to come: For example, high-tech airplane guidance systems worth more than $100,000 each were stolen in the spring of 1992 by a crime ring operating at Kennedy International Airport in New York and sold to a drug cartel for use on narcotics-smuggling planes. In the years ahead, all sorts of high-tech gear, such as medical equipment stolen from hospitals, will be sold on the increasingly international black market.

Manipulating Identities

Criminal organizations will hire the most-skilled computer hackers to penetrate targeted institutions. These hackers will change bank records, credit accounts and reports, criminal history files, and educational, medical, and even military records. The hackers will also sell identity-manipulation services to those who need a new persona but cannot get one legitimately. Anyone's private records may be invaded, copied, deleted, or removed for criminal purposes.

Future criminals may also be able to manipulate a person's genetic identity—a feat that will be increasingly desired, because of the growing use of genetic identification. Already genetic identification is being used by the U.S. military to assure that there will be no more "unknown soldiers." By the twenty-first century, genetic-based records will include a birth-to-death dossier of a person and will be *the* method of criminal identification.

However, with further advances in genetic engineering, an individual's genes may become manipulable in such a manner as to change the structure of his or her DNA. If so, criminal organizations will likely steal computer records of DNA to provide new identities for their own people or to clients who need one. These new identities will not only include the "paper identity" (birth certificate, driver's license, etc.), but—through bioengineering—the "physical identity" as well, including a DNA pattern that matches the individual being impersonated.

Building a Façade of Legitimacy

Criminal organizations worldwide currently use their profits from illegal activities to buy legitimate businesses. The Colombian drug cartels are thought to have major portfolios that include substantial holdings of stock in many of the *Fortune* 500 companies. Japan's premier criminal organization, the Yakuza, is believed to have major stock and real estate holdings around the world, including substantial investments the United States. And the Mafia has long invested in legitimate business enterprises.

By the next century, criminal organizations will not only own shares of multinational corporations, but manage them as well. Such a company will not be concerned with distinguishing between legal and illegal means of gaining an advantage over its competitors. A corporate computer hacker could be assigned to illegally obtain the technology, plans, formulas, intellectual property, and experimental information of the competitor. Data can be stolen outright or simply manipulated in a manner that causes major problems for the victim, such as placing incorrect information in a database or obstructing data.

Satellites will be yet another tool for tomorrow's criminals. Today, satellites make possible instantaneous communications all around the world; they also allow people and products to be tracked, help identify the best site for a particular activity, and the location and extent of a competitor's holdings. Satellite-imaging information services and communications networks are increasingly available on the commercial market. By the next century, criminal organizations will be able to afford their own satellites. For example, a drug cartel could hire its own team of scientists to launch a satellite that could be used as a secure information network for the cartel's drug trafficking and money laundering operations. Such systems could also be used to track couriers and shipments and act as an early-warning system spotting drug-enforcement agency operations.

With major organized-crime groups around the world already working together, it is likely that more than one group will become involved in the use of these satellite systems. Some organized-crime groups already have state-of-the-art equipment and communications systems, most of which puts law-enforcement technologies to shame. There is no reason to believe criminal organizations will not keep up with the latest, most-sophisticated technology. Their money will enable them to buy whatever they need to make themselves as invulnerable as possible. Satellite systems could conceivably be adapted to seize and redirect military weaponry, such as rockets or guided missiles, to use against government or law-enforcement forces.

The twenty-first century will see growing sophistication of criminal organizations, which will all be tied into larger networks devoted to meeting the public's demand for illegal goods and services. Technology and communications will allow crime networks to operate more efficiently and with greater impunity.

Sports gambling in the twenty-first century will be truly global. With their own satellite communications networks, criminal organizations will be able to operate from sites where law-enforcement agencies are sympathetic. Sporting events worldwide, from horse racing to school sports, will be fixed. In 1992, authorities discovered a $1-billion gambling ring operating out of the Dominican Republic that was involved in fixing sporting events in the United States. As criminal organizations refine and expand their networks, the Dominican ring will appear to have been a very small beginning.

Prostitution rings will use modern technology to coordinate global activities. The trade in young women from Africa, India, Pakistan, China, Thailand, and the Philippines for Yakuza and Chinese Triad brothels in the Far East will likely increase and expand into the Western Hemisphere, especially South America.

Organized-Crime Activities

Criminal organizations will also use their high-tech networks and information-based power to move into new areas, such as trafficking in newborn infants, sold to childless couples. If kidnapping fails to supply the market adequately, pregnant women may be seized, labor induced, and the child taken.

Given false documentation, stolen children may appear in the official records as the natural children of the individuals who bought them.

Fetuses are also becoming important in medical research and in treating certain conditions such as Parkinson's disease. Since religious, social, and political constraints restrict the supply, fetuses may also become subject to unlawful trafficking.

Waste disposal is another activity that may be increasingly pursued by crime organizations. Governments have not been—and will not be—willing to make the effort to fully enforce their own environmental regulations or to provide the personnel to do so. This leaves the door open for criminal entrepreneurs to provide waste-disposal services in violation of local laws. They will not hesitate to haul away toxic materials for illegal and dangerous dumping if the price is right. The Mafia has hauled hazardous industrial waste from New York and New Jersey and illegally dumped it in North Carolina. They have also dumped dangerous hospital waste in the Atlantic Ocean, and some of it has washed up on beaches.

An even more menacing opportunity for criminal entrepreneurs lies in the vast quantities of arms and nuclear materials that have become available with the shattering of the Soviet army and bureaucracy. Arms sales within the former Soviet republics are booming. Well into the twenty-first century, there will be a surplus of Soviet weapons. And more arms will flow from the downsized Western military forces. Criminal organizations will be able to supply the private armies of worldwide criminal networks, terrorists, hate groups, questionable regimes, independent crime groups, and individual criminals.

To make matters worse, a "nuclear mafia" has developed in the last two decades. Groups can acquire nuclear materials, mostly by theft, and then make them available to any regime or group with the money to purchase them. Germany has become the center of nuclear smuggling. According to one official, the problem is becoming so bad that Germany is in danger of becoming the global emporium for nuclear smuggling. By the next century, criminal groups will likely develop the ability to make nuclear weapons. Nuclear extortion will not only be a tool of irresponsible governments, but of criminal establishments as well.

265

Infiltrating Governments

In the years ahead, criminal organizations will control the governments of many countries, either directly or indirectly. In the new states of the former Soviet Union, organized-crime groups are tied closely to governments and essentially control economic systems. In other countries, such as Nigeria and Colombia, criminal organizations have virtually paralyzed the government. If members of the organization are arrested and tried, they receive special treatment and continue to run their organizations from prison.

The individual who becomes a part of a criminal organization in the twenty-first century will do so not because it's the only route to success, but because it offers the best opportunity for achieving wealth and power.

As members of criminal organizations become more educated, they will become more attuned to the ways of politics. They will become actively involved to assure that their interests are protected. Gaining greater power, they will become a force that world society will have to recognize and deal with.

Criminologists Must Study and Implement Natural Crime Prevention

MARCUS FELSON

Liberal and conservative approaches to crime reduction have led to ideological splits in criminology and to ineffective crime prevention. In the following viewpoint, Marcus Felson argues that various approaches to designing a more crime free environment have largely been ignored while the ideologues of crime control fight their meaningless battles for the control of crime fighting resources. Felson describes meaningful experimentation with crime prevention through environmental design and natural crime prevention in this viewpoint. These approaches have worked in a variety of settings and in a variety of cultures to help create a more crime free environment. To the extent that these crime prevention approaches can be implemented, they will reduce future reliance on get-tough and rehabilitation remedies for the crime problem. The author of this viewpoint argues that these

Marcus Felson, *Crime and Everyday Life: Insight and Implications for Society*, pp. 115-33, © 1994 by Pine Forge Press. Reprinted by permission of Pine Forge Press.

experiments provide much promise for the future. Marcus Felson is a criminologist at the University of Southern California where he serves as professor of sociology and senior research associate at the Social Science Research Institute.

QUESTIONS

1. What does the author mean by "situational crime prevention?" What examples does he give of this approach?
2. What does the author mean by "natural crime prevention?" What example of this can you think of that might reduce crime in your own neighborhood?
3. What agenda for the future does Felson recommend? Which social institutions in the community can play a part in crime reduction? How?

■ ■ ■

In 1961, Jane Jacobs' classic book *Death and Life of Great American Cities* documented the tragedy of urban renewal before anyone else realized what was happening. She explained why old urban neighborhoods, even if low in income, provided places for pedestrians, had vibrant lives, maintained local control of space, and protected people against crime. These neighborhoods were bulldozed to erect unnatural high-rise public housing complexes that became sterile environments and which had crime problems built into their design. Jane Jacobs remains a hero to students of crime prevention because she showed us how designing more crime is as easy as designing less. Her concept went beyond buildings themselves, including the entire urban environment and taking into consideration people using that environment. Her spark of creativity and freshness of thought might have enlightened U.S. crime policy for decades to come.

However, that was not what happened. Leadership fell into the hands of naïve ideologies, first liberal and then conservative. The first proposed to reduce crime by assuming that if government is good to people, then they will be good in return. The second proposed to reduce crime by assuming that if government is bad to people, then they will be good in return. Had either or both camps listened to Jane Jacobs, they would have realized that the issue is not how good or bad the government is to people but whether public places are designed and organized to allow people to control their own environments informally.

Around 1970, two other opportunities arose for crime policy to incorporate common sense. C. Ray Jeffery invented "Crime Prevention through Environmental Design" (CPTED; pronounced "sehp-tehd").... And Oscar Newman contributed landmark books about crime prevention, using such terms as *defensible space, natural surveillance,* and *community of interest.* Newman explained how crime could be prevented by creating buildings, environments, and communities that provided for interaction with and influence against crime.

Unfortunately, in the United States most public agencies have had little knowledge about or interest in designing out crime, preferring instead to wait until crime happens and then punishing the few people that can be apprehended. Nor is the academic world a center of interest in practical prevention. U.S. business has a much more enlightened attitude than government or universities, putting a good deal of effort into preventing crime by keeping offenders away from targets or otherwise reducing crime opportunities. Among researchers, the most creative bundle of prevention projects began within the British government's civil service system.

Situational Prevention: Experiments and Innovations

Great Britain's Home Office is roughly equivalent to the U.S. Department of Justice. Within this agency was the small Research and Planning Unit, located during the 1970s at Romney House on Marsham Street, a five-minute walk from Scotland Yard. There in 1973, Senior Research Officer Ronald V. Clarke had just completed a study of why youths abscond from borstals (American translation: why juvenile delinquents run away from reform school). In this study, the usual social science variables did not successfully explain the phenomenon. However, when Clarke took a look at the day of the week on which these events occurred, he found that most boys ran away on weekends when staffing and supervision were light. Because these were not prisons and staff members were not guards, their influence was more informal. Merely by being present, adults could prevent a certain amount of trouble, including absconding.

With these results, Clarke began to think of crime in general as the result of human situations and opportunities. In 1976, with Pat Mayhew, A. Sturman, and J. M. Hough, Clarke published *Crime as Opportunity*, and Clarke later became the unit's head. Under his leadership, several British researchers inside and outside the government created or discovered real-life crime prevention experiments. They adopted the following policy.

- Do not worry about academic theories. Just go out and gather facts about crime from nature herself (that is, by observing, interviewing offenders, etc.).
- Focus on very specific slices of crime, such as vandalism against telephones or soccer violence.
- Try to block crime in a practical, natural, and simple way.

They called their efforts *situational prevention.* From the 1970s to the present, many remarkable situational prevention studies have been carried out. A crime prevention unit was also established, and the two units contribute much of the systematic crime prevention work now available. We will now look at how the simple approach of situational prevention has been put into successful practice.

Trouble on Double-Deck Buses

We begin our illustration of situational prevention with the problem of vandalism against Britain's traditional red double-deck buses. The Home Office researchers learned that most of the vandalism was on the upper deck, usually in the back row, where supervision was least likely to occur. They also learned that the traditional British bus conductor had a major role in preventing vandalism. A bus conductor would ascend the stairs to the upper deck to collect fares and thus serve as a guardian against the crime of vandalism. One experiment put conductors back on buses that no longer had them. The experiment succeeded in reducing vandalism but had an unexpected result: Conductors were assaulted more often. This is an example of how crime prevention can sometimes backfire, solving one crime but leading to another. This also establishes that situational crime prevention is far from obvious, sometimes producing unexpected results.

Car Theft Prevention

Another interesting example of how crime prevention policy may not work quite right is seen in Great Britain's efforts to thwart car theft.

A Home Office study by Pat Mayhew, Ronald Clarke, and Mike Hough examined the impact of steering wheel locks on car theft. This study compared British experience with that of the former Federal Republic of Germany. Whereas the British enacted a law that only required steering wheel locks on new cars, the West Germans required that *all* cars—even old cars—have such locks installed by a certain date. In the British case, car thieves diverted their attention away from new cars and stole older models that lacked steering wheel locks. Thus the overall car theft rate did not decline. In West Germany the more comprehensive law produced a dramatic reduction in car theft across the board. This lower risk held for subsequent years.

This study indicates first that crime prevention can be accomplished without significant displacement to other crimes or other victims. Second, it teaches us that avoiding such displacement requires making some crime prevention efforts universal rather than piecemeal.

Motorcycle Theft Prevention

If the West German success in the case of car theft resulted from careful thinking, the same nation was successful with another crime prevention measure entirely by accident.

The West German government enacted a law that required motorcyclists to wear helmets to prevent serious injuries from accidents. After police began to enforce the law, the thefts of motorcycles declined precipitously. Many motorcycle thefts are for joyriding and occur on the spur of the moment. A youth who saw a shiny motorcycle and was suddenly tempted to steal it would usually not happen to have a motorcycle helmet and would decide not to commit the theft.

Several lessons can be learned from this example. First, we see that significant crime prevention can occur completely without planning. Second, the example demonstrates that fairly simple changes in rules or laws can have major significance for crime prevention. Third, we see that highly visible behavior (in this case, wearing a helmet while riding a motorcycle) can help produce controls. Fourth, this example found no evidence of displacement of prevented motorcycle crime to other vehicle thefts.

The two German vehicle theft examples achieved crime prevention by means of across-the-board laws enacted centrally. However, some crime prevention requires more "personal service," as the next example suggests.

Burglary Prevention

When Ken Pease studied burglary in British public housing, he noticed that some units were burglarized repeatedly. So when someone's home was burglarized for a first time, a prevention team focused its efforts on that particular unit to prevent a repetition. The team enlisted the residents of the five or six homes nearest the burglarized unit to keep an eye on it. The result was a lower burglary rate. The unit's success was far greater than the usual generally unfocused and ineffective Neighborhood Watch in the United States.

So far we have offered only British examples of situational prevention. Similar well-focused crime prevention is found in the following U.S. example.

Subway Graffiti in New York City

For many years, the subway trains of New York City were covered inside and out with ugly graffiti, surely among the ugliest anywhere. Moreover, the transit system was in chaos, ridership was dropping, and employee morale was low. Many efforts and policies had failed to correct the problems.

Then David Gunn became president of the New York City Transit Authority and announced the Clean Car Program. The aim of the program was to clean off graffiti immediately. This is important because it gave the graffiti painters no satisfaction in seeing their work travel around New York City. This removed the incentive and gave them no more reason to paint graffiti on subway cars. Compared to its previous experience, New York City's subway cars became largely free from major graffiti problems as a result of this program. One lesson of the program: Find out exactly what the offenders want and why they commit a particular crime. This information will guide the design of countermeasures.

Another subway system far distant from New York City prevented graffiti in fixed locations using a very different plan. . . .

The Displacement Issue

Displacement occurs when the crime prevented in one setting shifts to another setting. The goal of prevention is to reduce overall crime, not merely for one area to dump its crime problem onto another. In the steering wheel lock research, the motorcycle study, and other studies not presented here, Clarke and his associates have been able to demonstrate little or no displacement to other crimes or other settings when situational prevention is carefully conceived and executed.

We have offered several examples from different nations to demonstrate the utility of situational prevention not only in helping us think about crime prevention but also in finding real solutions to specific crime problems. We now turn to a more strategic and comprehensive approach to crime prevention: designing better environments.

Crime Prevention Through Environmental Design

A husband-and-wife team at Simon Fraser University, Pat and Paul Brantingham, began an important crime prevention effort in Vancouver, in the western Canadian province of British Columbia. This is an area with roughly the same climate and "feel" of Seattle, Washington.

Here the Brantinghams developed and applied CPTED (invented by C. Ray Jeffery). Forging relationships with local architects, planning boards, and police, they helped apply

CPTED in many settings. One of the most interesting developments in British Columbia is that the Royal Canadian Mounted Police began to train its officers in CPTED. For example, these "Mounties" are trained to read blueprints; they routinely sit on planning boards, examining detailed plans for new construction and making suggestions to help reduce the risk of crime. As a result, many new housing complexes, businesses, and schools in British Columbia apply principles of CPTED from the outset.

The following are examples of the sort of useful advice that these British Columbians can offer about crime prevention:

- Keep schools well away from shopping malls, so youths do not flock to the malls after school or at lunch time and become involved in theft, vandalism, and drug use.
- Make sure that school lunches are provided either at school or in local institutions with adults near, so youths do not go "out on the town."
- Plan carefully the routes that teenagers walk from housing developments to local high schools and back. Make sure these routes do not cross parking lots and thus invite vandalism against cars.
- When constructing public housing, make sure it is low-rise; avoid vast unassigned public space; avoid walls or solid fences that give burglars something to hide behind.
- Design housing for the elderly as a high-rise building with a glass-walled recreation room on the first floor. Thus the residents can keep watch on the doors.

Although this British Columbian approach does not conflict with the spirit of the British approach, there are some differences in emphasis. As Table 1 indicates, situational prevention focuses on a specific slice of a crime problem, plans in a more targeted fashion, acts more directly, involves business more than public agencies or police, reflects a psychological origin, and is linked to a "rational choice" theory of crime. This theory is summed up in the title of one of its books, *The Reasoning Criminal*, which examines how the offender thinks about a crime situation. By learning more details about the offender's thought processes, we might be able to figure out how to thwart illegal action before it even starts.

TABLE 1 Situational Crime Prevention Versus CPTED

	Approach	
	British Situational Prevention	*British Columbian CPTED*
Focus	specific crime problem	local environment
Planning concept	targeted	comprehensive
Action concept	act directly	act more indirectly
Police involvement	minimal	substantial
Work more with	business	public agencies
Origins	psychology	urban planning
Theoretical basis	rational choice	environmental criminology

The British Columbian approach uses CPTED, acts more indirectly, pays attention to comprehensive planning of local environments, and substantially involves public agencies and police. This reflects its origin in urban planning and is manifested in its theoretical term: *environmental criminology*. This theory has contributed the "geometry of crime," which traces an offender's normal route from work to school to home to entertainment. By planning locations of homes, schools, and recreation areas before a community is actually constructed, environmental criminologists can help to reduce crime levels in the community.

Although CPTED principles should be applied well before an environment is constructed, it is very often too late: The building already stands and a serious crime problem needs to be corrected. Sometimes changes can still be made to improve the situation. Here is a good example from across the Atlantic.

A Shopping Mall and Drug Market

The Netherlands combines the quaintness of dikes and windmills with some of Europe's highest population densities and crime rates. The Dutch Ministry of Justice has established local crime prevention offices and encouraged them to develop their own crime prevention projects. An interesting case in point is the effort to reduce a major crime problem in Utrecht's central-city shopping mall. There young drug addicts were hanging out, buying and selling drugs, using drugs on the premises, and committing predatory crimes in the vicinity. The authorities redesigned the mall to remove dead space and hidden corners, and they blocked private parts of the mall (such as service areas and offices) from public access. The effect of these efforts was neither to "wipe out crime" nor to displace crime to other locations. However, it did put a lid on the crime problem and helped reduce its worst manifestations.

Several examples so far have considered planning fairly large parts of a community. The following example demonstrates that it is possible to plan several components of quite a very limited environment: a small store.

Reducing Convenience-Store and Small Grocery Robberies

Small stores with late hours are very vulnerable to robbery, especially when located near freeways. In some cases employees or customers have been injured or murdered in the process. One large convenience-store chain, 7-Eleven, suffered staggering increases in the numbers of robberies during the 1970s. The chain's owner, the Southland Corporation, hired several convicted robbers, including Ray Johnson, and the Western Behavioral Sciences Institute to help redesign the corporation's retail stores with the intention of reducing the number of holdups. Sixty stores initiated the team's recommendations, and a control group of the same size did not. The control group experienced no change in robbery risk while the experimental group had a 30% decline in the number of robberies. These stores also reported major declines in nearby crime and in people loitering and harassing customers. The following are the stores' main innovations.

1. Display advertising that once covered all windows was removed so that would-be robbers would feel that they were more easily noticed from the street and thus subject to guardianship.

2. Cash registers were moved to the front of the store,

making them visible from the street.

3. Both registers and clerks were placed on a raised platform. This took the cash drawer out of the offender's line of vision and reduced temptation.

4. Special timed-access safes were placed beneath each register. These safes take in cash, especially large bills, but can release no more than $10 change every two minutes. This removed the target of the crime by making most of the money inaccessible.

5. Store properties were redesigned to eliminate all alley exits and to channel traffic to and from the streets out front. This helped customers better serve as guardians for one another.

6. Taxi drivers were encouraged to use the premises as a nighttime station at no cost and with free coffee and rest room privileges. This provided mild surveillance of the area at little cost.

7. Employees were trained to make eye contact with each customer on entry. This provided a more informal social influence against crime.

These 7-Eleven crime prevention policies have had the net effect of making stores more comfortable and safe for employees, customers, and neighbors, while avoiding the use of armed guards.

With the urging of Professor C. Ray Jeffery, the city of Gainesville, Florida, placed similar stipulations into a city ordinance and also required the presence of at least two clerks on duty late at night. The result was a decline in convenience-store robberies.

In most of our examples, crime prevention was the main motivating factor for the planning effort. Yet Tim Crowe of the National Crime Prevention Institute argues, "Good planning is good prevention and good prevention is good planning." His point is that a well-designed environment accomplishes its basic goals and simultaneously serves to prevent crime. Applying this principle to a small grocery or convenience store, a good design will not only reduce crime but also produce a better store in which customers enjoy shopping. No better illustration of this principle can be found than in the next example.

Disney World Is No Fantasyland

Clifford Shearing and Phillip Stenning have reported how Disney World organizes your visit in great detail. From parking lot to train to Monorail to park and back, activities are planned to minimize risk of accident or crime. Disney World follows this rule: Embed control in other structures so that it is barely noticed. For example, there is only one way to get into many exhibits: within a vehicle controlled by Disney personnel. Even when people are waiting in line, their wait is structured by railings that wrap each line of people back and forth. This encourages informal conversations and proximity of people in different age groups, thus reducing impatience and discouraging rowdiness by youths.

The most important lesson of Disney planning is that almost all visitors to Disney World are quite contented with the way their visit is managed and voluntarily comply. (Of course, people are not spending the rest of their lives in Disney World.) The lessons of this example are that crime prevention can be most effective when it is incidental, and that a well-planned and well-managed environment serves many human purposes along with security. . . .

From Many Specific Examples, a Few General Principles

We have seen contributions to crime prevention from Great Britain, Canada, the Netherlands, Sweden, the former West Germany, and the United States. Some of these efforts focus on specific crime problems (situational prevention), and other efforts focus on settings (CPTED). With either philosophy and in many different contexts, we repeatedly return to a simple but powerful idea: Crime can most often be prevented by following nature as closely as possible. This means avoiding so far as one can the use of the criminal justice system, armed guards, violence, and threats. Instead, we prefer to set up situations and environments in which acting legally feels like the normal and comfortable thing to do.

We call this *natural crime prevention*. It avoids a walled-off society and seeks more sophisticated means for avoiding crime. Those who construct walls around their backyards may not realize that this method has a tendency to backfire. Once an intruder has entered, the solid wall provides him with a screen for committing crime freely. Natural crime prevention suggests much less forbidding fences, affording significant visibility and thus reducing the temptation to intrude in the first place. For similar reasons, natural prevention recommends trimming hedges and the lower branches of trees so that offenders cannot readily conceal themselves.

Nor are guards with uniforms and guns necessary in most applications. It usually makes more sense for unarmed people to inquire politely, "May I help you?" when they notice someone wandering around with no legitimate purpose or for a receptionist or doorkeeper to offer assistance and thus provide a kinder, gentler, and subtler form of security.

Natural crime prevention includes (a) unplanned and informal crime prevention as it occurs naturally in everyday life and (b) planned crime prevention that imitates the former by skillfully designing human settings or activities so that crime opportunities are unobtrusively and nonviolently reduced. . . .

> Natural crime prevention may be described as the chunking and channeling of human activities, in imitation of nature, to reduce crime temptations and increase controls.

We have offered examples of such prevention from various settings in several nations. These examples provide some ideas for new crime prevention efforts.

Agenda for the Future

Many institutions in society can do much to reduce crime.

Improving Youth Programs

To begin, government and school programs for youths need to think more clearly about supervision aspects. . . . We suggest that youth programs can improve their chances for success by shifting to a tangible, situational definition of what is needed. A government jobs program for youths should be structured more carefully, locating jobs in mixed-age and mixed-sex settings, away from opportunities to commit employee theft, and with arrangements to go home after work. Afterschool activities for youths should seek to follow these same rules as well as fill most of the afternoon vacuum.

What Schools Can Do to Reduce Crime

Another area of policy disappointment is the limited success schools have in keeping youths out of trouble. Again we need to think more carefully about school activities as they are located in time and space. For example:

- start and end school later each day so that it more closely corresponds to parental work schedules,
- include more of the summer period within the school year,
- avoid excessive parks and landscaping right next to schools,
- keep smaller schools alive, and
- discourage "open campuses" where secondary school students can enter and leave at any time.

These suggestions are all designed to help restore natural and informal social control to schools and nearby settings, both during school hours and afterward.

What Colleges and Universities Can Do to Reduce Crime

Even though a campus is already built, it can make relatively small changes with surprisingly large consequences for security. A campus can:

- trim hedges and lower branches of trees,
- design out blind corners and block off less used parts of parking structures when there is no special need for them,
- put movement-sensitive lights in remaining blind spots,
- improve sign-in procedures for visitors to student housing,
- locate receptionists in places where they can better see who enters,
- assign security responsibility to someone in each building or section of a building,
- install new locks or key mechanisms on doors used more

often and limit key distribution,
- provide bicycle racks and get people to use them properly,
- organize bicycle check areas and provide attendants, and
- improve window protection to prevent illegal entry.

Gather the facts on a specific security problem before acting. For example, exactly *why* are graduate students or employees blocking the security doors open? Find out and then solve the problem rather than simply posting a sign demanding that they cease blocking the doors. In short, find the facts, use common sense, and do not be too conventional. Students who follow these rules can probably produce a better plan than anybody else for reducing crime on campus.

What Industry Can Do to Reduce Crime

Important contributions to natural crime prevention can be made by industrialists in the future. Even before products arrive at the store, they can be designed and manufactured in ways that reduce crime.

Clarke and Harris list numerous technical changes that the auto industry can contribute to help reduce auto theft:

- mark various valuable parts around the car with serial numbers;
- install high-security locks for steering column, doors, and hood;
- use flush-sill buttons that are difficult to pull up with a clothes hanger;
- strengthen window glass so that it is harder to break;
- protect the internal door-latching components;
- install hood-release catches; and
- program an audible reminder to remove keys from the ignition.

More expensive cars can also offer central locking and, when a break-in occurs, immobilize the engine through its electronic-management system.

The story of the Chevrolet Corvette provides a most interesting example of what the industrialist can do for crime prevention. Once the most stolen car in the United States, it now offers a small resistor embedded in the ignition key. When the key's resistance does not match the car's decoder, it cuts off the fuel injectors and the starter. This disables the car for a while. Only an electronics-sophisticated thief can defeat the system, which even then requires 15 minutes.

British Rover eliminates external door locks entirely, using an infrared transmitter to open the door instead. If windows are broken, this immobilizes the ignition system. The car's entertainment system is security coded; if removed, it can only be activated by a personal identification number.

Going beyond the automobile industry, inexpensive technology already exists to put a personal identification number into every new and valuable electronic item, such as a television set or videocassette recorder. The product will not work outside your home unless this number is entered. An item thus will be of no value to the thief. Industry can make a major contribution to society by designing and selling products that "go kaput" when stolen.

What Police Can Do to Reduce Crime

Herman Goldstein has coined the term "problem-oriented policing." Arguing that the goal of policing should be to reduce crime, not simply to arrest people, he has suggested first figuring out specific problems that need to be attacked and then targeting police action toward those problems. For example, if a drug house is generating most of the crime in an area, then it should be the target of action. The first step would be to find out who owns the property and make that person aware of what is going on there. Sometimes the landlord is willing to put an end to the problem by not renewing a lease.

In some cases, a drug dealer does business next to a pay phone, taking orders on the phone and handing drugs to customers as they drive by to pick up their orders. The police and the neighborhood can get the phone company to change the phone so that it will only call out and not receive calls, thus driving this specific illegal market out of business.

Many other examples and a good deal of experience is accruing in police departments and among other public agencies working with them. U.S. police are beginning to follow the example of the Mounties in seeking innovative opportunities to reduce crime. However, they are having some difficulty getting their minds off of arresting people. Will problem-oriented policing end up meaning nothing more than "targeting arrests"? Or will police begin to include in their repertoire a vast array of ideas for natural crime prevention?. . .

Summary

We have seen that crime prevention can be introduced incrementally into many parts of our society. The basic strategy is to imitate activity patterns of everyday life as already observed in nature. Included are chunking and channeling human activity to reduce temptations and increase informal control. Such efforts can reduce crime, up to a point, given the context of our current society.

Criminologists Must Promote Human Rights

ROBERT ELIAS

The author of this viewpoint asks why society persists in pursuing predictably ineffective crime policies in fighting crime. He argues that successful crime control must take human rights enforcement seriously. The government cannot promote war and injustice and, at the same time, convince individuals not to launch their own versions of violence, war, and crime. Rather than blaming offenders, institutions, or victims, criminology must study and diagnose inadequacies in the American political economy that induce crime. Repressive crime control policies must themselves be seen as crimes against humanity. Crime, according to the author, results from the violation of human rights produced by unjust political and economic arrangements. The place to start in creating a more crime free environment is to make sure that existing human rights standards are enforced and are upheld by our

Robert Elias, "Crime Control as Human Rights Enforcement." In *Criminology as Peacemaking*, Harold E. Pepinsky and Richard Quinney, eds. Bloomington: Indiana University Press, 1991. Copyright © 1991 by Harold E. Pepinsky and Richard Quinney. Reprinted by permission.

society. Elias argues that the U.S. should use the guidelines presented in the United Nations Declaration on the Victims of Crime and Abuses of Power which links the problems of crime and repression to reform criminal justice. This viewpoint represents a growing sentiment within criminology in the United States, Great Britain, and Europe. Robert Elias is chair of the Peace and Justice Studies Program at the University of San Francisco.

QUESTIONS

1. What is the relationship between crime and human rights, according to the author?
2. What examples does the author give for his claim that the political economy encourages conditions that lead to crime?
3. What steps would our politicians need to take to implement an approach to crime control such as the one recommended by Elias?

■ ■ ■

War and Peace

When the government declares another of its countless wars on crime or on drugs, criminology often provides logistical support for the resulting battles. This happens even though these wars are never won; indeed, we can easily predict that they'll be lost. Why do we pursue predictably ineffective crime policies? Why does criminology so often support those wars, thus promoting its own, professional failure? Instead of making *war*, crime control and criminology should be making *peace*.

The government has perhaps a strategic sense of this, having already appropriated the word "peace": At U.S. military bases, the new motto is "Peace" Is Our Profession. Likewise, in many areas, police officers are now "peace" officers. Nevertheless, military and law-enforcement policies remain virtually the same: they're still pursuing war, not peace.

What would crime control or criminology as peacemaking look like? What do we mean by peace? Over the four-decade history of peace studies, peace has come to mean two things: *positive* peace and *negative* peace. We're most familiar with the commonsense notion of negative peace, meaning an absence of violence and war. Here, crime control as peacemaking might resemble conventional crime policy (but with significantly different tactics): fighting crime either to prevent personal violence or to prevent crime "wars" such as those fought among drug dealers or mafia families. Crime policy typically fails to produce this kind of peace, perhaps because officials don't seriously want it, but also because it makes the wrong diagnosis and pursues the wrong strategies.

In part, crime policy fails because it ignores the second notion of peace. Positive peace describes not what government should prevent, but what government or the society should provide—*justice*: and not just criminal justice, but also political, economic, and social justice. You can't have peace if you don't have justice. Injustice is not merely unpeaceful in itself. It's also the source of further violence and war in any society, and it's the major source of the kind of violence and war we commonly call *crime*.

Most crime results from political, economic, and social injustices that the government or the society has failed or refused to prevent. In some circles, that injustice is called "repression": a violation of human rights. Thus, promoting peace is a matter of the government's not merely refraining from its own violence and war (and crime) but providing the conditions to persuade others against launching their own violence and war (and crime). Crime control can be successful only by taking human rights enforcement seriously.

Conventional Crime Control

Mainstream crime policy uses war purportedly to create peace. Yet as a process, its wars undermine both negative and positive peace: they use violence and rights violations as their major tactics. The need to win these wars rationalizes the use of illegitimate, but supposedly more effective, methods: We're told the police should no longer be "handcuffed"; rights must be sacrificed; our enforcement and punishments must be more violent. In the long run, crime will decline and peace will reign.

Yet the peace never comes: criminal violence keeps pace with escalating official violence.

Despite the wars, criminal victimization continues because conventional crime policy either ignores or misdiagnoses crime's sources. Officials argue that we don't or can't know the causes of crime, or they attribute it to what might better be viewed as crime symptoms. They blame offenders and institutions, even victims. Offender-blaming attributes crime to evil individuals or their inadequate families. Institution-blaming focuses on lax enforcement, inadequate resources, excessive rights, and judicial softness as the causes of crime. Victim-blaming faults victims for not taking precautions sufficient to deter crime. Predictably, crime-control strategies follow from these diagnoses. They're pursued; they fail.

Nevertheless, officials return to these diagnoses and strategies time and again. Criminology largely follows suit, adopting official definitions and perspectives. When officials go to war, criminology goes to war too. When confronting crime, government limits its scope; criminology does so too. The diagnoses made of what causes crime necessarily constrict the options for fighting it; make the wrong diagnoses and you'll likely pursue the wrong strategies. Conventional crime policy's repeated failure would seem reason enough to consider alternatives. Better yet, alternative diagnoses and strategies already exist.

Alternative Crime Policy

Blaming the System

An alternative crime policy would wage peace, not war. It would begin with a different diagnosis: Crime primarily results not from inherently or inevitably evil offenders, nor from institutional inefficiencies, nor from victim complacency. Rather, it's caused by adverse or destructive political, economic, and social conditions that induce crime across the spectrum of classes and races in American society. Instead of blaming offenders, institutions, or victims, this diagnosis blames the system, the existing set of U.S. political and economic arrangements. Inadequacies in the American political economy provide the breeding ground for most crime.

287

The economic system, for example, produces poverty, inequality, homelessness, hunger, and other victimization. It's not surprising that many poor people turn to crime, for economic gain or merely to vent their frustrations. The economy also promotes excessive materialism, competition, and consumerism. To get ahead and keep ahead, middle- and upper-class people commit crime too. If their wrongdoing was measured or enforced like poor people's crimes, it would amount to far more criminality and damage than the conventional crime we worry so much about.

The political system has its own inadequacies, induced partly by the economic system. Government officials widely commit crimes themselves, usually with little or no accounting, the Iran-Contra episode being only the latest example. Access to meaningful political participation is blocked for almost all but the very wealthy. Elections function more to tame the masses than to empower them. Despite talk about getting government off our backs, it steadily centralizes and grows. We're overwhelmed and alienated by our various public and private bureaucracies, including most of our workplaces. Government pays lip service to equality while tolerating or promoting racism, sexism, and classism. Whether in its domestic policy or its foreign policy, we learn by the government's official actions, if not by its pious rhetoric, that violence is legitimate.

In practice, we lack both political and economic democracy. Our system produces problems and conditions that breed crime far more than the things we usually blame. Societies with greater political and economic democracy have less crime and victimization. Even nations like those in Eastern Europe or like Cuba, which has little political democracy but greater economic democracy, have much lower crime rates than our nominally democratic capitalism.

Crime and Repression

But the problems of failed political and economic democracy are the sources of more than merely criminal victimization; the problems are themselves victimization. Human rights advocates would call these problems repression. International law requires nations to prevent or deal with these problems; and nations which fail to do so (particularly if, like the United States, they have the means) are human rights violators. These are crimes against humanity. Repression is crime. Crime is a human rights violation. Crime results from the violation of human rights produced by unjust political and economic arrangements.

Criminals are also victims, and, of course, offenders bear some responsibility for their crimes. But viewing criminals as passive automatons shaped by monolithic forces degrades offenders every bit as much as our conventional criminal process. And recognizing offender motivations does not excuse their crimes. Nevertheless, offenders act within an environment that often makes crime a viable alternative, a likely possibility, even a necessity. It's not an environment of lenience, as "law and order" advocates argue. (The United States has long had one of the world's highest incarceration rates and severity of punishments.) Rather, it's an environment of victimization, which beats people down, robs them of opportunities, and provokes their rage, frustration, and desperation. In response, they attack others; but their victims are much like themselves: Most victims come from the same backgrounds, and many of them have committed their own crimes for similar reasons.

It's politically convenient for officials to pit criminals and victims against each other. Protecting victims has justified our growing fortress mentality: increasing government powers and declining individual rights. Yet victim policy does not reduce crime; and arguably, pursuing crime control strategies that routinely fail, even encourage crime, makes victimization even more likely. Successful crime control relies not on promoting victims over offenders, but on recognizing how both are victimized and how the rights of both must be protected. Victims and criminals have the same interest: the protection of their human rights.

Alternative crime control strategies would follow from this diagnosis. It would require us to reduce or eliminate crime's systemic sources. We'd have to significantly restructure our political and economic system, bringing both much closer to democracy and justice. Thereby, we'd be promoting both positive and negative peace: a reduction in the violence the system and its major institutions directly produce, and a reduction in the violence committed by others in the society in reaction to injustice. By pursuing justice, we'd be pursuing peace; and we'd also be reducing the crime that now significantly impedes that peace.

Resisting Peace

Why does mainstream crime policy, which routinely fails, shun this alternative? It does so because it would clash dramatically with the American system's conventional political and economic practice both at home and abroad. To adopt alternative crime policies, we'd have to pursue crime control that really reduces crime rather than merely overseeing it. We'd have to stop manipulating or blaming victims, and take victimization (criminal and otherwise) seriously. We'd have to reject "democracy for the few" in favor of a more just political economy. We'd have to renounce our isolation from the world community and our rejection of international human rights standards.

Rogue Society

Let's examine, for example, U.S. human rights policy. The United States has long crusaded as democracy's champion at home and abroad. It's held up its own system as the democratic ideal and justified its foreign policy as helping others become more democratic. By now, it's hardly controversial to suggest that in practice the United States does neither. Even the pretensions of real democracy largely evaporated with Jimmy Carter, who at least pursued human rights rhetorically if not very vigorously in practice. Whether it's our increasing poverty, homelessness, inequality, and violence at home, or our promotion of brutal repression abroad, the victimization produced by the U.S. government and our other institutions hardly makes our commitment to human rights credible.

The United States is out of step with the world community. We pull out of United Nations' agencies while other nations commit themselves more fully. We're practically alone in rejecting the Law-of-the-Sea-Treaty's cooperative exploration of the oceans in favor of competitive exploitation. We defend the unconscionable marketing of infant baby formula while the rest of the world deplores it. We support pariah states like Chile, Israel, and South Africa while the international community condemns them. We increasingly reject and violate international law (and the jurisdiction of agencies like the World Court) while the rest of the world increasingly embraces it. We substitute military intervention for diplomacy when even the Soviet Union has rejected the practice. George Bush asks the U.S.S.R. to intervene in Rumania, and Mikhail Gorbachev says they don't do that kind of thing anymore. A few days later, the United States illegally invades Panama; and the Latin American nations, no lovers of Manuel Noriega, rightfully condemn us.

Human Rights Standards

Likewise, the United States exhibits a limited commitment to international human rights standards. By now, the world's nations have recognized, and most have ratified, three "generations" of human rights: political and civil rights; economic, social and cultural rights; and peace, development and environmental rights. The United States has ratified none of these standards. We've even shunned the Covenant on Political and Civil Rights, which comes closest to our narrow human rights definitions. Although this covenant embodies many of the things already in our own Bill of Rights, it adds other rights and, more menacing, threatens to make the rights substantially enforceable and not merely rhetorical. We'd have an international obligation to take these rights seriously. And instead of piecemeal, impermanent, and often unenforced rights protections, we'd be responsible for more honestly and equitably guaranteeing freedom of expression, political access, privacy, due process for suspects and defendants, and race and gender equality—rights that have instead declined in the last two decades (faster than they can be promoted) and are threatened even further by the Rehnquist Court.

Even more ominous for the American system would be accepting and protecting the second and third generations of human rights. Embracing economic, social, and cultural rights, for example, would force the United States to fundamentally change its political economy, which now acts systematically to deprive these rights for vast portions of the population. We can imagine why officials won't recognize the right to housing, employment, quality education, nutrition, good working conditions, comprehensive healthcare, and social and cultural equality. Similarly, the newest generation of human rights—the rights to peace, development, and a clean

291

environment—also clashes with the American system since this generation would condemn our persistent and far-flung military and economic interventionism, reject our vast nuclear stockpiles, and indict the corporate pollution of our environment.

Human rights covenants are treaties in U.S. and international law. If we were to ratify these treaties, they would become the law of the land under the U.S. Constitution. As such, the rights they contain would be legally enforceable in U.S. courts. We can imagine the threat posed to the American system by suits brought to demand that these rights be protected. Suppose claims were brought by our four million homeless Americans for their housing rights, or by our 60 million illiterates for their educational rights, or by our millions of jobless (50 percent in our ghettos) for their employment rights, or by our 30 million underfed for their nutrition rights, or by our millions of uninsured (50 percent of the population) for their healthcare rights, or by even millions more (such as those living near our 75,000 toxic dump sites) for their environmental rights. Or suppose U.S. citizens or foreigners sued to protect the rights of the millions of people victimized by the repression and economic deprivation our foreign policy exports to nations like El Salvador, Lebanon, Chile, South Africa, and many others?

Rights as Threats

Despite the rhetoric, the United States has been only minimally committed to protecting human rights. The few exceptions are politically motivated, such as the "demonstration elections" we've sponsored to help sanitize our client states. When we back away from the endless dictators we've either sponsored or installed, it's only after they've outlived their usefulness (such as Noriega in Panama) or where their popular overthrow is inevitable (such as Marcos in the Philippines). If popular revolution (such as in Nicaragua) threatens to seriously protect human rights and promote real political and economic democracy, we attack it.

A nation which tolerates and even promotes the victimization caused by repression can hardly be expected to respond differently to victimization caused by crime. Wars on crime and drugs, government-backed victim movements, and pious rhetoric about the "forgotten" victim in the criminal process achieve little for crime victims in practice. There's little evidence that officials ever thought they would.

We don't take crime and its victims seriously for the same reasons we don't take repression and its victims seriously; to do so would require fundamental changes in the American system, which would upset its prevailing concentration of power and resources. Undoing that concentration is the only hope for genuinely protecting and providing human rights; and short of that, crime and other victimization will continue unabated. The United States can't achieve peace if it's only willing to fight wars, especially since they're often launched not just against innocent foreigners, but also against its own people. Are U.S. wars, whether against domestic crime or foreign enemies, fought to promote democracy for the many or to preserve democracy for the few?

Taking Rights Seriously

Real crime control would consider rights not as an obstacle but rather as its major objective. Now, to fight crime, our "law and order" policy restricts and violates the rights of suspects, defendants, and the public; it further victimizes purportedly to end victimization. Indeed, alternative crime control would promote human rights fully: not just for suspects and defendants, not just to stem a growing police state, but also for the kind of political, economic, and social justice that would significantly eliminate crime's sources in the first place. An effective crime policy would recognize the relationship between criminal victimization and human rights victimization, not treat the two as separate and unconnected, and pursue a joint strategy designed to alleviate them both simultaneously.

How can this be done? We can begin, perhaps, by taking the lead offered by the United Nations Declaration on the Victims of Crime and Abuses of Power. Here the link has been made, despite U.S. resistance, between crime and repression. Like other declarations, its effectiveness depends first on getting as many nations as possible to ratify it; and the United States should be pressured to do so. Next, the U.N.'s Crime Prevention and Criminal Justice Branch must devise standards for the declaration's implementation; and criminologists, victimologists, and human rights advocates should contribute to this process. More generally, the United States should be pushed to get in step with the international community. It must ratify the human rights covenants. It must respect the sovereignty of other nations and peoples. It must recognize international law.

At home, the United States must take human rights seriously, implementing and enforcing them in both the political and economic realms. To do so requires not merely a more just legal system and less criminal government, but fundamental changes in the American system to undo its many obstacles to political and economic democracy. The United States must be held more accountable. Criminology and victimology can contribute by challenging prevailing assumptions about official benevolence and by adopting alternative definitions and perspectives on crime and victimization.

Of course, these objectives will not come easily. By now it should be obvious that formidable and fundamental changes will be needed to significantly reduce crime. A human rights perspective, however, gives us a new way of approaching the task ahead and, perhaps, a more powerful and symbolically acceptable mechanism for accomplishing it.

No doubt the obstacles will be compounded by official resistance to a substantive human rights movement. Rights will likely remain a threat to those unwilling to relinquish political and economic power, both at home and abroad. Our archconservative Supreme Court and foreign policy will be further impediments to taking rights seriously. Nevertheless, one wonders how long the United States can resist our rapidly changing world. With the walls of repression falling in Eastern Europe, and with incipient signs of democratic renewal in Latin America (despite U.S. policy), now is perhaps a historic opportunity. With renewed determination, perhaps we can launch a real human rights movement, beyond mere rhetoric, which emphasizes substantive protections of all human rights—a movement which will help reduce not only human rights victimization, but criminal victimization as well.

How can criminology work for peace? It can promote human rights—*justice:* the only effective path to peace, whether in our streets or among our nations.

FOR FURTHER DISCUSSION

Chapter 1

1. Think of a recent change in the law or in criminal justice policy that you have read about or heard about. What assumptions about crime and criminal offenders were made by those who advocated this change?

2. Does the change you thought about for the above question represent the wishes of those whose political ideology is on the right or on the left of the political spectrum? Does it represent one of the "crusading issues" of the ideological right or left?

3. Do you feel that criminologists should be limited to the study of adjudicated criminals or should they study any groups or individuals who do harm or present a danger to others, whether or not they have been labeled criminal? Why?

4. Can a society or a whole community be criminal? If so, what standards or criteria can be applied to make this judgment?

5. If criminologists charge that those who are in power or those who control vast economic resources are acting in a criminal manner and harming others, what consequences might this have for their ability to get research grants and to get the support of their professional peers?

Chapter 2

1. What does it mean to say that the law is a form of "social control"? What other forms of social control exist in your community?

2. What other functions does the law and the enforcement of criminal law provide your community?

3. Does the law and law enforcement serve the interests of the community as a whole or does it sometimes serve certain interests at the expense of others?

4. Are there activities which are now prohibited by criminal law which should be "decriminalized"? Which activities would you decriminalize if you had the power? Should these activities be regulated in some other way, or should they be tolerated and left alone by government?

Chapter 3

1. Does it make sense to you to say that society creates criminal behavior? How and why? Can criminality serve essential social functions?
2. Is crime caused by biological, psychological, social, economic, or political factors? Is it caused by some combination of these factors? Which are most important? Why?
3. Is the criminal normal or abnormal? Is crime learned in the same way as other behavior is learned? Defend your position.

Chapter 4

1. Is there something that you would do today that is illegal if you knew you would not be arrested and prosecuted for it? Do you think that most potential criminals think about this before they decide to act in a legal or criminal manner? Why or why not?
2. Can our resources be best utilized in crime control by targeting high-risk career criminals? What criminological research is this idea based on? Can future criminality be predicted? If so, how?
3. Are rehabilitation programs a good investment for crime control? What kinds of information would you want to have available about these programs before you decide to invest your tax dollars in them?

Chapter 5

1. How are changes in technology in our society likely to affect criminal opportunities in the future? Give an example of a new technology which creates new opportunities for crime.
2. How are technological changes likely to affect crime control in the future? Give an example.
3. How can crime prevention be improved by changing the patterns of our daily life and/or the design of our environment? Give an example of how this might be done in your community.
4. How is crime related to human rights? Can crime control and criminal justice be effective without achieving social justice? If not, how would we achieve social justice?

Suggestions for Further Reading

Chapter 1

Piers Beirne, *Inventing Criminology*. New York: State University of New York Press, 1993.

Piers Beirne and James Messerschmidt, *Criminology*. San Diego: Harcourt Brace Jovanovich, 1991.

Robert M. Bohm, "Crime, Criminal and Crime Control Policy Myths." *Justice Quarterly* 3:193-214, 1986.

————, "Criminology's Proper Role—A Rejoinder." *The Criminologist* 10, No. 5:4 and 8, 1985.

Steven Box, *Power, Crime, and Mystification*. New York: Tavistock, 1983.

Donald Cressey, "Criminological Theory, Social Science, and the Repression of Crime." *Criminology* 16:171-191, 1978.

Chris W. Eskridge, "Crime Management: Criminology's Proper Role." *The Criminologist* 10, No. 3:3-4, 1985.

Mark S. Gaylord and John F. Galliher, *The Criminology of Edwin Sutherland*. New Brunswick: Transaction Books, 1988.

Gilbert Geis and Robert F. Meier, eds., *White-Collar Crime: Offenses in Business, Politics and the Professions*. New York: The Free Press, 1977.

Don C. Gibbons and Peter Garabedian, "Conservative, Liberal and Radical Criminology: Some Trends and Observations." In Charles E. Reasons, ed., *The Criminologist: Crime and the Criminal*. Pacific Palisades, CA: Goodyear, 1974.

Jack P. Gibbs, "An Incorrigible Positivist." *The Criminologist* 4, No. 4:1-4, 1987.

Herman Mannheim, *Comparative Criminology*. Boston: Houghton Mifflin, 1965.

Jerome Michael and Mortimer Adler, *Crime, Law, and Social Science*. New York: Harcourt Brace, 1933.

Richard Quinney, *Critique of Legal Order*. Boston: Little, Brown, 1974.

Thorsten Sellin, *Culture Conflict and Crime*. New York: Social Science Research Council, 1938.

Edwin H. Sutherland, *White Collar Crime*. New York: Holt, Rinehart and Winston, 1961.

Edwin H. Sutherland and Donald R. Cressey, *Criminology*. Ninth edition. Philadelphia: J.B. Lippincott.

Ian Taylor, Paul Walton, and Jock Young, *The New Criminology: For a Social Theory of Deviance*. New York: Harper Colophon Books, 1973.

CHAPTER 2

Dan Baum, "Tunnel Vision: The War on Drugs." *ABA Journal*, March 1993.

William Chamblis, "A Sociological Analysis of the Law of Vagrancy." *Social Problems* 12:67-77, 1964.

George F. Cole, *The American System of Criminal Justice*. Pacific Grove, CA: Brooks/Cole, 1992.

Lawrence M. Friedman, *Crime and Punishment in American History*. New York: Basic Books, 1993.

Thomas J. Gardiner, *Criminal Law: Principles and Cases*. St. Paul: West, 1985.

Joseph R. Gusfield, *The Culture of Public Problems*. Chicago: University of Chicago Press, 1981.

John Hagan, "The Legislation of Crime and Delinquency: A Review of Theory, Method and Research." *Law and Society Review* 14:603-628, 1980.

Jerome Hall, *Theft, Law and Society*. Indianapolis: Bobbs-Merrill, 1935.

Oliver Holmes, *The Common Law*. Boston: Little, Brown, 1949.

C. Ray Jeffery, "The Development of Crime in Early English Society." *Journal of Criminal Law, Criminology, and Police Science* 47:647-666, 1957.

C. Ray Jeffery, Laura B. Myers, and Laurin A. Wollan, "Crime, Justice, and Their Systems: Resolving the Tension." *The Criminologist* 16, No. 4:1-6, 1991.

Herbert Johnson, *History of Criminal Justice*. Cincinnati: Anderson, 1988.

Mark A. R. Kleiman, *Against Excess: Drug Policy for Results*. New York: Basic Books, 1992.

———, "Neither Prohibition Nor Legalization: Grudging Toleration in Drug Control Policy." *Daedalus* 12, No. 3:53-83, 1992.

Arnold H. Loewy, *Criminal Law in a Nutshell*. St. Paul: West, 1987.

Raymond J. Michalowski, *Order, Law, and Crime*. New York: Random House, 1985.

David F. Musto, *The American Disease: Origins of Narcotic Control*. New Haven: Yale University Press, 1973.

Michael H. Tonry and James Q. Wilson, eds., *Drugs and Crime*. Chicago: University of Chicago Press, 1990.

CHAPTER 3

Reed L. Adams, "Differential Association and Learning Principles Revisited." *Social Problems* 20:458-470.

Robert Agnew, "Social Control Theory and Delinquency: A Longitudinal Test." *Criminology* 23:47-61, 1985.

Ronald L. Akers, *Deviant Behavior: A Social Learning Approach*. Belmont, CA: Wadsworth, 1973.

Rand D. Conger, "Social Control and Social Learning Models of Delinquent Behavior." *Criminology* 14:17-39, 1976.

Deborah W. Denno, "Human Biology and Criminal Responsibility: Free Will or Free Ride?" *University of Pennsylvania Law Review* 137:615-671, 1988.

————, *Biology and Violence: From Birth to Adulthood*. New York: Cambridge University Press, 1990.

Daniel L. Dotter and Julian B. Roebuck, "The Labeling Approach Reexamined: Interactionism and the Components of Deviance," *Deviant Behavior* 9:19-32, 1988.

Hans J. Eysenck and Gisli H. Gudjonsson, *The Causes and Cures of Criminality*. New York: Plenum, 1989.

David P. Farrington, Lloyd E. Ohlin, and James Q. Wilson, *Understanding and Controlling Crime: Toward a New Research Strategy*. New York: Springer-Verlag, 1986.

Walter R. Gove, *The Labeling of Deviance*. Beverly Hills: Sage, 1980.

Richard J. Herrnstein and Charles Murray, *The Bell Curve: Intelligence and Class Structure in American Life*. New York: Free Press, 1994.

Michael J. Hindelang, Travis Hirschi, and Joseph G. Weis, *Measuring Delinquency*. Beverly Hills: Sage, 1981.

Travis Hirschi, *Causes of Delinquency*. Berkeley: University of California Press, 1969.

C. Ray Jeffery, "Criminal Behavior and Learning Theory." *Journal of Criminal Law, Criminology, and Police Science* 54:294-300, 1965.

Marvin Krohn and James L. Massey, "Social Control and Delinquent Behavior: An Examination of the Elements of the Social Bond." *Sociological Quarterly* 21:529-544, 1980.

Rolf Loeber and Marc Le Blanc, "Toward a Developmental Criminology." In *Crime and Justice: A Review of Research*, Michael H. Tonry and

Norval Morris, eds. 12:375-473, Chicago: University of Chicago Press, 1990.

David Matza, *Delinquency and Drift*. New York: John Wiley, 1964.

Sarnoff A. Mednick, Terrie E. Moffitt, and Susan A. Stack, eds., *The Causes of Crime: New Biological Approaches*. New York: Cambridge University Press, 1987.

Walter C. Reckless, *The Crime Problem*. New York: Appleton-Century-Crofts, 1961.

Herman Schwendinger and Julia S. Schwendinger, *Adolescent Subcultures and Delinquency*. New York: Praeger, 1985.

Austin Turk, *Criminality and the Legal Order*. Chicago: Rand McNally, 1969.

James Q. Wilson and Richard J. Herrnstein, *Crime and Human Nature*. New York: Simon and Schuster, 1985.

Marvin E. Wolfgang and Franco Ferracuti, *The Subculture of Violence*. London: Social Science Paperbacks, 1967.

————, "Cesare Lombroso." In Hermann Mannheim, ed., *Pioneers in Criminology*, 232-291. Chicago: Quadrangle Books, 1960.

CHAPTER 4

Elliott Currie, *Confronting Crime: An American Challenge*. New York: Pantheon Books, 1985.

John J. DiIulio and Anne Morrison Piehl, "Does Prison Pay?" *Brookings Review*, Fall, 1991.

John Doble, Stephen Immerwahr, and Amy Richardson, *Punishing Criminals*. New York: The Public Agenda Foundation, 1991.

Phyllis Ellickson, "Helping Urban Teenagers Avoid High-Risk Behavior: What We've Learned from Prevention Research." In *Urban America*. Santa Monica, CA: Rand Corp., 1992.

David P. Farrington and Patrick A. Langan, "Changes in Crime and Punishment in England and America in the 1980s." *Justice Quarterly* 9:5-46, 1992.

Lois G. Forer, *The Rage to Punish: The Unintended Consequences of Mandatory Sentencing*. New York: W. W. Norton & Co., 1994.

Brian Forst, "Selective Incapacitation: A Sheep in Wolf's Clothing?" *Judicature*, October/November 1984.

Diana R. Gordon, *The Justice Juggernaut*. New Brunswick: Rutgers University Press, 1990.

Peter W. Greenwood and Allan Abrahamse, *Selective Incapacitation*. Santa Monica, CA: Rand Corp., 1982.

Christopher Jencks, "Is Violent Crime Increasing?" *The American Prospect*, Winter 1991.

Wendy Kaminer, "Crime and Community," *The Atlantic Monthly*, May and June 1994.

Gwen A. Kurz and Louis E. Moore, *The Eight Percent Problem: Chronic Juvenile Offender Recidivism*. Santa Ana, CA: Orange County Probation Department, 1994.

Patrick A. Langan, "America's Soaring Prison Population." *Science* 251:1568-1573, 1991.

Marc Mauer, *Americans Behind Bars: A Comparison of International Rates of Incarceration*. Washington, DC: The Sentencing Project, 1991.

Sean D. McCoville, *America's Correctional Crises*. New York: Greenwood Press, 1987.

Mark H. Moore, *Dangerous Offenders: The Elusive Target of Justice*. Cambridge: Harvard University Press, 1984.

Andrew von Hirsch, "Selective Incapacitation Reexamined," *Criminal Justice Ethics*, Winter/Spring 1988.

James Q. Wilson, *Thinking About Crime*. New York: Basic Books, 1983.

Marvin E. Wolfgang, Robert M. Figlio, and Thorsten Sellin. *Delinquency in a Birth Cohort*. Chicago: University of Chicago Press, 1972.

CHAPTER 5

Charles M. Bozza, "The Future of Diversity in America: The Law Enforcement Paradigm Shift," *Journal of Contemporary Criminal Justice* 8, No. 3:208-216 August 1992.

Michael C. Braswell, "Peacemaking: A Missing Link in Criminology," *The Criminologist* 15, No. 3, May/June 1990.

Paul J. Brantingham and Patricia L. Brantingham, eds., *Environmental Criminology*. Beverly Hills: Sage, 1981.

Robert J. Bursik Jr. and Harold G. Gramsick, *Neighborhoods and Crime: The Dimensions of Effective Community Control*. New York: Lexington Books, 1993.

Ronald V. Clarke and Marcus Felson, eds., *Routine Activity and Rational Choice*. New Brunswick: Transaction Books, 1993.

————, *Situational Crime Prevention: Successful Case Studies*. New York: Harrow and Heston, 1992.

Elliott Currie, "Confronting Crime: Looking Toward the Twenty-First Century," *Justice Quarterly* 6:5-25, 1989.

John J. DiIulio, *No Escape: The Future of American Corrections.* New York: Basic Books, 1991.

John E. Eck and William Spelman, *Problem-Oriented Policing in Newport News.* Washington, DC: Police Executive Research Forum.

David J. Evans, Nicholas R. Fyfe, and David T. Herbert, eds., *Crime, Policing and Place: Essays in Environmental Criminology.* London: Routledge, 1992.

C. Ray Jeffery, *Crime Prevention Through Environmental Design.* Beverly Hills: Sage, 1971.

Oscar Newman, *Defensible Space.* New York: Macmillan, 1972.

James Q. Wilson and Joan Petersilia, eds., *Crime.* San Francisco: Institute for Contemporary Studies, 1995.

Jock Young and Roger Matthews, *Rethinking Criminology: The Realist Debate.* London: Sage Publications, 1992.

Index